D0463417

CLAUDE M'KAY.
(*Photo by Cleary.*)

A FIERCE HATRED OF INJUSTICE

Claude McKay's Jamaica and his Poetry of Rebellion

WINSTON JAMES

VERSO

London • New York

First published by Verso 2000
© Winston James 2000
All rights reserved

The moral rights of the author have been asserted

Verso
UK: 6 Meard Street, London W1V 3HR
USA: 180 Varick Street, New York, NY 10014–4606

Verso is the imprint of New Left Books

ISBN 1–85984–740–4

British Library Cataloguing in Publication Data
A catalogue record for this book is available from the British Library

Library of Congress Cataloging-in-Publication Data
A catalog record for this book is available from the Library of Congress

Typeset by M Rules in Berkeley
Printed by R.R. Donnelley & Sons, USA

Frontispiece: Claude McKay, photograph by Cleary,
from the Collections of the National Library of Jamaica

To
Aunt Myrtle and Aunt Patsy
and to
Richard Hart and Cleston Taylor

CONTENTS

Part III: A Selection of McKay's Jamaican Writing

The Work of a Gifted Jamaican: An Interview with Claude McKay 165

Let me confess it at once. I had not in me the stuff that goes to the making of a good constable. . . . We blacks are all somewhat impatient of discipline, and to the natural impatience of my race there was added, in my particular case, a peculiar sensitiveness which made certain forms of discipline irksome, and a fierce hatred of injustice.

Claude McKay, 1912

ACKNOWLEDGEMENTS

This book is part of a larger project on the contribution and political evolution of Claude McKay. Over the years I have accumulated many debts which cannot be repaid but ought to be publicly acknowledged.

I am grateful for the courteous assistance that I received from librarians and archivists in the United States, Britain and Jamaica. I wish to thank those at the Beinecke Rare Book and Manuscript Library, Yale University; the British Library, especially its newspaper division at Colindale; Columbia University libraries, especially the Inter-library Loan Office; the Harry Ransom Humanities Research Center, University of Texas at Austin; the Lilly Library, Manuscripts Department, Indiana University, Bloomington; the Moorland-Spingarn Research Center, Howard University; the Public Record Office, Kew, Surrey; the Schomburg Center for Research in Black Culture, New York Public Library; the West India Reference Library, University of the West Indies, Mona, Jamaica. I owe a special debt to Mrs. Eppie Edwards, Deputy Director of the National Library of Jamaica, for the unfailing kindness and professionalism with which she has dealt with my many inquiries and requests over the years. Richard Smith efficiently and successfully chased down some of the items I was not able to ken myself in London. Cecil Gutzmore provided a similar service in Kingston. I am grateful to them both. Cecil and Carolyn Cooper also organized a seminar at the University of the West Indies, Mona, that allowed me to present some of the ideas contained in this book. I thank them, the Department of English, and the Centre for Caribbean Studies for sponsoring the event, and the participants for their comments.

Anthony Bogues and Robert Hill read an early draft in the form of a long essay and provided helpful comments. Indeed, it was Bobby who suggested that I publish it as a book in its own right. Professor Stuart Hall and the late Professor Eric Mottram of King's College, London, served as external examiners for the dissertation, a section from which this book grew. I drew strength from their enthusiasm for the project and benefited from their suggestions. I am sorry that Eric is not around to see this. George Lamming took the time to read a late draft and I value his generous comments. Varese Layzer copy-edited the book and helped in improving it. Faith Childs, my agent, has saved me much trouble by looking out for my interest.

I was moved by the kindness and hospitality of McKay's relatives in Clarendon when I, a stranger, arrived unannounced in their midst several summers ago. I am especially grateful to Mr. Hartley McKay, Miss Claudette McKay, and Mrs. Icelyn McKay Binger. I also owe a debt of gratitude to Rev. Luke N. Shaw, the pastor of Mount Zion baptist church, for granting me an interview and sharing documents about the history of his church with me. In London, McKay's niece, Mrs. Eloise McKay Edwards, was most generous with her time and memory. The late Carl Cowl, McKay's friend and last literary agent, was a great source of encouragement. He was equally generous with his time and knowledge. He never tired of talking about McKay and his milieu, and spoke of the man and his time not only with knowledge but great insight, too. He opened up McKay's world for me with a unique and unparalleled immediacy.

An active Marxist and Trotskyist right up to his death at the age of 93, Cowl had great sympathy for the political McKay that I have been trying to recover. I could always call him up or pop down to his Brooklyn apartment to talk McKay and share archival findings with him. I miss him and shall always treasure his friendship and generosity.

Much more than a public expression of thanks is, once again, due to Barbara. My extended family, too, will always deserve more than my gratitude. My parents, my brothers and sisters, and my uncles Teddy and Perton have provided invaluable support over the years. I also have to thank Rachel, Marcus, Luke, Anya and Millicent for the special joy that they have brought to their uncle's life. I hope this little book will one day help them to appreciate not only the work of Claude McKay, but also the culture and language of the land of their grandparents. Special thanks are owed two of my aunts, Myrtle and Patsy. Apart from being the beneficiary of their unceasing love and care, I have been privileged since childhood to witness their precious gifts in the use of our native tongue. Poets in their own right, they frequently entered my thoughts as I wrote this book. An mi know seh dem is livin proof dat dem fool-fool people no know wha dem a chat bout when dem seh dat fi wi Jamaican language impavrish an no ha no range. Mi auntie dem mek mi know seh when people chat dem saught a chat, a rubbish dem a chat. I therefore dedicate this book to my Aunt Myrtle and Aunt Patsy. I also dedicate it to two very special and unsung heroes of the Jamaican working-class movement, Richard Hart and Cleston Taylor, who also happen to be ardent admirers of Claude McKay's poetry. Dick and Cleston have never forsaken the Caribbean working class and, even in exile and old age, they have worked tirelessly and selflessly to promote its cause. Veterans of the Jamaican labor movement stretching back to the 1930s, in exile they founded together Caribbean Labour Solidarity in London some thirty years ago and, through thick and mainly thin, have remained steadfast in supporting the struggle of the poor and exploited in the Caribbean.

Dick and Cleston deserve to be better known, appreciated and celebrated. They will always deserve more and better than what I have to offer, but this is one way in which I can publicly express my admiration and appreciation of their efforts.

PROLOGUE

A t'ink buccra ha' jawed enuff.
Claude McKay, "Peasants' Ways o' Thinkin'," 1912

One of the most versatile and distinguished intellectuals to emerge from the African diaspora, Claude McKay (1889–1948) is most widely remembered, at home as well as abroad, as a poet. McKay would have preferred to have it this way. Despite his remarkable accomplishments as a novelist, essayist, social and political critic and activist, his identity as a poet was the one that was most precious to him, the one that he was proudest of, and the one that he felt most at home with. "Poetry had picked me as a medium," he once told Bernard Shaw, "instead of my picking poetry as a profession." A militant rationalist, McKay lost his Enlightenment poise when it came to explaining his poetic calling. "I was born to be a poet," he declared.[1] And he was deadly serious.

But even though it is widely known that McKay's poetic output began well before he left his island home—he began writing at the age of ten—and despite the fact that it is generally acknowledged that McKay was profoundly shaped by the Jamaica of his childhood and youth, no sustained and comprehensive analysis of his Jamaican poetry exists. His anthologies *Songs of Jamaica* and *Constab Ballads*, both published in 1912,[2] are more known *about* than really

known—even by McKay scholars.[3] And these scholars, especially
the literary critics, have drawn upon his autobiographical writings
and fiction more than his poetry in analyzing McKay's Jamaican
world and worldview.[4] The reason for this inattention is not readily
apparent. The relative unavailability of *Songs of Jamaica* and *Constab
Ballads*[5] and the linguistic challenges that they pose to those who do
not speak or understand the Jamaican in which they were written,
may help to explain why these volumes have attracted such little
notice. But whatever the reasons for their being ignored, *Songs of
Jamaica* and *Constab Ballads* have not received the attention they
merit. McKay's poetic output published in the Jamaican press, most
of which has never been anthologized, is even less known.[6] This is
unfortunate, for not only do his Jamaican poems constitute a large
and important portion of his *oeuvre*, they provide a window on
McKay's Jamaica and the infant stages of his political evolution.
And if we are interested in trying to understand the political
development of the young Claude McKay, as I am here, then, by
default, our primary and most precious documents for such
an undertaking are his early poems. For there are not extant
contemporaneous letters, essays, or even reportage of any real
substance by or on the young McKay before he left for the United
States in 1912—nothing to provide one with an *entrée* into his
political and inner life except his poems.

Autobiographical recollections exist—*My Green Hills of Jamaica*
most notably—but, by definition, these were written long after the
events they describe.[7] And along with genuine insights, such remi-
niscences also inevitably bring their attendant freight of silences,
forgetting, distortions and suppressions. Such writings are far from
valueless but for an understanding of McKay's political ideology
they cannot rival his contemporary writings, which took the exclu-
sive form of poetry.[8] If we reasonably assume that poems written in
1911 and 1912 are far more accurate guides to the poet's thoughts
and feelings at that time than the considered reminiscences of the
period—composed some twenty-five or thirty-five years later (*A*

Long Way From Home and *My Green Hills of Jamaica*)—then it follows that *Songs of Jamaica* and *Constab Ballads*, along with poems published by the author in the press, combine to constitute the unrivaled foundation for the understanding of the politics of the young McKay. Later autobiographical writings which reflect upon the pre-migration period of his life are helpful and will be used in my analysis but they are of marginal utility compared to the poetry. Accordingly, it is primarily through the examination of these artistic works that one is able to identify McKay's political preoccupations and to gauge his political sympathies and antipathies with any degree of reliability and success.

Fortunately, many of these texts, as I shall demonstrate, are political—versified commentary on social and political conditions and events—and are thus especially amenable to historical analysis. Apart from the pleasure that it provides, at least to this reader, McKay's poetry holds the key to a deeper understanding of the man and the Jamaican world in which he lived.

Many of the poems are disappointing in their form. But this failing—the preoccupation with rhyme, the inconsistency of poetic voice, and so on—is more than compensated for by McKay's acutely observant eye. But this is not meant to be a text of literary criticism; others are better qualified than I to carry out work under the protocols (whatever they may be these days) of that discipline. I am far more interested in the content. In the epilogue I do say something about the wider context within which any adequate discussion of form in McKay's Jamaican poetry ought to take place. It has been stimulated primarily by my dissatisfaction with the way in which the matter has been handled hitherto.

The ambition of this little book is modest. *A Fierce Hatred of Injustice* is aimed at illuminating the Jamaican world in which McKay lived, giving those who are familiar only with his post-Jamaican writings the wherewithal to recognize the continuities as well as the discontinuities with those and the products of his earlier years. Above all, it is aimed at shedding light upon the politics of the young McKay as they evolved while he was still in Jamaica. Finally, I also hope that the book stimulates further work in the highly fertile but inexplicably under-attended field of Caribbean intellectual and political life in the late nineteenth and early twentieth centuries.

PART I

BEGINNINGS

A JAMAICAN CHILDHOOD AND YOUTH, 1889 TO 1912

McKay was born in the remote and stunningly beautiful upcountry of Clarendon.[1] His village, Nairne Castle, comprising twenty families during his childhood, nestles in a lovely spot surrounded on almost every side by the serried, blue-green hills of central Jamaica. Though somewhat hilly, the land around Nairne Castle is kind to its inhabitants. Lush and fertile, its red soil is well watered by a river and small, gentle-flowing streams issue from the hills around. Clarendon's special qualities have long been recognized and praised. As early as the 1770s, planter-historian Edward Long, who owned a large estate not far from where Nairne Castle now sits, noted that "[t]he hills rise gradually in height the further we advance into the heart of the parish; yet here none so steep or barren, as not to be fit for culture of some sort or other. The vales between the hills and mountains are in general spacious, watered by some river, and enriched with fine caneland."[2] But over the centuries, the Afro-Jamaican peasantry, especially those who sought refuge in the island's interior after emancipation, have used the fecundity of the vales for far more than the cultivation of sugar, the planters class's crop par excellence. Thus, in Nairne Castle, the peasant's crop—bananas, coffee, oranges, mangoes, yams, sweet potatoes and a host of other fruits and vegetables—are cultivated and seem to grow as easily now as they did in McKay's time—"as if spilled straight out of the Hand of God."[3]

Perhaps it is only through seeing the countryside in the area McKay was born that one can acquire a true appreciation of why the poet celebrated it in song with such gusto and persistence. The physical beauty of McKay's Clarendon, which exceeded by far what I had previously imagined, is extraordinary—even for an island as extravagantly endowed with nature's splendors as Jamaica is. But nature does not always smile on Nairne Castle. Apart from the periodic fury of tropical storms and hurricanes, areas of the little village are peculiarly prone to flooding, especially after heavy rains. And the physical magnificence of upper Clarendon has always been marred by the social inequality determining access to the soil.

Born on September 15 1889, Claude was the last of eleven children born to Hannah Ann Elizabeth Edwards McKay and Thomas Francis McKay.[4] Eight of the children, seven boys and one girl, lived to maturity. An atypical family, the McKays were very dark skinned. In the islander's color scheme, which obtains to this very day, the McKays would be called "black", as opposed to not only "white," but also "light skinned" or "brown". One of the reasons the McKays stood out was the fact that they were black *and* relatively well-off, indeed prosperous. This was a rare combination, for they lived in a Jamaica in which the masses of black Jamaicans, especially the darkest ones, were not only poor, but often desperate.

McKay's Jamaica

During McKay's time on the island, the majority of its people were tested by the greatest hardship. Much of the suffering resulted from Jamaica's economic crisis in the late nineteenth century and the collapse of its economic mainstay, sugar. The sugar industry, the raison d'être for the British colonization of the island in 1655, lay prostrate. Outdone by Cuban and Brazilian cane sugar, substituted by beet sugar in Europe, and mercilessly exposed to international market forces by Britain's removal of tariffs against its rivals, King Sugar was well and truly dethroned in Jamaica by 1889.

In 1836 the price of Jamaican sugar stood at 41 shillings per hundredweight. It went up to as high as 48 shillings in 1840 but for the rest of the century it followed a sharply downward trend, falling to 11.25 shillings per hundredweight by 1900.[5] It was only with the First World War's inadverdent devastation of Europe's broad acres of sugar beet that an increase in the price of sugar occurred—and the favorable prices did not last much longer than the war itself.

The fall in the number of sugar estates on the island was even more precipitous. From 670 in 1836 the number dropped to an estimated 162 in 1890 and dwindled to 74 by 1910.[6] Between 1838 and 1890 Jamaica's annual sugar export fell by over 64 per cent.[7] Although there were many cases of amalgamation and consolidation of estates during the nineteenth century, the area under sugar cultivation nevertheless shrank considerably. Within the space of only a generation—between 1869 and 1900—it had declined by 45 per cent.[8]

But the decline of sugar was not evenly distributed across the island. King Sugar strategically retreated to the western plains of Jamaica while still maintaining a foothold in the flatlands of southern Clarendon, not far from where McKay was born. Under the whip of international competition, members of the island's ruling class embarked upon ruthless capitalist reorganization and rationalization.[9] Consequently, although the number of sugar estates substantially declined, the average size of the surviving ones increased by almost 60 per cent between 1880 and 1910.[10] Partly as a result of these changes, the average yield per acre also increased by over 24 per cent between 1846 and 1896. And with the amalgamation of the estates, the average output per sugar factory doubled between 1880 and 1910.[11] One consequence of this dialectic of decline was job losses. Between 1891 and 1911 male employment in the sugar industry fell by just under a third.[12] And this had repercussions far beyond the well-being of the unemployed: families and relatives relied upon the wages of the lucky ones who had work, one wage feeding many mouths.

During the last two decades of the nineteenth century, a new agricultural sector had emerged almost overnight, eclipsing sugar with astonishing rapidity. This was the "banana trade," as it was called. Introduced into Jamaica in the sixteenth century, the banana was a humble but valued fruit cultivated primarily by slaves on their provision grounds and by their descendants, the black peasantry, in the post-emancipation era. The Gros Michel, introduced from Martinique in the nineteenth century, quickly emerged as the most successful variety.

To flourish, the banana needs fertile soil with vegetable mold along with good rainfall and drainage. It therefore thrived in the "black soils" of Portland, St. Mary, St. Thomas, and St. Catherine— areas with the heaviest rainfall, the eastern parishes of Jamaica.[13] Up to the late 1870s, the banana remained an essentially peasant crop. According to Lord Olivier, a former governor of the island, banana cultivation was "despised as a backwoods 'nigger business,' which any old-time sugar planter would have disdained to handle, or, if tempted by undeniable prospects of profit, would have thought an apology was required."[14] Thus in 1879, only one large estate was under banana cultivation.[15] However, large-scale banana cultivation began the following year. Jamaican merchants and professionals "whom their neighbours regarded as cranks," Olivier tells us, moved into the "nigger business" on a grand scale;[16] fourteen of St. Thomas' eighteen sugar estates had changed over to banana cultivation by 1899.[17] There was money to be made. In the fertile up-country of Clarendon, Thomas McKay and many of his peasant neighbors became deeply involved in banana cultivation. In subsequent years, McKay's eldest brother, Uriah Theodore (known to all as U. Theo), would leave his profession as schoolmaster and become a banana grower and agent.

The revolution in banana cultivation and marketing was initiated by an American, Lorenzo Dow Baker, who, unburdened by the historical snobbery of sugar cultivation, had proven in 1871 the feasibility and profitability of large-scale banana cultivation and shipment to the United States. By the 1880s, acutely aware of the profits to be made, Baker was busy purchasing and leasing thousands of acres in eastern Jamaica for the cultivation and export of bananas. Others were to follow in Baker's footsteps in the banana trade, but the Bostonian and his corporate creations, the Boston Fruit Company (which later developed into the notorious United Fruit Company), were not to be denied. Beneath his beatific New England smile was the mind of a ruthless and shrewd capitalist.[18] But it was not only his capitalist rivals who were punished and vanquished by Baker: the peasants of eastern Jamaica suffered an historic defeat at his hands. Baker had friends in high places: he was aided and abetted by the colonial state and Joseph Chamberlain's policy of encouraging large land-holdings in the British Caribbean.[19]

The area under banana cultivation in 1894 was just under half that under sugar cane. But within only six years, the acreage of banana plantations exceeded that of sugar. The rise in banana cultivation was meteoric. From 2,000 stems in 1869, Jamaica was producing in 1900 an astonishing 8,248,000 stems of banana.[20] In 1870 sugar accounted for 44.5 per cent of the island's export earnings whereas banana claimed less than one tenth of 1 per cent of such earnings. By 1900 banana had become the island's most important agricultural export earner, bringing in more than three times the amount earned by sugar, and almost double the combined earnings of sugar and rum. Ten years later banana furnished more than half of Jamaica's export earnings, three times the amount sugar and rum together brought into the island.[21] By 1911 banana employed

77 per cent more people than the sugar industry did.[22] The island was the world's premier producer of bananas for over two generations, from 1876 to 1929, when it fell behind Honduras.[23]

However, as intimated, the consequences of the expansion of banana cultivation under Baker's de facto hegemony were not all happy ones. With initially high prices, Baker lured the peasantry of St. Mary, Portland and St. Thomas into agreements to exclusively supply his company with bananas. Having captured the market, he then controlled the prices.[24] Baker instructed his agents to bargain hard with the peasant producers. And by insisting that the producers bring their fruit to the ports, he not only avoided the cost of transportation, but also adroitly obviated the risk and cost of damage—such as the all too common bruising—of the bananas en route; the suppliers, the small peasants, would bear these burdens. Baker was profoundly aware of the powerful position that he had successfully maneuvred himself into: "You need not make any extra exertion for bananas," he told his son. "Tell the people if they wish to sell their fruit they must bring it down." Baker briefed his agents to accept only top-quality bananas, and to reject all fruit deemed below his prescribed standards. "Never mind what people say," Baker told his son, "throw it back on their barrels, let them suffer for it if they will not mind you."[25]

In addition, Baker's Boston Fruit Company and later the United Fruit Company, through their various acquisition of land, significantly contributed to the raising of the price of land beyond the reach of the peasantry. Indeed, some were reduced to becoming tenants on Baker's estates.[26]

But Baker's impact on the peasantry and agro-proletarians did not end there: the rapid expansion of banana cultivation and the extensive irrigation it demanded meant that malaria—a disease carried by mosquitoes which breed in stagnant water—became more prevalent in the eastern parishes. Indeed, according to one authority: "the extension of banana cultivation to some of the areas . . . made malaria a *typical* disease of banana workers.[27]

While Thomas McKay and his family were successfully climbing the island's socio-economic ladder, the vast majority of the Jamaican peasantry were losing their footing on its brittle lower rungs, falling deeper into poverty and despair as the nineteenth century wore on. And Thomas's ascendancy was not unrelated to the decline of his neighbors.

In his pioneering study of land transactions in Jamaica between 1866 and 1900, Veront Satchell has shown in laudable detail the mechanisms through which the peasantry was systematically squeezed during this period. The 1860s marked the expansion and consolidation of peasant holdings, the partial result of the Morant Bay uprising of 1865. This peasant expansion occurred in spite of the fact that through the removal of "squatters" there were numerous losers amongst the peasantry.[28] Small holders (those in possession of land five acres or less in size) were sold public land—"crown land," land which came under the control of the state—at five times the price paid by large landowners (those with over five hundred acres.) Indeed, while large properties were sold at an average of 8 shillings per acre, small lots attracted prices of 45 shillings per acre.[29] This was partly due to the fact that from the 1870s to the 1890s the colonial government had a policy of selling land in large tracts, which the peasantry, needless to say, could not afford. And so when small units came on the market there was fierce competition between members of the peasantry to acquire them.[30] Thus only a quarter of the lots sold in the 1870s were under fifty acres, and in the 1880s just one-sixth were holdings under fifty acres.[31] The land procured by the peasantry was far less fertile, more hilly and less accessible than that acquired by the merchants and planters. Furthermore, the expansion of crown land inflicted a devastating blow upon the peasants. It artificially reduced the supply of land, thus increasing its price. Between 1867 and 1912 some 240,000 acres had reverted to the colonial government as crown land. This vigorous consolidation was concentrated at the very end of the century—more than half the total area had reverted to the Crown during the seven years between 1894 and 1901.[32]

Given these policies and trends, it comes as no surprise that by the mid 1890s eighty-one individuals had become the owners of no less than 97 per cent of the area of rural land offered by the government for sale. A similar dynamic of expansion and consolidation of large plantations at the expense of small holders occurred in private land transactions over the same period.[33] It was not surprising either that by the end of the nineteenth century the peasantry was acquiring considerably less land than it had been in the 1860s. They were boxed in by corporate capital and a resurgent plantocracy. With the exception of parts of the Windward Islands, this was characteristic of the anglophone Caribbean at the turn of the century. Woodville Marshall describes the period as one of "saturation," when the peasantry in the entire area failed to expand its holdings and, indeed, experienced contraction in a number of instances, including in Jamaica.[34]

With the boom in banana cultivation, it became more and more difficult for small holders to acquire land in the banana parishes. By 1900 four landholders, including Baker, came to acquire over 65,000 acres of land in the principal banana parishes.[35] In addition to this, the colonial government had offered 76,800 acres of land (79 per cent of which was in Portland and St. Thomas) to an American syndicate, the West Indian Improvement Company, for extending the island's railway by 116 miles.[36]

Thus although the McKays did not live in one of the premier banana parishes, Thomas McKay's extensive acquisition of land during this period of contraction of the black peasantry was decidedly against the general trend. According to Claude McKay's account, Thomas McKay was also one of the indirect beneficiaries of the misfortunes of the poorer people. "He was always ready to snap up a piece of land that was for sale through the death of its owner or its being encumbered by taxes."[37] Between 1869 and 1900, the colonial regime ejected and repossessed from so-called "peasant squatters" some six thousand acres of land in the parish of Clarendon alone. Clarendon had by far the largest area of land repossessed in this way of any parish, accounting for more than a third of the national total. Moreover, during the same period, of Jamaica's fourteen parishes, Clarendon had the largest number of peasant squatters ejected—just under 29 per cent of the island's total.[38] Clarendon was perhaps the most favorable area in Jamaica for one in Thomas McKay's position and with his ambition: bargains were to be had if one got to the encumbered peasants a step ahead of the bailiff.

By the time Claude McKay left Jamaica in 1912, his father had established himself as a relatively prosperous, progressive commercial farmer with at least one hundred acres of fertile land. By this time also, Thomas McKay had his own little sugar mill, one of the coveted Chattanooga mills, so called because they were built in the Tennessee town of the same name. He also had his own boiler and sugar house in which he manufactured sugar; he had earlier acquired his own dray and mules for transporting his produce to far-off markets.[39] Thus, from being an illiterate and humble road mender at the time of his marriage in 1870, Thomas McKay, through his exertions, shrewd business sense and primitive accumulation in the Clarendon countryside, had transformed himself by 1912 into a prosperous capitalist farmer. Although Claude McKay would always describe himself as a son of the Jamaican peasantry, by the time he left the island his family's economic position defied such definition.

If the McKays were a breed apart from the Clarendon peasants by whom they were surrounded, even more remote was their economic position from that of the Jamaican proletariat. Thomas had come out of that world but, by the time Claude was born, he had long escaped its harsh confinement.

In 1838—the year slavery finally came to an end (with the close of the apprenticeship system)—an agricultural worker could expect to earn between 7 and 14 pence for a day's labor. In 1890 the figure was between 9 and 21 pence and in 1910 the range was 6 to 18.[40] *Nominal*—not to mention real—agricultural wages remained stagnant over three generations. The African Jamaicans had left the realm of chattel slavery only to enter a world of wage slavery—with hardly any wages at all.

During the Kingston dock workers' strike of 1895, one of these black proletarians wrote to the *Gleaner* to plead his case, that of his striking comrades and his class:

> I ask you to occupy a space in your paper concerning the striking of the labourers. We the labouring classes do strike for higher wages, for we are under the advantage of the Agents of ships. We asked for more wages so that we may be able to sustain ourselves and our families in a respectable manner. We have to support our families, pay rent, and tax and water rates. Our Island will increase more. It will enable us to spend more, and the merchants will receive more, for we will be able to pay our tax, and in a better way. We won't be having to trouble the Governments often for coffins, and hole for the burial of the dead; we will be able to bury them ourselves if we get suitable wages. The Alms House won't be having so much paupers on the list. All those owing from the want of more wages. Look at our sister island of Trinidad, where the labouring classes are getting 5 [shillings] per day and feeding, then why we Jamaicans can't do the same, we are not behind hand, we been suffering a long time under the tyranny of small wages, so it is time now we look around ourselves . . . We mean to be determined for good wages, in our Island—and everybody will inherit the benefit thereof. Three and two shillings are no pay at all for a working man. There are more stealing going on now than if we were getting good wages, if we got good pay, there is no need for us to steal; but on account of the wages is so small, we have to steal, we are going to prison and disgrace ourselves.[41]

Some twenty years later, E. Ethelred Brown, an educated black man who emerged from the Jamaican peasantry, summed up the depth of oppression and poverty that the masses of his compatriots had sunk to. He acknowledged that some progress had been made since emancipation but the majority of laborers, the men and women and children who till the banana fields and work on the sugar plantations, are no better off than previously. These are still beasts of burden, still the victims of an economic system under which they labor not as human beings with bodies to be fed or clothed, with minds to be cultivated and aspiring souls to be ministered unto, but as living machines designed only to plant so many banana suckers in an hour, or to carry so many loads of canes in a day. After seventy-eight years in this fair island, side by side with the progress and improvements . . . referred to, there are still hundreds and hundreds of men and women who live like savages in unfloored huts, huddled together like beasts of the field, without regard to health or comfort. And they live thus, not because they are worthless or because they are wholly without ambition or desire to live otherwise, but because they must thus continue as economic slaves receiving still the miserable pittance of a wage of eighteen pence or 36 cents a day that was paid to their forefathers at the dawn of emancipation.[42]

Brown was by no means alone in the articulation of such views. There were others, including, as we shall see, McKay's eldest brother and mentor, U. Theo McKay, as well as the young Claude himself.

But despite the protests, poverty and hunger stalked the land. The constraints placed upon the poor and the working class by their powerful white overlords were formidable. Wages were kept down partially through the planter class's importation of indentured laborers from India and China. Tied to the plantations through harsh labor contracts, they lacked the bargaining power of the former slaves. When Jamaican workers tried to escape to Panama to work on the canal, and to find work in Cuba, Costa Rica and elsewhere, the authorities placed obstacles in their way, taxing them and demanding deposits conditional for departure. Hundreds of thousands, however, made the sacrifice and escaped to what they regarded as greener pastures—which were not so green after all. Others sought a new life in Kingston only to find appalling conditions there too.

In keeping with the general trend of the time, the proportion of the island's labour force employed in agriculture—including the peasantry—declined. From an estimated 68 per cent in 1871 it fell to just over 58 per cent by 1911. At the same time those employed in "domestic service" increased from 10 to 15 per cent.[43] These developments reflected the disruptive effect of agrarian capitalism in the late nineteenth century. While powerful enough to disturb, uproot and displace the peasants, capitalist transformation in the countryside was insufficiently dynamic to absorb and transform them into fully fledged agrarian proletarians. And in the absence of a rapidly expanding manufacturing sector to absorb their labor power, many of the displaced peasants and rural workers reappeared, especially in the towns, as domestic servants, as petty traders, as prostitutes and, of course, as the chronically unemployed—that category that Marx described as the "lazarus-layer" of the working class—those mercilessly disgorged and thrown to the winds by capitalist upheaval.[44] In 1891 less than one in five female workers in Kingston and St. Andrew (Jamaica's largest urban center) was a domestic servant, by 1911 it was one in four, and by 1921 it was nearly one in three.[45] According to economist Gisela Eisner,

> [t]he large increase in female domestic servants was no evidence of a high standard of living enjoyed by a small sector of the community. On the contrary, it was the response of a much wider community to the needs of surplus rural population. By the end of the century the custom had grown to provide shelter, food and training to "school-girls" in return for service. This cheap labour supply enabled far lower income groups to enjoy personal services than is usually found in more fully developed societies.[46]

But considerably less reciprocity inhered in such arrangements than Eisner suggests. Abuse and exploitation more typically defined the lot of domestic servants. Employers quite often took advantage of the economic vulnerability of domestics. This is a subject that McKay, who lived in Kingston at the time, had much to say about. In late- and post-Victorian Jamaica even relatively humble persons indulged in conspicuous consumption and keeping-up-with-the-Joneses at the expense of their domestic servants. "It will be apparent," one contemporary observed in 1913, "that if out of a population of less than nine hundred thousand, most of whom serve themselves, the number of domestics is forty thousand, almost everybody who has the slightest pretensions to be considered anybody employs a servant. In fact, you are not respectable if you have not a servant. That at least is one law of Jamaica life."[47]

As was the case in the number of domestic servants, so also the growth in petty traders did not mean a general increase in prosperity. On the contrary, as people became more desperate, many turned to petty trading, especially in the urban areas. Black, working-class Jamaican women figured prominently in this practice and, like their sisters in domestic service, the number of female petty traders increased dramatically during the period, doubling between 1891 and 1911.[48] They became more visible than ever in Kingston and McKay wrote some of his finest poems about them.

Despite the revolt of the Jamaican peasants at Morant Bay in 1865,[49] one of whose main contributory causes was the conspicuously unfair taxation system, such a system was to remain essentially unchanged during McKay's time in Jamaica, and indeed well into the twentieth century. Between 1870 and 1910 custom-and-excise duties—regressive *per se* (they are exacted regardless of income) but made doubly so by the higher rate imposed on items consumed by the masses—accounted for between 70 and 80 per cent of government revenue. There was no income tax. In the 1890s the tax on housing was so designed that "the heaviest burden [fell] on the poorest class." As Eisner noted, "If the criterion of a just system of taxation is ability to pay then the Jamaican system could not be called just. The same rate of duty was payable irrespective of income and no attempt was made to single out for higher taxes the commodities consumed or property owned by the better-off."[50]

There was virtually no access to healthcare for the overwhelming majority of people. Doctors were few and far between, and they charged exorbitant fees. It therefore comes as no surprise that given the conditions under which ordinary people existed—including the abysmally low wages paid to workers—that their health deteriorated.

Infant mortality increased by more than 21 per cent between the mid 1880s and 1910.[51] In 1910, 70 per cent of the population suffered from hookworm.[52]

Legitimate avenues for protest were few. In the aftermath of the Morant Bay revolt, the Jamaican Assembly abolished itself to suppress parliamentary protests of the type articulated by George William Gordon on behalf of the poor. The governor exercised absolute power under the Crown Colony system implemented in 1865. In 1884 the terms of rule were modified, allowing for an elective element, but the governor retained a majority in the legislature and executive branches of government. Thus the right to vote was introduced but it was tightly restricted and therefore ineffectual, as it was meant to be.

Thomas McKay was a member of that rare species of men in *fin de siècle* Jamaica: an African prosperous enough to qualify to vote under this highly restrictive franchise. The financial qualifications to vote were so prohibitive that of a population of 600,000 only 9,176 were registered voters in 1884—a mere 1.5 per cent of the population. In 1901, when the population was estimated at 756,000, there were only 16,256 registered voters—hardly an improvement.[53] The franchise, clearly skewed in favor of merchants, landowners and attorneys (the majority of whom were European and Levantine in origin), worked against the Africans who comprised the majority of the population. Among the non-Europeans, the "coloureds" (meaning those of "mixed" descent) were wealthier than the "Negroes" (Africans) and, somewhat like the whites, were disproportionately represented by votes. They made up less than a fifth of the population but accounted for over a third of all the registered voters. In 1886 the black portion of the Jamaican population was conservatively estimated to be more than three fourths yet only half the registered voters were black Jamaicans. In contrast, the white population, which amounted to just over two out of every hundred inhabitants, accounted for more than thirteen of every hundred registered voters. And this was so even though many of the whites who were qualified did not bother to register, and, of those who registered, few bothered to vote.[54] (They probably calculated, and not incorrectly, that their vital interests were well taken care of without the charade and inconvenience of going to the polling station.) While less than one in every hundred black Jamaicans was eligible to vote, more than two of every hundred coloureds and seven of every hundred whites were registered to vote.[55]

As if the veto power of the British governor, and the cabal of oligarchs around him, were not enough, black Jamaicans were disenfranchised even further after 1893 as literacy tests and hard times knocked them off the voter registration rolls. From a peak of 42,266 in 1893–94, the number of registered voters declined to 16,256 in 1901, to 8,607 in 1905–06. And in 1910–11, the year before McKay left for the United States, there were only 27,257 voters out of a population of 831,383.[56]

Women were not allowed to vote in Jamaica until 1919. Before the bill was passed into law, the Governor, Sir Leslie Probyn, suggested that the vote should be given to women only with "safe and rigid qualifications."[57] When the franchise was conceded to women in May 1919, they had to be 25 years old (one member of the Legislative Council had proposed 30); men had to be 21. While one of the qualifications for men to vote was the paying of taxes, or rates, on real property amounting to no less than ten shillings per year, women were required to be paying such taxes amounting to no less than two pounds.[58] On the grounds of their sex alone women were banned from running for public office, local or national. Whereas men who had registered before 1893 need not be literate to vote, all women had to be. Needless to say, the vast majority of black Jamaican women were thus denied the right to vote. And this was the object of those who agitated for women suffrage, including the white women who made their voices heard.[59]

Universal adult suffrage did not come until 1944; only after the masses had revolted, shaking the colonial edifice of Jamaica to its very foundations, frightening their overlords into making political concessions.[60] Thomas McKay, then, was one of a tiny minority within a tiny minority. This status no doubt contributed to the quiet self-confidence of Thomas and his family.

The McKays

The McKays made extraordinary social advances in less than a generation. From the small plot of land Hannah Ann's father gave the couple on their marriage, the McKays accumulated more than one hundred fertile acres by the time Claude left the island in 1912—as well as livestock, drays and the sugar mill. The couple, proud and aspiring, ensured that all their children got a good education. They were successful: all their children barring one, who pursued farming, became professionals and white-collar workers. Over the years several of them made it into *Who's Who in Jamaica*. Their success was reinforced in the subsequent generation.

Despite their relative wealth and independent economic base, the McKays still came up against the colorism that prevailed in Jamaica at the time. Unlike the black poor and most of the less well-heeled emergent black middle classes, the McKays spoke out. Shielded by their material resources, it was relatively difficult for their enemies, including the white oligarchy, to punish them.

Thomas and Hannah McKay, their dark skin notwithstanding, enjoyed the highest respect of their community in rural Clarendon as members of the "respectable peasantry."[61] McKay tells us that Thomas was "something of a village leader, as they have in Africa." Because he was "a very just man," instead of going to court, villagers would often ask Thomas to arbitrate and settle their differences; his rulings were generally obeyed. Mr. McKay was very strict about the law and "hated" dishonesty and trickery.[62] A deeply religious man, he served as a deacon in the local baptist church—a position of great prestige within the community. Claude McKay recalled that, although his mother was in her forties, all the villagers called her "Mother Mac . . . a great mark of love because only certain native women are honoured with this distinctive title." Mrs. McKay was also a church leader, directing the women's prayer meetings. Women often visited the McKay home to discuss church business with her.[63]

McKay loved and admired his mother deeply and she him: "I was the baby of the family and the favourite of my mother."[64] (Indeed, there is some indication from McKay's own writings that his mother spoiled him as a boy.)[65] A certain sadness overshadowed their relationship, however, as McKay wrote almost forty years after Hannah Ann's death: "One thing I do remember sharply is that my mother was ill and it was generally said that she became ill right after I was born."[66] He never said so explicitly, but McKay evidently felt personally responsible for his mother's illness and early death: a burden he never relinquished. In *Banana Bottom*, McKay's novel of Jamaican peasant life, the mother died at the heroine's birth. "The village folk said that she had killed her mother. That was the way the black peasants referred to a child that survived when the mother had died giving birth to it."[67]

Carl Cowl, McKay's friend and last literary agent, said that McKay also felt guilty because not only did his mother die early, but McKay was not at her bedside when she died. Young Claude had left his mother for a short time to go to the field and she died before he returned. It was always with self-recriminating anguish that McKay remembered the circumstances of his mother's death.[68] He devoted a number of fine poems to her memory and when he went to America his first works were published under the nom de plume of Eli Edwards, a masculinization of his mother's maiden name, Elizabeth Edwards. "My Mother" tells the story of Hannah Ann's last moments:

> Reg wished me to go with him to the field;
> I paused because I did not want to go,
> But in her quiet way she made me yield
> Reluctantly,—for she was breathing low.
> Her hand she slowly lifted from her lap
> And, smiling sadly in the old sweet way,
> She pointed to the nail where hung my cap;
> Her eyes said: I shall last another day.

But scarcely had we reached the distant place
When o'er the hills we heard a faint bell ringing,
A boy came running up with frightened face,
We knew the fatal news that he was bringing.
I heard him listlessly and made no moan,
Although the only one I loved was gone.[69]

"I always thought my mother was very beautiful," he wrote. "She was round faced and brown skinned with two plaits of curls one on each side of her head." She was also "a wonderful person:"

She was especially nice to the young girls who had produced babies out of wedlock. She used to give them food and clean rags. These girls were likely to be snubbed by the older married women who were in the church and considered themselves very respectable. Although my mother was a deaconess in the church, she treated those girls just as she would anybody else.

McKay underlined the virtuousness of his mother: "Perhaps the quality most prominent in my mother was her goodness. She loved people and believed in being kind to everybody."[70] She "didn't care very much about what people did and why and how they did it. She only wanted to help those who were outcast, poor and miserable."[71] His brother Thomas, who became an Anglican pastor, remarked to McKay twenty years after his mother's death, "I hope you have not forgotten God and you are following dear mother's footsteps."[72] McKay's letter responding to his brother has not survived but he might well have told him that he had forgotten God many years earlier—McKay had become a proselytizing freethinker while a teenager—but that he had always attempted, however unsuccessfully, to follow in his mother's footsteps.

McKay's attitude towards his father differed radically from the warmth that he felt for his mother. In his autobiography he often contrasts his parents—invariably to his father's disadvantage. The warm, generous and loving mother is juxtaposed with the cold, remote, "very stern and upright" father who "believed in justice, a kind of Anglo-Saxon justice." All the children preferred Mrs. McKay, "who was so much more elastic and understanding. . . . My father, however, was a Presbyterian Calvinist. A real black Scotchman. We boys wondered how his education could have made him that way. He was so entirely different from all our colored neighbors with their cockish-liquor drinking [sic] and rowdy singing . . . So top-lofty, one might say."[73] While Mrs. McKay always took the children's side in dealings with her husband, Mr McKay was not averse to meting out corporal punishment to his children.[74] Claude McKay showed he knew how to confront authority—not for the last time.

> I could not reconcile myself to the fact that even though I was fourteen years old, my father wanted to whip me. I was very impertinent and said to him one day: "You cannot whip me, sir. I am a man." He promptly tied me to a post and dropped my pants. He went to get his strap. When I saw him coming I started to curse and use every swear word that a small boy could think of. My father who was a deacon of the church was so shocked that he said: "I can't whip the boy. Why he's gone crazy!" He left me tied there and went off to the fields. It was the last time he ever tied me up or laid a hand on me.[75]

It would be a mistake to deduce from all this that McKay did not respect his father although he may not have loved or even liked him. But the evidence suggests that McKay's depiction of the relationship with his father in *My Green Hills of Jamaica* was more negative than it was in reality.[76] In his correspondence with other members of his family, especially U. Theo and his sister Rachel, McKay consistently asked after his father.[77] He repeatedly requested a photograph of him, and his siblings promised they would send one. "I will try to send you [father's] picture," U. Theo told him in April 1929. But in August of the same year U. Theo wrote: "I saw father about three days after I got your letter and . . . he said that he has not heard anything about money for photograph." "You will soon get father's photo," his sister Rachel informed him in December 1929. "Thanks for the photographs," Claude wrote in August 1932 to Nancy Cunard, who was on a visit to Jamaica. "Sorry you did not get one of Father. Been asking my brother for one for three years."[78] One does not seek so assiduously and persistently the photograph of a father one detests.

McKay did respect his father. He was proud of the old man's remarkable accomplishments and principled positions. And he acknowledged that Thomas did his best—if only in his own peculiar way—for his eight dark-skinned children in a society riddled with colorism, if not downright racism.[79] Thomas was ambitious for his children and made it very clear to his seven sons: "I am not educating my boys for any of these village girls no matter how pretty they might be. . . . I never did run around with girls and I've never known another woman besides your mother. And God helping me, never will." He kept his word, even though he survived his wife by twenty-four years. But his sons had different ideas: "All of us went after the village girls."[80] McKay relates with admiration and pride his father's bold stand against a hypocritical Scottish missionary:

> Mount Zion was a Baptist church. The Baptists are very strict about drinking, smoking, dancing and, as they feel, about other sins. Many of the members had accused this Scotchman of being a heavy smoker; but father who was the head deacon had always said he should not be accused unless the thing could be proved. The Scotch minister, like all the other Baptist preachers, always preached regularly against smoking and drinking and the like. Then one day when father went to visit him in his library he found the place full of smoke. Father said, "It is true then what people say about your smoking?" The Scotchman without batting an eye said that he was not smoking. Father said: "How can you say you are not smoking when we are enveloped in the fog of hell?" So father told him that he wasn't going to bring any charges against him but that he should give up the ministry and leave Mount Zion.[81]

The Scotsman refused. Thomas resigned as deacon and stayed away from church. The villagers rallied round him, most of them boycotting the church. Mount Zion "went down to the devil. And the mountain country became a hell for that missionary. Even the children jeered at him along the roads when he went riding by."[82] Meetings were held by the villagers with the church hierarchy to resolve the crisis. The missionary stoutly refused to heed the congregation's demand and even abused his status of titular head of the Mount Zion church school by firing the local teacher and replacing him with his own wife. Children and parents revolted. Parents sent their children to other schools, even though the other schools were several miles away. To make matters worse, the missionary began doing "things that no other minister had ever done," including embezzling missionary funds for his own use.[83]

Another large members' meeting was convened with the Baptist ministers from the surrounding area all in attendance. The white ones especially urged the minister to leave because "he was bringing a bad name upon all the white clergy." The missionary's wife, who by this time had already sent their two sons off to Canada, decided to leave her husband and take the two remaining children with her. His wife had got on well with the villagers and found herself in an invidious and uncomfortable position. With the pressure piled up on him to the rafters and his wife now threatening to leave him, taking the children with her, the minister finally threw in the towel. The whole affair had lasted no less than five years.[84] On the morning of their departure, the missionary's wife went over to the McKays and she and Hannah Ann "mingled their tears." But when the missionary approached Mr. McKay to shake hands and say goodbye, Mr. McKay said, "I will not shake your hands because they are dirty; and a dirty white hand is the same to me as a dirty coloured hand. *No sir*, I will not shake your hand." So the missionary left. Another minister was appointed, this time a coloured man who had been educated at the Calabar Institution. Thomas went back to the church and was made deacon again.[85]

For McKay, not only did these events symbolize the sturdy character of his father, but they also demonstrated the power of collective action. The struggle for Mount Zion left a profound impression on him. It is not insignificant that the anecdote is told twice: in *A Long Way From Home* and again, a decade later, in *My Green Hills of Jamaica*. McKay was to support the boycott of the Canadian-owned trams in Kingston after a particularly unpopular fare increase in February 1912. His poem on the subject, "Passive Resistance," published in 1912, anticipated the militant defiance of

"If We Must Die" and other poems of protest written in the United States.[86] The example of the Mount Zion battle also echoed in McKay's strong and public support of the boycotting of racist retailers in Harlem during the Depression. The white storeowners in Harlem, whose businesses were concentrated on 125th Street, explicitly refused to employ black people in any except the most menial positions. "Don't Buy Where You Can't Work" became the slogan. Of all Harlem's black intellectuals, McKay provided the most vigorous and passionate defense of the boycotters. He paid a heavy price for this. He was criticized by the left and the right, black and white. George Schuyler, a prominent Afro-American journalist, was among those who accused McKay of being a black fascist. McKay, like the congregation of Mount Zion decades before, remained steadfast.[87]

McKay provides us with other vignettes of his father and their complex relationship. He recalls his father's tenderness on hearing that he had escaped the terrible Kingston earthquake of 1907. In the aftermath of the devastation, McKay took a dray back to Clarendon. He met up with his father near May Pen.

> It was night and he [Thomas] had been calling out to the different drays to see if I was on any of them. Finally he spotted the one which carried me. I remember the drayman stopped and I got off. My father hugged and kissed me. It gave me the strangest feeling—my father's beard against my face—because I had never before been kissed by him. He was always a very stern man; but now he must have felt that I'd escaped from something terribly tragic as he held me in his arms.[88]

Although he frowned upon some of the customs of the peasants— especially the boisterous tea-meetings—the puritanical Thomas never forgot his African roots: "Sometimes when he became angry with us boys for any foolish practice he would say to us: 'Your grandfather . . . was a slave and knew how cruel the white man could be. You boys don't know anything about life.'" He was also a "wonderful teller of African stories," as was Hannah Ann an accomplished teller of anancy stories, the African-derived Jamaican folktales.[89] Of the West African customs his father told, McKay recalled one in particular: "I vividly remember his telling us that when Ashanti mothers gave birth to albino babies they were regarded as types who were mixed up with magic and thus caused bad luck, so they were exposed to die."[90]

Thomas McKay, however, vigorously rejected the magico-religious practice of obeah. (Claude McKay may have exaggerated when he wrote: "My father's family and the Constable's our cousins, were the only two in our village which did not practice the magic of obeah.")[91] What is clear is that McKay heartily approved of the rationalist premise underlying his father's skepticism of the obeah-man. Thomas used to say that "one could be hurt only by being poisoned, or through some other physical contact with an enemy."[92]

McKay also wrote with undisguised awe about his father's stoicism and puritanical behavior. The son linked these qualities to Thomas McKay's amazingly robust constitution—even though he was "as lean as a greyhound"—and astonishing longevity:

> I remember that my father besides his mules and horses had two milch cows, and my mother and we kids, between us, had a flock of Shaggy goats; but father did not drink cow's milk or goat's milk. He preferred the milk that came from the dried nut of the coco-palm tree. The coconut was grated, the milk strained from it, and put into coffee. It gives the coffee an entirely different taste from that of either goat's or cow's milk, or cream. It is delicious indeed, if you acquire the taste. My father would drink about a pint of coffee with coconut milk and go to work all day and return only in the evening for dinner.
>
> People used to say that he would ruin his health; but my father knew what he was doing. I remember, too, he would never touch a drop of anything that came out of a bottle, even plain soda pop. At Christmas time, my brother used to bring home or if he did not come, would send two bottles of Moet and Chandon. Mother and the older boys used to drink it with the orange wine and Port wine with which we celebrated Christmas. Father never touched it and he lived until he was ninety-eight. Mother died at fifty-three. None of us boys are like our father; all of us do all the things that he wouldn't do, without any regrets[.] Only my sister lived up to his standards of austerity.[93]

The old man may have been more emotional than his son knew. In a letter sent to Claude in August 1927, his sister Rachel wrote,

"Our heart pines and yearns after you; especially your aged father who believes that the Lord has heard his prayers in allowing him to hear from you before he dies." U. Theo had also told McKay that his father would have loved to see him before he died. Although McKay never returned to see his father, when the old man died in 1933 he willed to his youngest son the family home and "the lands around it," while Rachel was allowed to live there until her death.[94]

U. Theo

Although McKay recalled his parents well, the most influential figure in his formation, including his intellectual formation, was his eldest brother, U. Theo. U. Theo's stature as an intellectual, a political activist and McKay's teacher, in the widest sense of that term, has not been accurately estimated before.[95]

My own research suggests that there are serious shortcomings in the existing depiction of U. Theo and the role he played in McKay's life. U. Theo McKay had the greatest impact upon his little brother and Claude McKay cannot be properly understood without a prior understanding of his older brother. It is for these reasons that one needs to re-examine the life of U. Theo McKay and the influence he had upon McKay.

Born on March 23 1872, U. Theo was over seventeen years McKay's senior. He was a graduate of the most prestigious teacher-training institution in Jamaica—arguably the most highly regarded of such institutions in the British Caribbean at the time—Mico College, in Kingston. U. Theo excelled at Mico where he studied from 1891–96. According to *Who's Who in Jamaica*, he passed "first in Honours" and "also in other subjects." He received a broad academic training in the natural sciences, mathematics, music and the humanities; Claude recalled that he had a "very sound grounding" in Latin and French. It is probably true that for the time and place, as one writer remarked, it was the best education available.[96]

U. Theo became one of the island's most distinguished schoolmasters. Something of a Renaissance man, he loved cricket, reading good literature, playing the piano, and he was renowned as a choir-master. McKay vividly recalled his organizing a choir in Clarendon that performed Handel's *Messiah* to national acclaim. U. Theo also kept abreast of current affairs, subscribing to a large number of foreign journals and newspapers in order to do so. He moved with confi-dence and ease between the classes. He loved a good conversation and in *Who's Who* listed "Political and Economic discussions" among his recreations.[97] Unlike his little brother, who was always shy and never enjoyed speaking in public, not even to recite his own poems, U. Theo was an accomplished orator. Indeed, a distinguished con-temporary claimed that he was "one of the ablest speakers in Jamaica."[98] "One of the smartest of the elementary teachers of the island,"[99] he left the profession before retirement age and became a large-scale farmer, living and working near the family seat at Nairne Castle.[100]

When Claude was seven, his parents entrusted his upbringing and education to their distinguished eldest son, who at the time was a schoolmaster in Mount Carey, near Montego Bay. It is not clear why Thomas and Hannah, along with U. Theo, decided to do this, but such practices were relatively common in Jamaica at the time.[101] When U. Theo went back to Clarendon to farm, McKay, who was about fourteen, returned to his parents' home and finished his sec-ondary education at a nearby school.

Not only was U. Theo a second father to Claude, he also served as his little brother's political mentor. A committed freethinker and socialist, U. Theo had an impressive library. By the age of ten young Claude, much to his brother's delight, took to reading U. Theo's books. U. Theo encouraged McKay's untrammeled intellectual curiosity. When U. Theo's wife, who was very religious, saw Claude reading Haeckel's *The Riddle of the Universe*, she said it was a bad book and tried to stop him. "Let the boy read what he likes," U. Theo told her.[102] As Claude got older, ever reading more and more of his brother's library, U. Theo "loosened up," becoming as much a friend and intellectual sparring partner as a big brother. When Claude took to reading the freethinkers, U. Theo was "very happy." He started to tell Claude about the lives of the great free-thinkers of the times such as "Thomas Huxley, [Charles] Bradlaugh, the great Parliamentarian, Mrs. Annie Besant and Mr. John Robertson—also a Parliamentarian." Claude reported that he then "started to read the freethinking books with greater interest and saw and thought of life solely from the freethought angle."[103] The brothers had long conversations about rationalism, literature, politics and the larger issues of life. This must have contributed immensely to the development of McKay's clarity and rigor of thought, for U. Theo had nothing but contempt for sloppy thinkers. McKay grew up to have even less patience than his brother for poor reasoning. This became most evident in later years.

It was during those years with U. Theo that Claude took his first steps toward both rationalism and socialism. By his early teens, he was, as he put it, "a hard little agnostic;"[104] a few years later he signed up to be a member of one of the world's leading freethought organizations, the Rationalist Press Association, based in London.[105] Fabian Socialism went hand in hand with his rationalism for many of the socialists that he read and admired were also rationalists—Annie Besant is a prime example—and many of the Victorian rationalists were equally well known as socialists. Thus when McKay wrote in 1945 "I had imbibed Fabian Socialism with my mother's milk,"[106] what was true of his Fabianism was also true of his militant rationalism.[107]

By the time that he returned to live in Nairne Castle with his big brother and sister-in-law Claude had become a committed free-thinker in a sea of believers; not only that, he began proselytizing: "soon I began talking to the younger set . . . boys of my age, some older and some younger. Many of them believed as I believed. We went to my brother for enlightenment and instruction. Soon there was a young crop of agnostics way up there in the hills of Jamaica."[108]

McKay's education was to continue in Clarendon for the next couple of years. Although he was no longer formally taught by U. Theo, their intellectual relationship continued. U. Theo's interest in music flourished and when he organized a local choir of national repute, Claude proudly participated in its activities.[109]

Not long after his return, events in Nairne Castle severely tested McKay's intellectual resolve as a rationalist and brought him even closer to U. Theo. A wave of religious revivalism hit the Clarendon hills and other parts of Jamaica in 1906. Claude and U. Theo stood firm while the local villagers fell like tenpins to the spiritual allurements of a small, fiery Welshman "who had a personal friendly way of appealing to people, talking to them and singing." Unlike previous revivals which lasted a few days, this was the first McKay encountered that lasted "for weeks and months." Mount Zion was set alight: "life was one long excitable thrill from seven o'clock in the morning until long after midnight." By the time the Welshman reached Nairne Castle he had accumulated a fervent band of followers. "Strong, husky men who had not been in church for years would suddenly break down babbling like babies and be taken to the penitent form to kneel and pray and to confess and rejoice in a new life." With lively singing interspersed with the missionary's beckoning to the onlookers ("Come to Jesus. He wants you. He waits for you. Come to Jesus now.") the tally of the converted grew rapidly. Even the vibrant young lovers of the Clarendon hills would confess their sins, seek forgiveness and surrender to the Lord. McKay's father "was right in it," as was his mother and all his brothers except, of course, U. Theo. "The rumour got around that I had been trained in ungodliness. This was why I resisted going to the penitent form." There was uncharacteristic menace in the air of the little village. "All the people" were angry with U. Theo. "They prayed for him in the church . . . prayed for God to convert him. But in their prayers there was a menacing tone as if they would like to lynch him. When they met him in the street they would not speak to him. They felt that he was the child of Satan while they were the holy children of God." Confident of his militant rationalism, U. Theo took it all in his stride and harbored no hard feelings against these "simple country people who laboured under the illusion that they had seen God personally and were talking to Him day and night." The villagers concluded that U. Theo's education was "something more of a compact with the devil than real education."[110]

In time, Nairne Castle settled down to its usual, rustic pattern. The bad feelings quickly evaporated into the Clarendon sky and the rationalists had the last laugh:

> After the first wave of excitement was over in the beginning weeks of the revival, it was discovered that scores of our young girls were *enceinte*. On this occasion, however, the young men who had committed the acts admitted to them. So there were many marriages . . . revival marriages we called them, because in many cases there was nothing of the usual merrymaking and high feasting. The missionary just got a cheap ring and married the offenders.[111]

It was after the revival that McKay set to work, cultivating his agnostics. But for a time, he had to endure the anguish of isolation and hostility directed at him and his brother for swimming against the tide and holding fast to his convictions. This was not the last time that he would find himself in such a predicament but it was the first time that he became acquainted with the price of following the lonesome road.

In discussions of McKay's intellectual and political development, U. Theo's role is invariably diminished and that of Walter Jekyll (whom we shall encounter soon) exaggerated. But McKay himself always credited his brother for his early intellectual and political development. "All I know I learnt from him," McKay told the *Gleaner* in 1911, less than a year before his departure for the United States.[112] In *My Green Hills of Jamaica*, McKay writes that when he was growing up, being his brother's brother was something that gave him a lot of joy.[113] U. Theo loved his little brother too and was pleased and proud of the young man's accomplishments. He keenly followed his progress from afar after McKay left Jamaica.[114] When his other brothers bad-mouthed Claude for not writing often enough, U. Theo always defended his errant little brother-son.[115]

U. Theo was an integral member of the extraordinary second generation of freeborn, educated, African Jamaicans. The advanced guard of this generation, which included U. Theo, became organic intellectuals of the black masses. They advocated land reform to ease the plight of the landless poor, protested against the exploitation of black labor, agitated against Indian indentureship, which undermined the wages and working conditions of black laborers, fought racism and colorism in all their guises, called for the improvement and extension of Jamaica's road and railway networks to help the peasantry and rural folk, demanded the enhancement and expansion of educational opportunities for the black masses and they lobbied the colonial authorities in London when they could not get local redress for their many and sundry grievances. By the turn of the century, the People's Convention, the National Club, and the Jamaica League had become the most important of the organizations created to press their demands. Teachers and preachers figured most prominently among this new generation of outspoken black Jamaicans.[116]

Though he shared their general ideals, U. Theo stood apart from his peers in two important respects: he was a socialist and a militant rationalist. To be sure, he was not a revolutionary socialist,[117] but he was to the left of the Fabians, for whom he nonetheless had great admiration. (Jamaica's Governor, Sydney Olivier, and Annie Besant were two of the Fabian Socialists he admired the most.) U. Theo advocated a progressive income tax scheme—at a time when incomes were not directly taxed at all in Jamaica. Taxes were levied but they were indirect and obscenely regressive (as discussed above). Thus U. Theo gave qualified support to the Income Tax Bill that was under discussion in 1919 because "it [might] eventually touch the pockets of the rich men."[118] He was also among the first Jamaicans to call for self-government[119] and he supported equal rights for women. During the heated debate that raged in the press between 1918 and 1919 over a bill proposing the enfranchisement of women, U. Theo was one of only a handful of black men who spoke out in favor of the measure—unequivocally:

> Woman has proven herself as capable as man in the management of affairs, and it is only hide-bound conservatism for which the twentieth century has no use that would oppose the measure. No less a savant than John Stuart Mill advocated the enfranchisement of women years ago, and the justice of her claim has grown with the years.[120]

In marked contrast to U. Theo, the two most prominent black men in the legislative council, D. T. Wint and J. A. G. Smith, opposed the bill.[121]

Unlike most of his distinguished black contemporaries engaged in the agitation of the time—men such as Dr. J. Robert Love, Rev. C. A. Wilson and Rev. A. A. Barclay, who were all men of the cloth— U. Theo was a freethinker who strongly believed in the power of reason and science over faith. He had little time for the Christianity of his parents and the magico-religious beliefs of the Jamaican masses; they were all so much mumbo-jumbo to him—and he was not afraid to say so publicly. "I believe in independence," he wrote in a 1929 letter to his brother, "especially intellectual independence, which prevents one from accepting theories however respectable traditions may make them. I still stand a free man, where revealed religion is concerned. Try as I may I cannot but regard the teachings of priest and prophet as anything but superstition."[122] He never shied away from speaking his mind but unlike Claude he did not believe in proselytizing, only in living by his own conscience. Claude wrote that his brother had "great respect" for religious people and though he was an agnostic, remarkably, he served as a lay reader in an Anglican church when he lived in Mount Carey. "[U. Theo] always said to me that an agnostic should so live his life that Christian people would have to respect him."[123]

Like his father, U. Theo was black, proud and independent. In a letter to his younger brother in 1930, he wrote: "I have never wanted anything from the white man save recognition. I mean by that a fair field and no favours."[124] His stout defense of the "small man," his admiration of the working class and his loyalty to his humble roots were a matter of public record. He was an inveterate writer of letters to the press and in 1912, he wrote to the *Jamaica Times* about the exploitation of Clarendon laborers engaged in road-building: "In every work or great enterprise dealing with human progress the horny-handed son of toil is an indispensable unit." He argued that mental and manual labor are "inter-dependent, the one . . . as essential as the other." In his letter, U. Theo wrote tenderly:

> We see the son of labour, the horny-handed son of labour, jacketless, begrimmed with dirt and saturated with honest sweat. Sometimes he is coarse in his expressions and his argument is punctuated by oaths and fiats and sticks and stones, but as you watch the shovel making the dirt fly, the pick levelling the rock, the "borer" drilling with persistency a hole in the rock, the barrow going backward and forward the whole day through while the rays of the sun beat down on him mercilessly, a wave of admiration for such a one passes over you. A man like this should get the reward of his labour. . . . And oftentimes he is in some way or another cheated out of what is his by right.[125]

From these general observations, he moved on to the specific problems of the local laborers. "The work on the New Roads and on [the new railway line] in Clarendon furnishes many cases in which [the laborer] has not been rewarded for his toil. Surely it won't be long before the horny-handed sons of toil are given ample protection, for every day the world is awakening more and more to their great importance."[126]

Never one to pull his punches, U. Theo was at the center of a 1918 *cause célèbre* because of the firm stand he took against government interference in the activities of the Jamaican Agricultural Society, a farmers' educational and pressure group. In the tumultuous aftermath of the First World War, the colonial authorities were particularly anxious to silence oppositional voices and the JAS was one of the institutions within which the peasantry could organize and speak its mind, despite the involvement of some large farmers. The expression of discontent within the JAS against the state became so intense that the government attempted to proscribe political discussion at branch meetings. Pressed by the colonial government, the Board of Management of the JAS—comprising some of the largest land-owners—issued a circular in November 1918 to the individual branches telling them, in the words of U. Theo, "the subjects they have right to discuss at their branch meetings." U. Theo wrote to the *Gleaner*,

> I sincerely hope that every branch society in the island will say to the Board of Management "Hands Off." . . . The branch societies are popular organisations; they are not under government rule; they are free and independent, and the Board of Management has no power on earth to dictate to them. These societies are used as clubs, as meeting places where the members discuss all sorts of subjects acceptable to them, and at these meetings they are learning citizenship, learning to take an intelligent interest in their own affairs, learning to think for themselves; finding out those who are seeking their own interests.[127]

As far as U. Theo was concerned, the branches of the JAS were unparalleled in their "splendid educative work among the mass of the people . . . and it would be a sorry day when any reactionary is allowed to scotch progress in this direction." He, for one, would not be afraid to fight in defense of the political autonomy of the branches. He concluded the letter with fighting words:

> [T]he time has come when we are thinking for ourselves and can see through the veil of self-interest, and the most they can do is to use their power and influence in crushing those who dare to speak, but as a man can die but once, there seems to be nothing to fear in this.[128]

The same defiance animated his brother's famous sonnet, "If We Must Die," written under the emergency conditions of anti-black pogroms in the United States less than a year after U. Theo's letter.[129]

During the 1920s, U. Theo continued to speak out, becoming increasingly nationalistic. In 1922, on a platform of the Jamaican People's Association, U. Theo went beyond the aims of that organization by explicitly calling for Jamaican self-government. His nationalist call came sixteen years before the formation of the People's National Party and a generation before a semblance of self-government was won in 1944. As one of the first Jamaicans to call for such a constitutional arrangement, U. Theo McKay should be counted among Jamaica's first nationalists. Not surprisingly, his remarks generated considerable public debate, not to mention censure from the colonial "elite."[130]

U. Theo was on the platform at a Universal Negro Improvement Association meeting that Marcus Garvey himself chaired and spoke at on New Year's Day, 1928.[131] Garvey had arrived on the island on December 10 1927 after his release from prison and deportation from the United States. The meeting took place at the Ward Theatre in Kingston. U. Theo lived in Frankfield, rural Clarendon, and would have had to make a special effort to participate. He must have had strong sympathy for Garvey and the UNIA. But by August 1929 U. Theo had altered his position considerably. He wrote to his younger brother:

> Garvey is having a big convention here during the month of August. He appeared in court as witness in a case which one Marks has against the UNIA, and I must say from the evidence he gave he cut a very sorry figure. He was the little, sniffling, dodging-the-issue, mean-hearted, little-minded fellow and his bigness was eclipsed by his semi-truths. I think he has gone down immensely. I am not a Garveyite and never will be but I must confess to a secret desire that the man may eventually show himself to be *somebody*. I do not think he can rise to the occasion. He publishes a paper here[,] the "Blackman"[,] which is just a dirty rag. When I see the chance he has of doing something and making a name and uplifting those who believe in him[,] I can assure you that I feel that the man is his own enemy.[132]

U. Theo carried on his civic activities during the 1930s. Through his work with the Frankfield Citizen's Association and the Clarendon Old Boys' Association he was accredited with helping to develop a sense of nationalism within the parish. In 1932 the *Gleaner* called his the one district in the island with "national spirit" and U. Theo ("Mayor of Frankfield") the "gospeller in the promotion of a national feeling." According to the report, the motto of U. Theo and his co-workers was "For the good that we can do."[133]

Walter Jekyll, U. Theo and McKay's Political Education

The impression is often given that after McKay left Clarendon for Kingston in 1909 or early 1910 there was little contact between him and U. Theo and that he passed over, as it were, to another mentor, Walter Jekyll. One is also led to believe that there was no contact between Jekyll and U. Theo but nothing could be further from the truth. It is evident from the surviving correspondence between the two brothers that they were in contact even after McKay left and that U. Theo knew Jekyll.[134]

Walter Jekyll was born into an upper-class family in Surrey in 1849. A Cambridge graduate, Jekyll is said to have excelled in music, literature, languages and philosophy. After university he was ordained by the Church of England and served for a number of years, including a stint as chaplain in Malta. But in the great contest between religion and science that rocked intellectual life in late Victorian Britain, Jekyll opted for science and renounced Christianity. He had been a friend of Robert Louis Stevenson and "almost certainly," it has been plausibly claimed, lent his name to that author's famous character.[135] Jekyll came to Jamaica in 1895 and when Claude McKay met him, Jekyll had just written the first authoritative documentation of Jamaican folk songs and stories, *Jamaican Song and Story*, published in London by the Folklore Society in 1907.[136]

By all accounts, Jekyll lived a simple life in Jamaica, collecting stories and songs from the peasantry, reading and writing books and translating others—most notably Schopenhauer—into English (he apparently knew six European languages). He was to deepen McKay's knowledge of German philosophy and poetry: "Besides [Schopenhauer, Kant, Nietzsche and Hegel] he had translated some poems from Goethe, Schiller and Heine. . . . Mr. Jekyll always read the German, deep and sonorous, before he translated it into English for me." They read and discussed Berkeley, Hume and Spencer, among others.[137] Jekyll also improved McKay's French.

It has been suggested that Jekyll was gay and that, even though they may not have developed a physical relationship, a "homoerotic component most likely underlay" the relationship that Claude had with him.[138] This may very well have been true, but the quality of the supposed evidence of this—even allowing for the obvious difficulty of acquiring this type of information—is far from satisfactory. There is in fact no evidence to say that Jekyll was gay. We do know that McKay, after he left the island, had homosexual as well as heterosexual relations, but this tells us nothing of the relationship he had with Jekyll in Jamaica. Walter Jekyll was an ascetic man—a fact abundantly testified to by McKay and others—and was rather asexual, with perhaps some misogynistic tendencies.[139]

McKay provides a snapshot of Jekyll's politico-philosophical perspective:

> Mr Jekyll hated the British Empire but he used to say, "What is there to take its place, Claude? The Germans are still too young and arrogant; they will never do."
>
> He was disillusioned with British liberalism, yet he did not believe in socialism or any of the radical parties of the day. He always said to me that the British upper class would know how to handle radicals and that Lloyd George, who was the famous liberal radical then, would finish up as a lord. He was a great follower of Leo Tolstoy, and a pessimist. Mr. Jekyll was also something of a Buddhist and did not think that the world could be reformed. He used to say that the politicians would fool the people all the time, until the end of time. He was a member of the English upper class and knew that class thoroughly.[140]

Jekyll's best friend at the time was the private secretary of King Edward VII; his eldest brother was a "governor of India," writes McKay. Other members of his family were in politics or bankers in the City of London. Gertrude Jekyll, one of Britain's leading landscape gardeners and a prolific writer on gardening, was Jekyll's older sister. According to his brother, Jekyll suffered terribly from asthma and spent several winters in Jamaica in the 1890s, avoiding the damp British weather. Jekyll loved Jamaica and decided to settle there after his mother died in 1895. Jamaica also had another attraction for

Jekyll. It provided him with the scope to live the quiet, unencumbered life he sought. Herbert Jekyll reported that Jekyll found the restraints of British society "irksome to him and preferred to live his own life and follow his own pursuits unmolested."[141] McKay wrote that Jekyll turned his back upon English society and decided "to live like a peasant except for his books" in Jamaica.[142] What McKay was too polite to write (for once) was that Jekyll could afford it: no Jamaican peasant could afford to follow Jekyll's "peasant" lifestyle; if they could, they would no longer have been *peasants*. Jekyll was in the very privileged position of not having to work, and did not: he had a substantial private income to finance his fantasy life in Jamaica.[143] McKay was overly indulgent in his portrait of this rather eccentric aristocrat. Some fourteen years earlier when McKay depicted Jekyll as Squire Gensir in *Banana Bottom* he was perhaps more accurate in his portrait when he declared in a telling sentence: "The peasants were his hobby."[144]

McKay registered the aristocratic class snobbery of Jekyll. "In spite of his gentleness and otherworldliness, he possessed a curious kind of class pride. In fact he was strangely proud of his class." One weekend, Sydney Olivier, the Fabian Governor of Jamaica mentioned earlier, visited Jekyll while McKay was there. Towards the end of the evening, Olivier asked to stay overnight.

> Evidently he relished the simplicity of Mr. Jekyll's surroundings and wanted to stay for a night instead of . . . staying in some hotel in the Blue Mountains. . . . But Mr. Jekyll said to him quite sharply: "There's no place for you to stay." The Governor nodded towards me and said: "But he stays here." Mr. Jekyll replied: "But he is my special friend."

After Olivier left, Jekyll "raved." McKay had never seen him in such a temper. "That's English middle-class bad manners. No person of my class would ever say that to me." McKay said, "But Mr. Jekyll, how can you tolerate me? I am merely the son of a peasant." "Oh," Jekyll replied, "English gentlemen have always liked their peasants, it's the ambitious middle class that we cannot tolerate."[145]

When Jekyll died U. Theo suggested that McKay write "a short tribute of him and send it to me and I would see it published in the

Jamaican press. I do think he has been really good to you and it would be fitting for you to do so if time will allow." In ending his letter, U. Theo remarked: "I hope that one of your books will deal with Jamaican life, altho there may not be much money in it as your audience may be restricted."[146] McKay set his next book and arguably his best novel, *Banana Bottom*, in rural Jamaica. It was dedicated to Walter Jekyll. (And, alas, U. Theo was right: *Banana Bottom*, published in New York at the height of the Depression, was a commercial flop.) While we may never know what U. Theo thought of it, we know he contributed to its construction by providing McKay with background information.[147] "I am glad," wrote U. Theo, "that the materials I sent you proved of some use to you and the compiling of your last volume and I hope that you shall earn enough from literary efforts to put you beyond the pale of want and that before long you will pay us a visit when we will give you the welcome which you have so richly earned."[148]

Political differences undoubtedly existed between the brothers. They differed in the 1920s over their estimation of the influential Jamaican journalist, Herbert De Lisser.[149] While U. Theo, perhaps mellowing with age, claimed that "it is not in our blood to be revolutionists,"[150] the younger McKay was politically and spiritually nourished by the memory—regardless of how questionable the oral history might have been—of his ancestors' defiant stance on the auction block. And while the younger McKay became increasingly critical of British imperialism, the older brother counselled that it was the best that there was at the time (as had Jekyll):

> [Y]ou have travelled widely and have gained experience which I have had no chance of getting, so your judgement must be worth infinitely more than mine, but at present, I do hold that the British Commonwealth of Nations with all its most glaring faults is the best national organization in existence.[151]

Walter Jekyll's education was "acres broader" than U. Theo's[152] but McKay's formative years were spent under the personal and educational guidance of his brother. Until he left Clarendon at the age of twenty, U. Theo was effectively the only teacher he had ever had.[153] McKay first met Jekyll when he was eighteen and did not see him on a regular basis until about 1910, when he was twenty-one. This more frequent contact in Kingston was interrupted when McKay went to Spanish Town and joined the constabulary force. After joining the force, he spent at least six months in Spanish Town, where he was trained and first served as constable, and was transferred to Half Way Tree in Kingston. He left the country not long afterwards. In short, the level of contact and the intensity of interaction between McKay and Walter Jekyll do not compare to those between McKay and his brother. Jekyll's influence has been exaggerated in the literature.

This exaggeration is partly based on McKay's own portrait of Jekyll in *A Long Way From Home*. But it was only after Jekyll's death in 1929 that McKay began to extol Jekyll's role in his intellectual formation. McKay did not attend Jekyll's funeral; he apparently did not write a tribute to Jekyll for the Jamaican press, as his brother had requested, in 1929 (if he did write a tribute, it was not published). It is possible that McKay may have overcompensated for these shortcomings after 1929.

An audit of the value McKay placed on his brother's contribution to his intellectual formation, however, puts U. Theo in an unrivalled position. In an interview published in the *Gleaner* in October 1911, for instance, McKay—elsewhere described as reticent, diffident, modest to a degree, monosyllabic—was asked to clarify whether the famous U. Theo McKay was his brother. "Yes, and all I know I learnt from him." Jekyll is thanked for his "kindness" in helping to bring out *Songs of Jamaica*, but there is no other mention of Jekyll by McKay in the interview.[154] In a 1918 autobiographical sketch in *Pearson's Magazine*, and again in 1923 in *Negroes in America*, U. Theo and Jekyll are acknowledged but precedence is given to U. Theo.[155] And as late as 1927 McKay accorded Jekyll only one sentence in an autobiographical sketch: "An English gentleman who was collecting Jamaica folklore became interested in my dialect verses and helped me to publish my first book, *Songs of Jamaica*."[156]

Banana Bottom, published in 1933, was dedicated to Jekyll. The character of Squire Gensir was based on Jekyll, as McKay himself writes in a prefatory note to the novel. The other post-1929 mention of Jekyll and U. Theo occurs in *A Long Way From Home* (1937) followed by a little essay in 1945.[157] *My Green Hills of Jamaica*, finished less than a year before his death, has richly textured portraits brimming with love, warmth, generosity and humor, of both U. Theo and Walter Jekyll but he attributes to U. Theo the primary role in his education.

With the sun going down on his life, McKay wrote that "There was one thing that gave me a great deal of physical and mental joy. That was the fact that I was my brother's brother."[158]

Becoming a Constab

Though he was a somewhat mischievous boy, McKay was also bright, performing exceptionally well at school. When he left school, he had no set idea about a career. He knew, however, what he did not want to do. He did not want to become a teacher or a preacher as most of his brothers had become. McKay eventually decided to become a craftsman, and he won a government scholarship to a trade school that the colonial authorities had recently established in Kingston. But the devastating earthquake of 1907 that centered on Kingston reduced the school to rubble. Miraculously unhurt, McKay left Kingston, returned to his village, then went to Brown's Town in the neighboring parish of St. Ann, where he was apprenticed to a cabinetmaker. Reluctant to reveal the secrets of his craft, Old Brenga,[159] as he called his master, taught him little.

When his mother became fatally ill, McKay abandoned his apprenticeship and went back home to help nurse her. Because he was the baby of the family and his mother's favorite, he gave up trade with little objection from his family.[160] After her long struggle—including several very close calls—with her "cardiac trouble," Hannah McKay died in December 1909. This was McKay's greatest loss. "The only one I loved was gone," he declares in "My Mother,"[161] and in another poem written on the tenth anniversary of her death, "December 1919," he writes:

> 'Tis ten years since you died, mother,
>   Just ten dark years of pain . . .[162]

McKay left Nairne Castle for Kingston in the same month of his mother's death, as if nothing was left in Clarendon to keep him there. Not even "de loved, de hallowed spot/Where my dear mother rest," of which he wrote in an early poem, could detain him.[163] He had no specific intention of going to Kingston apart from getting closer to Walter Jekyll, with whom he corresponded about his poetry from the time they met at Old Brenga's in St. Ann. The relationship between McKay and Jekyll was born out of a flippant remark of Brenga's. Knowing Jekyll was a man of letters he introduced McKay to him one day, joking, "Here I have an apprentice who write poetry." To Brenga's amazement, Jekyll expressed a genuine interest in seeing McKay's poems and agreed for them to be sent to him, as McKay had none with him.[164]

Jekyll regarded McKay as an exotic novelty at first, a member of a somewhat peculiar, talking-horse-like species, "a Negro who was writing poetry."[165] Bernard Shaw, a childhood literary hero of McKay's, had a similar reaction when McKay, with uncharacteristic, even *hadj*-like reverence, visited him at his home in London in 1919: "It must be tragic for a sensitive Negro to be a poet. Why didn't you choose pugilism instead of poetry for a profession? You might have developed into a successful boxer with training."[166]

Jekyll's interest in McKay as merely "a literate phenomenon among the illiterate peasantry" was to alter. Jekyll also became "keen" about McKay's intellectual development and in his verse as "real" poetry.[167]

> He read my poetry. . . . Then he laughed a lot, and I became angry at the laughing because I thought he was laughing at me. All these poems

that I gave him to read had been done in straight English, but there was one short one about an ass that was laden for the market—laden with native vegetables—who had suddenly sat down in the middle of the road and wouldn't get up. Its owner was talking to it in the Jamaican dialect, telling it to get up. That was the poem that Mr. Jekyll was laughing about. He then told me that he did not like my poems in straight English—they were repetitious. "But this," said he, holding up the donkey poem, "this is the real thing. The Jamaican dialect has never been put into literary form except in my Annancy stories. Now is your chance as a native boy [to] put the Jamaica dialect into literary language. I am sure that your poems will sell."[168]

McKay's reaction was understandable. "I was not very enthusiastic about this statement, because to us who were getting an education in the English schools the Jamaican dialect was considered a vulgar tongue. It was the language of the peasants. All cultivated people spoke English, straight English."[169]

McKay's response could hardly have been otherwise. The ethos of colonial education was to inculcate into the colonized—the conquered—the superiority of the metropole and its culture. As Frantz Fanon demonstrated in *Black Skin, White Masks*, language constitutes one crucial and strategic site of struggle.[170] The acquisition of and facility with the language of the imperial power are signs, as well as prerequisites, of social elevation. France and Portugal were perhaps the most explicit of the colonial powers on this question, providing special privileges in their colonies to natives who mastered the European tongue. This was and is nothing less than a calculated policy of cultural genocide, systematic *deracination* in both senses of the term—uprooting and whitening: "Wherever colonialism is a fact the indigenous culture begins to rot."[171] For the aspiring colonial, the culture of the "mother country," becomes what Mervyn Alleyne terms the "target culture."[172] According to the ethos of colonial education, there was no beauty, no nobility, no history, no culture, in short nothing of any worth—barring the natural resources and markets for the metropolis manufactured goods—in that which existed locally.

The task of the colonial educator, then, in the far-flung hinterland of Empire was to elevate the hapless colonized—"Ham's children," "the Natives," "the Wogs"—from their pathological condition, to lead, coax, cajole and coerce them out of the long night of their heathen darkness into the clear light of day of Western civilization. Colonial education inculcated black inferiority. How else could it persuade black people to relinquish and malign their own culture? Force alone could never work. Commander Bodilly, an Englishman stationed in Jamaica as a resident magistrate, spelled this out as recently as the early 1930s in an interview: British rule in the colonies depends upon a "carefully nurtured sense of inferiority" in the governed.[173]

Colonial domination, direct as well as indirect, is never devoid of local collaboration. This is the key to its longevity: it imbues in the colonized a sense of its indispensability—"But what is there to take its place, Claude?"—a natural, reified permanence.[174]

After the money he took with him from Clarendon to Kingston ran out, McKay worked in a match factory, "but the hours were long and there was no fun in it." He made a new friend who had been kept a long time by the "most beautiful" prostitute in Kingston. His friend was "fed up" like him and "wanted to get away from it all." They both decided to go to Spanish Town and join the Jamaica Constabulary, the police force. That is how McKay recalls his joining the force.[175] But the real story, although still unclear, appears to be different and more painful. In a 1911 interview with the *Gleaner*, McKay was "very reticent as to why he joined the Force. It is said that the underlying cause is a pitiable love story. I hear he has poured out poem after poem on this subject, but he would not discuss the matter." "I cannot touch the public with my heart," McKay told his interviewer, W.A. Stephenson, "it would be of no interest to them."[176] The ache in his heart that drove him to the police force remains unidentified. (It is by no means evident in his extant poems.) Why McKay thought he could gain solace in the constabulary remains a mystery.

McKay tells us that when he and his friend got to Spanish Town the recruiting officer told them that they were a little too short, but the officials liked them and allowed them to join.[177] The real reason the officials allowed them to join is probably less flattering: the constabulary was understaffed and in 1910 and 1911 (the years McKay served) the force failed to reach its targeted size.[178]

From the outset, McKay hated life in the force. With Jekyll's help, he managed to get out of it within seventeen months of joining, serving from June 1910 to October 1911, instead of the five years he had signed up for.[179] His experience in the police force traumatized him and deepened his radicalization. But although McKay "despised" the institution and his time there, it provided him with invaluable knowledge and insight into Jamaican society and class structure. It pervaded the tone and content of much of his early poetry, furnishing the bulk of the material for his two volumes of verse, *Songs of Jamaica* and *Constab Ballads*. (Walter Jekyll provided detailed annotations of the poems published in the first volume, and a useful glossary to those in *Constab Ballads*—as well as being instrumental in their publication.)

Having narrowly escaped from the clutches of the force, McKay returned to the balming streams and beautiful hills of Clarendon. He decided to study scientific agriculture so that he could help his people. In July 1912, he sailed from the northeastern Jamaican seaport of Port Antonio for Charleston, South Carolina, and continued by train for Booker T. Washington's Tuskegee Institute in Alabama. Over the remaining thirty-six years of his life, in addition to living in different parts of the United States, he traveled widely, restlessly perching for varying periods in Britain, Russia, Germany, France, Spain and Morocco. Desperately homesick while living in London in 1920, he explicitly promised to return to Jamaica:

> I shall return to loiter by the streams
> That bathe the brown blades of the bending grasses
> And realize once more my thousand dreams
> Of waters rushing down the mountain passes.

> I shall return to hear the fiddle and fife
> Of village dances, dear delicious tunes
> That stir the hidden depths of native life,
> Stray melodies of dim-remembered runes:
> I shall return. I shall return again
> To ease my mind of long, long years of pain.[180]

But McKay never made it back to Jamaica. He died an exile in Chicago on May 22 1948. Almost exactly a year later, on June 16 1949, U. Theo McKay died from injuries suffered in a car accident.[181]

Growing Up

McKay was a freethinker, a rationalist and member of the Rationalist Press Association in London, a militant and proud child of the European Enlightenment. He lived with his brother from the age of seven in a household that engendered and nourished such a world-view. Contrary to the belief of some commentators, he was never formed by religion.[182] By the time he returned to Clarendon with his brother at the age of fourteen he was a proselytizing freethinker. Prior to his conversion to Catholicism in 1944, his atheism was one of the most powerful and enduring threads of continuity in his outlook on life. He spent a great deal of time and effort attacking religion, especially Protestant Christianity. Not even his somewhat idealized peasants in his last novel, *Banana Bottom*, escaped censure on this score.

Accompanying his rationalism was socialism, Fabian Socialism, to be precise. McKay explained this by pointing out that Jekyll was "a Buddhist and something of a Fabian. The governor of the island, Lord Olivier, was the statistician of the Fabians and the friend of Bernard Shaw." McKay recalled that U. Theo also liked Olivier's book, *White Capital and Coloured Labour*, which was first published by the Fabian Society in 1906 in its "Socialist Library" series.[183]

McKay also strongly identified with, respected and indeed loved the Jamaican peasantry. Significantly, one of the motives behind his going to America in the first place was to study "scientific agriculture" in order to be able to serve and be near the peasants of Jamaica.[184] His respect for these small black farmers is illustrated by two examples he gave of their interaction with supposedly British experts.

Agricultural instructors were sent by the British colonial authorities to spread the wonders and benefits of modern science. Governor Sir Henry Blake, who established the Jamaica Agricultural Society in 1895, was not optimistic about the chances of success: "What the ultimate result will be I cannot say. A black population not very intelligent and saturated with suspicion of any attempt to interfere with their crude and wasteful system is not easily influenced."[185]

Before planting, the peasants would clear the land. Two to three weeks later, they would burn the shrub, grass and other debris. Generations of Jamaican peasants had done things by this tried and proven method but the agricultural instructors knew better. They protested against the burning of the debris, saying that it should be ploughed under to enrich the soil. "Well," reported McKay, "some of the peasants followed their advice and when they did their planting, the leaves of what they had planted were consumed by worms as soon as they had grown a few inches. Those who insisted on burning this debris found that their planting had developed very healthily. The agricultural instructors made their mistakes." McKay distinctly remembered one of the instructors telling a peasant that the young cocoa plant he had uprooted would not grow. "The peasant insisted that it would and planted it. The next year when the instructor returned, he found a flourishing cocoa tree."[186] So much for "crude and wasteful systems."

McKay's celebration of the peasantry at times, however, became excessive. "No Jamaican peasant," he declares, "imagines he is inferior to anybody but God."[187] In another passage in *My Green Hills of Jamaica*, McKay explicitly objected to the way townspeople looked upon country folk. Anticipating the surprise, condescension—if not total incredulity—with which most people would react to the idea of a group of committed freethinking peasant children in turn-of-the-century Jamaica, he went on the offensive:

> People who are born and grow up in large towns and cities have a tendency to imagine that people from small towns and villages are naturally stupid and unintelligent. There is no greater fallacy. Personally I believe that the masses of the cities are woefully less intelligent than people who make up the population of a country town or a village. The country or small town man may not be as slickly dressed but somehow he does use his brains to think. I have known so many city people from truck driver to professor who just cannot think at all.[188]

He praised the openness, tolerance and generosity of spirit that he believed characterized the Jamaican peasantry. "Yes, the country people *are* wonderful," he told Nancy Cunard. "They just have *no idea* of the hard and fast moral standards of Europe and America. Any really fine-minded person could live among them in *any way* he pleases."[189] Cunard, who visited the island in 1932 to gather material for her remarkable compendium, *Negro: An Anthology*, like so many visitors before and since, fell under the spell of the Jamaican peasantry. She lends support to McKay:

> [T]he Jamaican Negro peasant is particularly energetic; this comes out most visibly in any chance conversation . . . . In no sense ever an *abruti* by the encompassment of the economic horizon, Jamaicans are as full of curiosity concerning the rest of the world as they are of talk, mother-wit and logic. A most lovable and interesting people. They give you a great sense of the *justice* in them. They are subtle, their minds work at such a slant angle (and how apparent this is in the very shortest exchange of words, and in their famous proverbs) that you have the impression no other people in the least like them exist in the world. . . .And they are a beautiful race, or rather, blend of black races. The women's hair is done in a wealth of twists and knobs and knots and curls—a perfect series in which no two seem alike in style but all suggest direct parentage to Africa. Their manners are exquisite; a lusty, strong and dignified people without the least trace of any of the surface "inferiority" or exterior hesitancy that has been beaten and pumped into some of the American Negroes by the bestiality of the American whites.[190]

McKay tells us two stories, recalled some forty years after the fact, which reveal the presence of exemplary black figures other than the ones already mentioned.

We gather from McKay that the most effective doctor his ailing mother ever had was not white, but black. McKay wrote that when he was sixteen, his mother became "desperately ill." He remembered coming home from school, finding the house full of people, many of them weeping, for his mother seemed to be paralyzed. "She could not talk, and seemed as if she did not want to talk. They had discovered her in a dead faint in the kitchen and brought her to her room where she was lying like a dead person in the great carved mahogany four-poster bed which had belonged to her father."

Instead of the white family doctor, they called in a black doctor who was relatively new to the area. Described as a "very black man," the new doctor was born in Barbados and educated at Edinburgh University. (The people admired him very much, said McKay, "as they do anything foreign that is any good.") A close friend of U. Theo's, the doctor prescribed some medicine for Mrs. McKay and ordered that the gable ends be boarded up. McKay recalled that U. Theo and the doctor had "quite a controversy" over the gable ends. "My brother said that we were living in a tropical country and it would be better for the people to live in tents and hammocks than in closed houses." However, Thomas McKay followed the doctor's advice. Having plenty of boards, he had the gable ends boarded up, "and surprisingly enough my mother was well again in a few weeks."

McKay remembered the old quadroon woman who had delivered most of the McKay children saying to his mother, "You have had a wonderful escape, Anna. That new doctor is surely a wizard." Four years later, Mrs. McKay was not so lucky when she was once again dangerously ill. The Barbadian doctor, following in the footsteps of many Caribbean professionals, had by then left for the United States. The white family doctor, who was living ten miles away, was called but would not attend to Mrs. McKay. He sent word saying that there was nothing he could do and that "Her battle with life is ended."[191]

At the time of his mother's death, the minister at Mount Zion was white. However, "one of our brilliant young Negro preachers, a Presbyterian whose name was Barkley, and a member of the legislative council, had visited mother when she was ill. She had indicated that she would like to have him preach the funeral sermon."[192]

The final point that I would like to emphasize is this: McKay was privileged in having been exposed to different facets of Jamaican life. He came from the peasantry and knew that world intimately. He had also lived the life of a member of the Jamaican black middle class, especially when he lived with his brother near Montego Bay. U. Theo's, however, was a first-generation black middle class household that remained loyal to, interested in, and unforgetful of its humble beginnings.[193]

A confident young black man, Claude interacted easily with white people. As he told his friend James Weldon Johnson many years later, he grew up on "equal terms" with white, mulatto and black children of a certain class because his father was a big peasant and "belonged."[194] In his communication with, and observation of them, he knew that they did not possess a monopoly on intelligence or knowledge or beauty. He knew that they were human beings and not gods, and he acted accordingly.

Through living in Kingston as a factory worker, and later serving as a member of the police force in Spanish Town as well as in Kingston, McKay became acquainted with the plight of the urban working class and the desperation of the black poor of Kingston. He also took advantage of the opportunity to observe "higglering," the marketing end of peasant economic activity, in urban Jamaica, and especially in Kingston. McKay also encountered at close range the vicious species of colorism and class snobbery that the "brown" (light-skinned) middle class carried on in both Spanish Town and Kingston. As a constable, he learned about the colonial police force and the nakedness of its class rule and corrupt practices. His membership on the force radicalized him and he learned to detest the institution.

Perhaps the most remarkable feature of McKay's early years is the extent to which he lived on the borders, intersections and within the interstices of many worlds. Though of the peasantry, he was sufficiently separated from it to see that class with clear eyes. A member of the black middle class of Mount Carey, he never forgot his peasant past and his perspective of the middle class was profoundly informed by his blackness. McKay joined the police force, but never felt at home within it. Back in his village, he never felt at home: his success as a poet had robbed him of the relaxed warmth of village life.

When he returned home, he was treated like a "little personage."[195] He never liked it. (McKay was always a rather shy person, something his critics have never appreciated. He always genuinely hated the limelight, although he never let that stop him from speaking out.) In truth, the restlessness, the wanderlust so evident during his period of exile, was there from the age of seven when he joined the world of U. Theo at Mount Carey. Once he left the world into which he was born, the black Jamaican peasantry, he never knew peace. This inquietude and deep loneliness was given creative expression.

The knowledge and experience of these different spheres were to be brought together and drawn upon in McKay's Jamaican poetry. The young poet's political and social analyses were sharply articulated in his two anthologies published in 1912. A critical engagement with these volumes, along with other poems published in the Jamaican press, will therefore constitute the fundamental basis for our coming to terms with the politics of the young Jamaican, enabling us to plot the trajectory, from its very point of origin, of Claude McKay's political thought.

PART II

AN ANALYSIS OF McKAY'S JAMAICAN POETRY

2

SONGS OF LAMENT, SONGS OF PROTEST: AN INTRODUCTION

"Let me confess it at once," begins the twenty-two-year-old McKay,

> I had not in me the stuff that goes to the making of a good constable; for I am so constituted that imagination outruns discretion, and it is my misfortune to have a most improper sympathy with wrongdoers. I therefore never "made cases," but turning, like Nelson, a blind eye to what was my manifest duty to see, tried to make peace, which seemed to me better.
>
> Moreover, I am, by temperament, unadaptive; by which I mean that it is not in me to conform cheerfully to uncongenial usages. We blacks are all somewhat impatient of discipline, and to the natural impatience of my race there was added, in my particular case, a peculiar sensitiveness which made certain forms of discipline irksome, and a fierce hatred of injustice. Not that I ever openly rebelled; but the rebellion was in my heart, and it was fomented by the inevitable rubs of daily life—trifles to most of my comrades, but to me calamities and tragedies. To relieve my feelings, I wrote poems, and into them I poured my heart in its various moods.[1]

This 1912 preface to *Constab Ballads* is almost uncannily true of the man McKay was for the remaining thirty-six years of his life, as if it were a declaration of intent, a credo to live by. McKay's "improper sympathy with" wrongdoers is one of the hallmarks of his work. Prostitutes, "good-hearted bums," vagabonds and the motley outcasts of polite society inhabit, and inhabit with dignity, all his novels and many of his poems.[2]

The poems in *Constab Ballads* illustrate McKay's preface. But McKay's Jamaican language poems were not all concerned with explicitly political subjects. McKay was primarily a lyric poet. He also had an unusual range. Able to write in the most wistful and delicate manner about childhood, nature and rural life, he could also, in the next breath, summon up a fiery ball of words, blazing with rage. Few poets have expressed different and contrasting moods—sorrow and happiness, rage and ecstasy—as effectively as McKay. This rare capacity was noticed before he left Jamaica[3] and soon after his arrival in the United States. James Weldon Johnson, one of McKay's most discerning admirers and a loyal friend, wrote that "Reading McKay's poetry of protest and rebellion, it is difficult to imagine him dreaming of his native Jamaica and singing as he does in 'Flame Heart' or creating poetic beauty in the absolute as he does in 'The Harlem Dancer,' 'Spring in New Hampshire,' and many another of his poems. Of the major Negro poets he, above all, is the poet of passion. That passion found in his poems of rebellion, transmuted, is felt in his love lyrics."[4]

Songs of Jamaica and *Constab Ballads* are McKay's entry onto the literary stage. They constitute—like the breaking voice of an adolescent boy—the young Jamaican's stammering but eloquent maturing political voice. In these eighty-eight poems (including the ten published in the press) McKay's lifelong concern with race, color, class, justice and injustice, oppression and revolt are all given expression. We also see McKay's feminist sympathies publicly expressed for the first time. Indeed "A Midnight Woman to the Bobby" (in *Songs of Jamaica*) and "The Apple-Woman's Complaint" (in *Constab Ballads*) are often read as documents of state oppression and class difference, when they also clearly constitute powerful works of protest against the oppression of women qua women. It is in these 1912 collections that the origins of McKay's memorable female characters—Latnah (of *Banjo*), Crazy Mary and Sue Turner (of *Gingertown*), and Bita Plant (of *Banana Bottom*)—are to be found.

Still, McKay's most spirited and eloquent protests were directed at class (and thereby racial) oppression and at racial (and thereby class) oppression, and at the very imbrication of the two in the Jamaica in which he lived. McKay threw in his lot with the Jamaican oppressed and exploited, and in particular the peasantry and the urban poor of Spanish Town and Kingston where he served as a policeman. But McKay's worldview (at that point in his life) contained discernible and relatively sharp contradictions, tensions reflective of the social forces where he lived. We are left in no doubt as to what McKay was *against*, the objects of his social protest. But as to what he was *for*, beyond generalities, we are far less clear—and so was he. Perhaps it is to expect too much of McKay, or any artist, to present a clear alternative to the object of their social criticism. Some, even on the left, have argued that the proffering of alternatives is not and should not be the role of the artist.[5]

McKay juxtaposes the rural and the urban, where the rural is generally depicted positively and the urban is depicted as an alien, somewhat forbidding and almost diabolical world. But McKay's views of country life were not entirely positive, nor was he entirely dismissive of the urban environment. His attitude to both town and country were ambivalent. At a more prescriptively ideological level one finds more than a hint of Fabianism in his work—gradual social reform within the existing capitalist framework. *Songs of Jamaica* was dedicated, after all, to the island's governor, Sydney Olivier, a leading Fabian intellectual. Despite this, however, McKay's protest was far more radical and pointed than any vision he may have had of an alternative to the *status quo*. He was still searching ideologically.

Here was the Schopenhauerian intellectual pessimist with the

rebel heart of the optimist; here was one of Jamaica's first national-
ists declaring his love for the "Mother Country," Britain; here was
the proud African espousing Social Darwinism. Granted, there were
distinctive tendencies in the movement of his thought, but also
present were these far from trivial contradictions; one of the chal-
lenges of this work is to account for them.

3

THE WORLD OF THE STRUGGLING PEASANT

McKay had a detailed and intimate knowledge of the peasant's life; he always regarded and described himself as a proud child of Jamaica's black peasantry. He witnessed enormous upheavals in the rural proletarian and peasant classes—the secular and precipitous decline of sugar, the seductive but dubious rise of the banana as an export crop, the conspicuously widening inequalities in the distribution of the land, the economic dislocation expressed in rural to urban migration, the working-class flight to Panama. All of these turbulent developments of the time were chronicled, reflected, analyzed and interpreted in his poems.

Songs of Jamaica opens with "Quashie to Buccra." Quashie and buccra are antipodes of Jamaica's social world: the black country bumpkin, the peasant, the subaltern, and the symbol of power, superordination, the oppressor, the white man.[1] Here Quashie is giving buccra a piece of his mind:

> You tas'e petater an' you say it sweet,
> But you no know how hard we wuk fe it;
> You want a basketful fe quattiewut,
> 'Cause you no know how 'tiff de bush fe cut.[2]

The peasant complains that the white man simply devours the fruits of his labor without giving any thought to the effort put into their cultivation. Moreover, there is the constant haggle over the price, the persistent attempt to get the sweet potato for as little as possible—a "basketful fe quattiewut," that is, for one and a half pence. The peasant enlightens buccra about the stark hardship involved in the cultivation of the potato—the prickly plants that have to be negotiated or cleared with the cutlass, his enduring the prolonged, merciless and roasting rays of the sun ("hot like when fire ketch a town"), the predations of the nieghbor's pig which is borne without complaint "sake o' we naybor tongue." But quashie is not pathetic. He is proud of his work:

> De fiel' pretty? It couldn't less 'an dat,
> We wuk de bes', an' den de lan' is fat;
> We dig de row dem eben in a line,
> An' keep it clean—den so it *mus'* look fine.[3]

McKay is revealing the difficult production process, as it were, of the sweet potato as a commodity, a commodity that the rich whites consume without serious thought about how it reaches their plates. Through the growing division of labor, the gap between the acts of production and consumption widens, and capitalist relations of production, as Marx persuasively demonstrated in *Capital*, become alien, "estranged" from consumers. Individuals, especially those who are not involved in the cycle of production itself, consume without a sense of the processes of production/creation. (this condition existed in some pre-capitalist class societies but becomes even more pronounced under capitalism in tandem with the increasing division of labor and the development of the productive forces.[4]) Quashie provides buccra (and us) with an overview of the lifecycle of this commodity, the role of labor power in the process of its creation, from planting to reaping. In so doing he outlines the value of labor in the enterprise and also how the peasants are cheated of their hard work through low prices.

In "Hard Times" the troubles of the peasants are also given voice:

> De mo' me wuk, de mo' time hard,
>   I don't know what fe do;
> I ben' me knee an' pray to Gahd,
>   Yet t'ings same as befo'.
>
> De taxes knockin' at me door,
>   I hear de bailiff's v'ice;
> Me wife is sick, can't get no cure,
>   But gnawin' me like mice.[5]

The peasant's children went to school without a "bite fe taste," despite the fact that he has worked

> like a mule,
> While buccra, sittin' in de cool,
> Hab 'nuff nenyam fe waste.

On top of the inequalities, the crops are failing: "De peas won't pop, de corn can't grow." Yet there is the hard perseverance of the peasant: "I won't gib up, I won't say die."[6]

The inequalities seen from the perspective of the peasant are also powerfully represented in "Fetchin' Water," where the tourists are observed watching and thinking that the rigors of peasant life are somehow exotic:

> Watch how dem touris' like fe look
>   Out 'pon me little daughter,
> Wheneber fe her tu'n to cook
>   Or fetch a pan of water:
>   De sight look gay;
>   Dat is one way,
>   But I can tell you say,
> 'Nuff rock'tone in de sea, yet none
> But those 'pon lan' know 'bouten sun.[7]

The boy coming up the hill with a gourd full of water is also the target of the tourists' gaze. The boy feels the "weight," the burden of the load, while the tourists "watch him gait," no doubt admiring his "natural" balance, his "natural" rhythm:

> It's so some of de great
> High people fabour t'ink it sweet
> Fe batter in de boilin' heat.[8]

The hardship of the life of the peasant child is also graphically depicted in "Retribution" which describes boys required to catch the mules and the donkey before nightfall. The task is not easy "for de whole o' dem can run," and the field is the domain of formidable grass-lice:

> Grass-lice dat mek you trimble long time more
>   dan when you meet
> A man dat mean to fight you who you know you
>   cannot beat;
> Dem mek you feel you' blood crawl from you' head
>   do'n to you' feet . . .[9]

There is no tongue-in-cheek humor in "Two-an'-Six," but pathos, finally relieved by hope. In these fifteen stanzas, McKay describes a day in the life of a peasant, Cous' Sun. It is "Sateday," a market day, and he gets up early: "de stars are shinin' still."[10] He's off to market with a lot on his mind:

> Cous' Sun sits in hired dray,
> Drivin' 'long de market way;
> Whole week grindin' sugar-cane
> T'rough de boilin' sun an' rain,
> Now, a'ter de toilin' hard,
> He goes seekin' his reward,
> While he's thinkin' in him min'
> Of de dear ones lef' behin',
> Of de loved though ailin' wife,
> Darlin' treasure of his life,
> An' de picknies, six in all,
> Whose 'nuff burdens 'pon him fall:

> Seben lovin' ones in need,
> Seben hungry mouths fe feed;
> On deir wants he thinks alone,
> Neber dreamin' of his own,

But gwin' on wid joyful face
Till him re'ch de market-place.[11]

It is a bad day for sellers of sugar—it is going at "tup an' gill" (two and a half pence) per quart. And despite the fact that the tyrannous market for sugar is already ruling in their favor, the buyers still take advantage:

Sugar tup an' gill a quart,
Yet de people hab de heart
Wantin' brater top o' i',
Want de sweatin' higgler fe
Ram de pan an' pile i' up,
Yet sell i' fe so-so tup.[12]

Sugar was selling for only "two-an'-six" (two shillings and six pence) a tin. Dejected, Cous' Sun makes his way home without even making the usual stop at the candy store to buy the children sweetmeats. When he gets home

. . . de children scamper roun',
Each one stretchin' out him han',
Lookin' to de poor sad man.

Oh, how much he felt de blow,
As he watched dem face fall low,
When dem wait an' nuttin' came
An' drew back deir han's wid shame![13]

His wife kisses and consoles him. She is determined to

Cut an' carve, an' carve an' cut,
Mek gill sarbe fe quattiewut';
We mus' try mek two ends meet
Neber mind how hard be it.
We won't mind de haul an' pull,
while dem pickny belly full.[14]

Sun's spirits lift. He and his wife get down to the business of counting the takings for the day and calculate their financial obligations and

A'ter all de business fix',
Was a princely two-an'-six.[15]

The accuracy of this poem to reality has been corroborated by the anthropological research conducted by Martha Beckwith in the 1920s: "[W]hen money is plentiful and prices high, much coin changes hands at the market and provision stores." When the market is low, the peasants resort to bartering, "but always in terms of money value." She recorded the chorus of what the peasants call a "hard time" song that is remarkably similar to McKay's own poetry.

> Annotto can't sell, the price is unfair,
> Pimento a blossom and drop.
> Hard time, hard time,
> Hard time a carry the day.
> Hard time, hard time,
> For they won't put cramouchin' away.[16]

In "Whe' Fe Do?" we have the clearest evidence of Schopenhauer's philosophical influence on the young McKay. There is no way out of the troubles of peasant life here, so 'whe' fe do?'—what can we do?

> We've got to wuk wid might an' main,
> To use we han' an' use we brain,
> To toil an' worry, 'cheme an' 'train
> Fe t'ings that bring more loss dan gain;
> To stan' de sun an' bear de rain,
> An' suck we bellyful o' pain
> Widouten cry nor yet complain—
>   For dat caan' do.
>
> .   .   .   .
> We'll try an' live as any man,
> An' fight de wul' de best we can,
> E'en though it hard fe understan'
>   Whe' we mus' do.
>
> For da's de way o' dis ya wul';
> It's snap an' bite, an' haul an' pull,
> An' we all get we bellyful—
>   But whe' fe do?[17]

"We' Fe Do?"is the most pessimistic of McKay's Jamaican poems and, with one exception,[18] perhaps of the poet's entire oeuvre.

Schopenhauer was one of Walter Jekyll's favorite thinkers, and Jekyll had translated and edited a volume entitled *The Wisdom of Schopenhauer as Revealed in Some of His Writings.* Although McKay had made an earlier acquaintance with Schopenhauer through U. Theo's library, Jekyll undoubtedly deepened McKay's knowledge and appreciation of the philosopher: "Mr. Jekyll was translating Schopenhauer and I read a lot of his translation."[19]

"Life is a task to be worked off," Schopenhauer declared, "in this sense *defunctus* is a fine expression."[20] To him, human existence is a synonym for "work, worry, toil, and trouble."[21] Were it not for necessity and the intense pleasure derived from sex, it is doubtful that human beings would want to reproduce themselves as a species because of the inherent suffering that the task of life is constituted by. Were procreation "a matter of pure rational deliberation," would not "everyone feel so much sympathy for the coming generation that he would prefer to spare it the burden of existence, or at any rate would not like to assume in cold blood the responsibility of imposing on it such a burden?"[22] Human existence is "a uselessly disturbing episode in the blissful repose of nothingness. . . . [L]ife on the whole is *a disappointment, nay a cheat.*"[23] The whole business of living was worse than disappointing: "The world is just a *hell* and in it human beings are the tortured souls on the one hand, and the devils on the other."[24]

But McKay's cheerless philosophy in "Whe' Fe Do?" cannot be completely attributed to his encounter with Schopenhauerian philosophy through Jekyll's ideology or directly through his own reading. The worldview of the peasants themselves might have showed him as much, as with their fatalism in relation to natural disasters such as hurricanes, floods and droughts—not infrequent visitors to the island when McKay lived there.[25] There was also an affinity and homology between the conjuncture within which McKay wrote and Schopenhauer's melancholic philosophy. At the time of these poems, the Jamaican people were experiencing unspeakable hardship, with almost no prospect of relief in sight. For the overwhelming majority of peasants and workers, *fin de siècle* Jamaica *was* a rather hellish place—a place very much like Schopenhauer's world, where it was not inappropriate to put one's hands on one's head and ask the gods "Whe' fe do?"

Although Schopenhauerian motifs may be found from time to time in McKay's writings in the United States as well as when he lived in Europe, such pessimism was generally foreign to his outlook. McKay endured sadness, sorrow and loneliness, but he never committed himself to a philosophy of disillusionment with life and the world. He revelled in the adventure of living. From time to time he slipped into desperately dark moods but he also knew how to laugh. Max Eastman, a close friend of McKay's, wrote about the "ironical and mischievous" side of the man. In a biographical sketch (which happened to be as revealing about himself as about McKay) Eastman observed: "His laughter at the frailties of his friends and enemies, no matter which—that high, half-wailing falsetto laugh of the recklessly delighted Darky—was the center of my joy in him throughout our friendship of more than thirty years."[26] McKay also had more than a little sympathy for hedonism; *Home to Harlem* and *Banjo* make that clear. Like Jake, the protagonist of his novel *Home to Harlem*, "Sometimes he was disgusted with life, but he was never frightened of it."[27] His characteristic posture was a combination of defiance and struggle.

McKay's world of the peasant is not all struggle; neither was the peasants' actual world a one-sided experience of unmitigated hardship. They also knew community, an ordered pattern of existence (albeit one increasingly disturbed by the expansion of agriarian capitalism) camaraderie and systems of mutual support as well as of gossip, quarreling, inequality and predial larceny. McKay wrote hardly a negative word about the Jamaican peasantry. We would have to wait some thirty years before some of the unpleasant aspects of peasant life would be questioned in *My Green Hills of Jamaica*. For the moment, McKay's rural folk would only be censured, half-jokingly, for being "too bad" and for believing in obeah—and then it was not specifically the peasantry but black people in general, "naygur," who were criticized.[28] After McKay joined the police force and worked in Spanish Town and Kingston and was exposed to the harshness of urban life as an enforcer of the law, not even these criticisms would escape his lips. His Clarendon hills would become his rural idyll.

4

CONSTAB BLUES:
BLACK CONSCIOUSNESS AND
BLACK SOLIDARITY

In *My Green Hills of Jamaica*, written in the premature evening of his life, McKay vividly recalled his first visit to Kingston as a child accompanied by U. Theo's wife. He was struck by the size of the city, "so many times larger than the little village where my brother taught school." His sister-in-law had gone to the city to shop and they visited its main thoroughfares. He remembered going to the stores on Harbour Street, King Street and Orange Street. "I gazed with wonder at the stores, thinking they were so large and beautiful. Years later I was just as overwhelmed and bewildered when I first arrived in New York City."

McKay remembered his first ice cream, bought by his sister-in-law from a Kingston vendor. He also remembered that on his very first trip to Kingston he vomited on the train when the trees "seemed to be rushing by as we rode along." He could not eat lunch on the train "but when I got off and we drove through the city I was so excited that I did not care about eating."[1] This is the beginnings of McKay's fascination with cities. Over the years, as he traveled in the United States, Europe and North Africa, McKay grew to love some cities more than others, but he developed a strange and powerful attraction to metropolises in general that abided with him for the rest of his life.

The discussion of his attitude towards cities is one of the weakest elements of the critical literature on McKay. Critics have registered what they see as his negative position about cities at the expense of noticing the enormous thrill he always got from them— especially from large cities such as New York. The critical literature is littered with remarks that miss McKay's nuanced ambivalence towards urban life. How can a critic square McKay's alleged "antipathy for the city"[2] with, for example, this passage reporting his feelings as his ship approaches New York harbor on its way back from Europe in 1921?

> Like fixed massed sentinels guarding the approaches to the great metropolis, again the pyramids of New York in their Egyptian majesty dazzled my sight like a miracle of might and took my breath like the banging music of Wagner assaulting one's spirit and rushing it skyward with the pride and power of an eagle.
>
> The feeling of the dirty steerage passage across the Atlantic was swept away in the immense wonder of clean, vertical heaven-challenging lines, a glory to the grandeur of space.
>
> Oh, I wished that it were possible to know New York in that way only—as a masterpiece wrought like a searchlight, making one big and great with feeling.[3]

The critic Jean Wagner, a thorough researcher, must have known better, for his notes on McKay[4]—made during the research for his book—include the opening poem to a remarkable but still unpublished collection which McKay entitled "Cities."

> Oh cities are a fever in my blood,
> And all their moods find lodgement in my breast,
> Whether they sweep me onward like a flood
> Or torture me as an unwanted guest,
> With wormwood flavoring my scanty foods,
> I love all cities, I love their changing moods.
>
> I love all cities, I love their foreign ways,
> Their tyranny over the life of man,

> Their wakeful nights and never-resting days,
> Their mighty movements seeing without plan,
> Their pavement stones on which the broken fall,
> Their damning wickedness: I love it all.[5]

It should come as no surprise that this poem is nowhere to be found in the book itself—nor is it even referred to.[6] Instead, the section "Rejection of the City" features this bold thesis: "Hatred of the city is one of the principal motifs in McKay's . . . poems."[7] McKay's attitude towards cities was ambivalent, but he loved them more than he hated them.

The foregoing is aimed at bringing into focus a questionable orthodoxy in McKay criticism which has obfuscated an important dimension of McKay's Jamaican poetry. A more careful reading of his Kingston and Spanish Town poems, written while in the constabulary, reveals that his experience of those cities cannot be separated from his experience on the police force. He saw the urban environment on the beat, so to speak. Those poems hitherto viewed as writings about Kingston are in fact less about Kingston per se and primarily about the travails of a reluctant black policeman serving in Jamaica in 1910 and 1911. McKay's Kingston, would have been in all likelihood, a very different place had he not been in uniform. His policeman's badge gave him access to forms of life in the city that he otherwise might not have encountered at all, and certainly not encountered with the same degree of frequency and depth of familiarity. Indeed, prior to his entering the police force, all of his references to Kingston were favorable ones.

Before the 1907 earthquake, McKay very much enjoyed his stay in Kingston. "The change from the hills of Clarendon to the city of Kingston was stupendous," he wrote. His cousin, with whom he lodged for part of his stay in the city, looked after him and saw to it that he had a good time. "My cousin knew many of the better class girls from the villages who were working in Kingston as clerks and maids. They all came to his apartment and of course I was impressed by their stylish dress and hairdo. We went to concerts in Queen Victoria Park and to the beaches where we swam."[8] McKay wanted to stay in Kingston but the earthquake's destruction of the trade school and its mangling of the infrastructure of Kingston meant that he had to find a tradesman to train with in the countryside. Still he was reluctant: "I wanted to stay in Kingston for a year because I liked the glamour of the city, and I thought that in the meantime I could find what trade I wanted to take up."[9] McKay summed up this period in Kingston with the following words: "I was very happy."[10]

How do we reconcile these words with the poetry in *Songs of Jamaica* and *Constab Ballads*? The reconciliation is relatively straightforward but it is only so if we step outside of the poems and examine them in their proper context. Kingston had certainly undergone changes between 1907 and 1910, but it was not Kingston that had changed as much as the position that McKay occupied in the city and the vantage point from which he viewed it.

In contrast to the young, aspiring apprentice that he was when he first moved to Kingston in 1907, in 1910 McKay was a policeman, a hated "red seam," as the peasants, alluding to their uniform, derisively dubbed members of the constabulary. His poems in *Constab Ballads* are directed against the police much more than at the city of Kingston. These poems were not entitled "urban blues," partly because they were not. But they could be easily described as "constab blues." The poems tell of the hypocrisy of the police force ("Papine Corner," "The Apple-Woman's Complaint"),[11] of the class snobbery and abuse of power in the force ("Pay Day," "Flat-Foot Drill," "The Apple-Woman's Complaint," "A Labourer's Life Give Me"),[12] of petty corruption there ("A Recruit on the Corpy," "The Bobby to the Sneering Lady"),[13] of mindless callousness ("De Dog-Driver's Frien'").[14] (It is never said, but it is nevertheless true that these poems also tell of the incidental friendship and camaraderie that developed in the force, especially in the early part of McKay's tenure.)[15]

The most valuable aspect of these poems, read as indices of McKay's political evolution, is that he expresses even more explicitly than in his earlier poems in *Songs of Jamaica* his empathy with the black oppressed, including Kingston's poor. His unhappy experience in the force pushed him to what we may call an openly black nationalist position where he felt part of the black masses of his Jamaica—those who in Jamaican (as opposed to American) parlance would be described as black (as opposed to "brown," "mulatto," or "light-skinned") and "Negro" (as opposed to "colored" or "mixed"). These were literally the darkest members of the black population who crowded the lowest rung of the social ladder. Thus, to identify with this group also meant identification with an economic category or class—black proletarians and, more generally, poor people in the city and in the countryside, the peasantry and agro-proletarians. One therefore has the conceptual linking, indeed imbrication, of race and class in the young McKay's thinking. This connection with the black masses is brought out most forcefully in "The Bobby to the Sneering Lady" and in "The Heart of a Constab."

In "The Bobby to the Sneering Lady," the policeman narrator is called to the home of a member of the white or "light" upper middle class of Kingston. She wants the police to arrest her (black) servant girl (for reasons unspecified in the poem) although she has already beaten the girl. The policeman tells the woman that although he is an enforcer of the law he has feelings too. He refuses to arrest the girl:

> Our soul's jes' like fe you,
>   If our work does make us rough;
> Me won't 'res' you servant-gal
>   When you've beaten her enough.[16]

The woman accuses the Bobby of being the servant's friend and threatens to report him for refusing to arrest her. He acknowledges that his inspector is "flinty hard" and that he would lose a "few days' pay" or be locked in a cell, were she to lodge a complaint against him. But such "pains and losses" are nothing new to him; he has been fined heavily in the past for petty violations of the police code of conduct. His superiors are keen and zealous in the imposition of fines, as such money is used to build up the reward fund—out of which rewards are ostensibly given to constables for meritorious work.[17] But the policeman will not be disloyal to his "own" poor black people:

> Ef our lot, then, is so hard,
>> I mus' ever bear in mind
> Dat to fe me own black 'kin
>> I mus' not be too unkind.[18]

In "The Heart of a Constab," the policeman narrator sorrowfully and regretfully reflects upon the heavy personal price he has paid for joining the force. He feels the pain of his rejection by those whom he regards as his people; he hates the fact that he has effectively betrayed them:

> Oh! where are de faces I loved in de past,
>> De frien's dat I used to hold dear?
> Oh say, have dey all turned away from me now
>> Becausen de red seam I wear?
>
> I foolishly wandered away from dem all
>> To dis life of anguish an' woe,
> Where I mus' be hard on me own kith an' kin,
>> And even to frien' mus' prove foe.
>
> Oh! what have I gained from my too too rash act
>> O' joinin' a hard Constab Force,
> Save quenchin' me thirst from a vinegar cup,
>> De vinegar cup o' remorse?

He had entered the force with honest intentions, to carry out "pure honest toil"; the experience proved otherwise. "But no, de life surely is bendin' me do'n,/Is bendin' me do'n to de death." Most agonizing is his own people's rejection of him:

> 'Tis grievous to think dat, while toilin' on here,
>> My people won't love me again,

My people, my people, me owna black skin,—
De wretched t'ought gives me such pain.

He resolves to follow his conscience and leave the force.

But I'll leave it, my people, an' come back to you,
I'll flee from de grief an' turmoil;
I'll leave it, though flow'rs here should line my path yet,
An' come back to you an de' soil.

For 'tis hatred without an' 'tis hatred within,
An' how can I live 'douten heart?
Then oh for de country, de love o' me soul,
From which I shall nevermore part![19]

"I . . . joined the Jamaican Constabulary . . . despised it and left," McKay wrote years later.[20] His 1932 volume of short stories, *Gingertown*, contains an incongruous, hybrid and remarkable text called "When I Pounded the Pavement." Not strictly a tale of fiction, not straight autobiography either, written in the first person, it stands in sharp contrast to the other eleven stories in the volume. The story is based upon his experience in the force and is substantially autobiographical. It tells of a sensitive black policeman trying to withstand the pressure to "make cases"— arrest, charge, prosecute, win conviction—however unjustly they may be made. The protagonist yearns to leave the force without making a case: "Nothing could please me more and my peasant friends and relatives who abhorred my profession."[21] The peasants' attitude to the police is described and explained in the following terms:

As a son of peasants, I also had in my blood the peasant's instinctive hostility for police people. In spite of night marauders who rifled their fields and stole chickens and goats, the peasants liked the police less than the thieves. When the thieves were caught, it was invariably the peasants who did [so] themselves and brought them to justice. The "red seams" . . . always distinguished themselves in other ways that were hateful to the peasants. They always butted in on family feuds and quarrels and made arrests when such troubles might have been easily settled by our old heads. And on popular marketing days, mostly Saturdays, when the peasants crowded the towns with their stuff, drinking rum and making merry with the rough obscene vocabulary of the fields, the uniformed police would pounce on them for disorderly conduct and thus take most of the money they made out of their pockets.[22]

One of the narrator's friends and fellow policemen was also put under pressure for not having made a case. He quickly made one in order to get his superiors off his back.

While he was on his beat he was accosted by a street girl that we both used to visit in common. She teased him a little for doing patrol duty, and he arrested her for "obstructing a constable on his duty." The girl had thought it was all a joke. But when the court fined her ten shillings with twenty-one days imprisonment, her smiling turned to a terrible howling.[23]

For the narrator, this was more than he could take and remain in the police force. "The last thread of feeling attaching me to the place had snapped and all my desire now was to get out and away from it."[24]

McKay, goes on to illustrate how the black police force was used to stifle black advancement. Mr. Klinger, a white official working in the colonial bureaucracy in Kingston, uses a black police constable to arrest the lover of his female domestic servant. At Klinger's insistence, the policeman arrives at his home early and unobtrusively, then waits until the "intruder" is in the maid's shed at the back of the house. The lover, a black man, is duly apprehended while in bed with the girl and arrested for trespassing. It transpires that the lover is also a candidate for the legislative chamber. "I learned later that his opponent, a European, was a friend of Mr. Klinger's; some said he was even a relative."

I had to arrest him. He dressed himself and I took him to the lock-up. The next day his father bailed him out. And he was front-page news, photograph and all. When the case was tried he received a maximum sentence. Six months in prison and twenty-one strokes of the tamarind switch. Convicted as a common criminal, his political career was broken. But I think that what broke him most of all was the switch. Policemen holding him down on a block and taking down his pants and whipping him for sleeping with a girl.

It was my first and last case. Before I could make another I managed to obtain my discharge from the constabulary.[25]

The evidence suggests that it was experiences such as this one, however fictionalized, which honed McKay's black nationalist consciousness and sensibilities.

McKay's portrait of the force and its oppression of poor black people is amply buttressed by contemporary reports in the Jamaica press. The following, for example, was carried without comment by the *Gleaner* in 1913. It reads, in full: "Charged with trading on the Lord's Day—selling curios to tourists on Sunday last, David Roberts was in the Police Court yesterday fined 5 [shillings] or 7 days [in jail]. He was prosecuted by Sergt.-Major Black who asked that he be made an example of."[26] The fine of five shillings amounted to more than a week's wages for a highly skilled worker at the time. Roberts probably had to spend seven days in jail and the jails were notorious for their inhumane conditions.

The authorities were determined to see to it that tourists to the island were not inconvenienced in any way. One Thomas Campbell was arrested in Kingston for begging from tourists. He represented himself in court for he obviously could not afford and was not provided legal support. He explained that he was from the country, new to the city, and did not know it was illegal to beg. "You are a perfect pest to the unfortunate people [the tourists]," Justice Burke told Campbell and sentenced him to six strokes of the tamarind switch. In the same session of the Police Court, Burke fined Jacob Jones ten shillings and six pence or fourteen days in jail for using indecent language in the presence of tourists.[27] Such cases were not uncommon:

Piloted by a "limb of the law," John Hylton, a blind old man, found his way into the Police Court dock yesterday forenoon, to answer a charge of soliciting alms.

Hylton, who is well known in Kingston, has for a good many years been deprived of his sight, and thus depends on charity for daily sustenance. Not long ago, in his wanderings around the city seeking alms, Hylton used to be guided by a faithful member of the canine tribe which, with a string attached to its neck and held by its blind master, would lead him safely out of danger.

The dog has died and now Hylton depends on his stick and the kind assistance of more fortunate folks.

On Saturday last, Hylton was in King Street, where he hailed each passer with his usual cry: "Pity the blind." Constable McEwan was nearby and he was called upon by one of his superior officers to take the man in charge. The crowd which gathered was a sympathetic one and there were cries of "Shame!" but the law had to be carried out.

When the case was brought up a Mr. H.A.L. Lake spoke up on behalf of Mr. Hylton. He had known Hylton for a number of years and thought it "pretty hard to expect a man who had lost his sight and had no means of getting support to do anything beside seeking alms." Lake thought that "if His Honour admonished and discharged the defendant, he would be sufficiently punished." But the magistrate said that he would remand Hylton in custody for "a few days" and so Mr. Hylton was sent to jail.[28]

McKay's anguished days in the police force haunted him and lingered in his memory. Some twenty years after leaving the constabulary he confessed to a friend that, "Being a cop, even though it was for a short time, was one of the few things that I ever did that I profoundly regretted."[29] By "frankly writing" the story "When I Pounded the Pavement," "I have expiated," he wrote. But McKay was far too sensitive a person to effect such an easy expiation, and his remark lacks persuasion. He was, however, able to recognize that although he "loathed" it, "the experience was interesting."

A final note: there is a striking incongruity between the note of dedication in *Constab Ballads* and the content of the book itself. The note reads: "To Lieut. Col. A.E. Kershaw, Inspector-General of Constabulary, and to Inspector W.E. Clark, Under Whom the

Author had The Honour of Serving, This Volume is Respectfully and Gratefully dedicated." It appears, at least from McKay's own explanation in a private correspondence, that the dedication was the combined result of Jekyll's manipulation (he sponsored the volume) calculated *realpolitik* and genuine regard. This is how McKay explained the anomalous dedication:

> I never could stand [*Constab Ballads*] because for one thing it was dedicated to the Inspector General whom we all (constabs) disliked. But the Englishman who sponsored the publication thought it was "good taste" to give the Inspector General the dedication especially as he was trying to get my discharge from the service. I wanted the dedication to go solely to Inspector Clark whom we all liked.[30]

McKay and his colleagues did have genuine fondness for Clark. The new recruits suffered more directly at the hands of the lower ranking officers, especially the drill sergeants, a number of whom were apparently confused and cruel light-skinned men who had nothing but contempt for the dark-skinned beat policemen who came mainly from the countryside. "Flat-Foot Drill" effectively depicts the verbal abuse that the raw recruits suffered at the hands of these colored underlings of empire. The poem presents the barked admonitions and insults of the black recruits by a drill instructor. To the instructor, the recruits are hopelessly stupid and clumsy:

> 'Tention! keep you' han's dem still,
> Can't you tek in dat a li'l?
>   Hearin' all, but larnin' none.
>
> But seems unno all do'n-ca',
>   Won't mek up you' min' fe larn;
> Drill-instructor boun' fe swea',
> Dealin' wid you' class all day,
>   Neber see such from A barn.

The attack upon the "class" background of the country recruits becomes even more brutal and dense:

> Right tu'n, you damn' bungo brut'!
>   Do it *so*, you mountain man;
> Car' behin' de bluff lef' foot,
> Seems i' frighten fe de boot!
>   Why you won't keep do'n you' han'?

The ferocity of the insults cannot be fully appreciated without a proper understanding of some of the language used. *Bungo* is translated in McKay's glossary to *Constab Ballads* as "black African," but this does not fully impart the meaning of the term. In Jamaican it was synonymous with nincompoop, very black, ugly, stupid, a country bumpkin.[31] (It still carries a negative connotation in Jamaica despite the fact that the Rastafarians, following the practise of the African-derived Kumina religion, have tried to invert and subvert its racist implications.) The drill instruction thus added charge to the already potent insult by describing the recruit as a "damned bungo brute." To call the recruit "mountain man" is to further enforce, if not repeat, "bungo brute." When the instructor shouts "Car' behin' de bluff lef' foot,/Seems i' frighten fe de boot!" he is surmising that the foot is frightened of the boot and suggesting that the recruit is used to going barefoot and is flummoxed by the experience of having to move with something on his feet—for *bluff* means clumsily large.

The instructor will brook no explanation, let alone protest: "Shet you' mout'!" he yelled, "A wan' no chat!" He suggests that it is only because they are now, for the first time, eating decent food provided by the police force ("nyamin' Depot fat") and having a bed to sleep in instead of bare mats ("so-so mat") that they have the strength and pluck to talk back at all. But he will soon put them back in their place:

> A mean fe pull you' tongue,
>   Wonder when unno wi' fit
> Fe move up in-a fus' squad,
>   Use carbine an' bayonet!

But he resolves to make these bungo men into constables despite their grievous failings—even if he has to drive them insane: "Wait dough,—unno wi' larn yet,—/Me wi' drill you ti' you mad."[32]

In "A Labourer's Life Give Me" McKay creates a response to the drill instructor. The narrator here expresses his regret at having joined the force and wishes he could return to the land.

> If I'd followed a peasant's career,
>   I would now be a happier lad;
> You would not be abusing me here,
>   An' mekin' me sorry an' sad.
>
> Fool! I hated my precious birthright,
>   Scornin' what made my father a man;
> Now I grope in de pitchy dark night,
>   Hate de day when me poo' life began.
>
> To de loved country life I'll return,
>   I don't mind at all, Sir, if you smile;
> As a peasant my livin' I'll earn,
>   An' a labourer's life is worth while.[33]

Ellen Tarry, an Afro-American writer who became close friends with McKay during the last decade of his life, thinks that McKay's experience in the constabulary had enduring effects upon him. One of McKay's Jamaican friends told Tarry that when the poet was on the force, his immediate superior, "a stern, uncompromising, sometimes unreasonable task-master, was a mulatto." Tarry believes that the "indignities—real and imaginary—which Claude suffered at this man's hands left their mark."[34] (In sharp contrast to the drill instructor of "Flat-Foot Drill," Inspector Clark was regarded as tough but fair, and McKay wrote two poems which said so: "Though often you have been our judge,/We never owed you one lee grudge,/For you were always fair . . .".[35])

McKay fired a parting shot at the drill sergeants as he left the police force. He concluded his preface to *Constab Ballads*, a book that was published after he had sailed for the United States, with the following words:

> As constituted by the authorities the Force is admirable, and it only remains for the men themselves, and especially the sub-officers, to make it what it should be, a harmonious band of brothers.[36]

It is doubtful that McKay truly believed that the constabulary was admirable as constituted. As with this dedication, this part of the preface may reflect Jekyll's sentiment rather than McKay's. And like the dedication, it might have been a calculated way of currying favor with the top brass in order to gain his discharge. If he did indeed believe that the force was admirable, if only in its formal arrangements, he certainly did not reveal it in his poetry.

It is just as well that McKay had left the police force at the end of 1911, for early in the new year Kingston's uneasy peace was shattered by a popular uprising that was unprecedented in the city's history. In the end, the primary target of the people's fury was the police.

The whole affair started innocently enough. On February 17 1912, the Canadian-owned West India Electric Company that operated Kingston's tramway services, announced that it would no longer offer seven vouchers for two shillings but six. This amounted to a more than 14 per cent increase in the cost of travel. The residents of Kingston were outraged. Their representatives on the city council and in the legislative council protested to the governor and the company on their behalf. The mayor of Kingston was especially angry with the governor for having allowed the increase without any prior consultation with the people's local representatives. In its reportage and editorials, the *Gleaner* was more critical of Governor Olivier than it was of the West India Electric Company.

The people took matters into their own hands by refusing to buy the two-shilling voucher and instead buying two-pence vouchers one at a time. Moreover, they expanded the protest by paying in farthings. The protest soon escalated to more ingenious ways of inconveniencing the company in order to force it to back down.

One man started the practice of putting one farthing in the box and then handing the conductor a two-and-six-pence piece to take the remaining seven farthings from. These and other obstructionist tactics soon came to be called "passive resistance" with the practitioners "passive resisters." They managed to slow the progress of the conductors to such an extent that many people were not asked for their fares before they reached their destination. The company's income was reduced and the conductors' inconvenience maximized.

The resisters now began to ask for receipts verifying payment and transfers, to which they were entitled but had never previously demanded from conductors. Remarkably, the company did not have the receipts requested nor did they have the transfer slips. They also did not have enough farthings to provide change for the passengers. The company sent to England to get more farthings to counteract the resisters, but one ingenious group of citizens (a "syndicate," the *Gleaner* called it) attempted to amass as many farthings as possible to frustrate the company's move. As the protest continued, drivers and conductors were forced to stop trams when passengers refused to pay without receiving receipts. This frustrated the remaining passengers who demanded refunds, since they were not taken to their destinations. The police were frequently called by conductors and road masters working for the company, but the police refrained from arresting the resisters, perhaps fearful of being attacked by an enraged citizenry. Two members of the Kingston middle class were arrested, however, after Harry McCrea, the deputy inspector of the constabulary and head of the Kingston police called up reinforcements, including mounted policemen, when one passenger, Caulville Heath, refused to pay without a receipt. F.A. Judah, a member of a well-known merchant family saw the incident and remarked: "Why should a man who has done nothing wrong be arrested?" For this, McCrea asked for Judah's name and address. Judah refused and he too was arrested. McCrea quickly became the most hated man in

Kingston. The *Gleaner* attacked him, the mayor and Kingston's council called upon the governor to dismiss him, as did H.A. Simpson, the city's popular representative in the legislative council. The crowds booed and jeered Inspector McCrea whenever he appeared.[37]

The protest was genteel and good-humored. For a week, Kingston basked in a carnivalesque mood as the passengers and the people as a whole felt their strength and noticed the company's growing discomfiture. According to the newspapers, the prime movers behind the "passive resistance" were young men, mainly clerks, who depended upon the trams to get to and from work in the commerical area of the city. The conductors suffered the most as they were increasingly frustrated in the execution of their work. "For God sake, Sir, caut [sic] you behave yourself?" one exasperated conductor asked a passive resister.[38] But soon, they too resigned themselves to the situation, many not even bothering to collect the fares.

By the end of the first week of protesting, the little people of Kingston started to take a greater hand in the protest. The management of the West India Electric Company grew more and more irritated, but instead of relenting by rescinding the fare increase, it pressured the government to intervene on the company's side, it chided the *Gleaner* for supporting the resisters, it insulted the mayor in a most disrespectful manner, and it called upon the forces of law and order to take action. McCrea was happy to oblige and the police beat up a group of working-class protesters on the night of Saturday, February 24. The mounting violence of the police was met with the violence of the Kingston poor. The latter sought revenge the following night in the downtown area of Kingston.

The violence intensified on Sunday night and reached its climax on Monday night. The city leaders' call for calm had gone largely unheeded. Three of the company's streetcars were damaged and another was commandeered by the crowd, who drove it down

Orange Street and then onto the foot of King Street where it was set on fire and partially destroyed.

The stoning of policemen meanwhile intensified and the force was placed on the defensive for the first time. Inspector Kershaw had the temerity to drive into one of the hot spots at the corner of Orange Street and North Street. He reported that his vehicle was "followed by a shower of stones." When he turned the corner he found two of his sub-inspectors and a small party of policemen "bombarded by a hurricane of bricks and stones from the yards on both sides of the street." His men made repeated charges, but as they could not get to close quarters and as they were nearly all injured he "ordered a retreat to Barracks which was carried out."[39]

The crowd laid siege to the main police station in Kingston that night and they were dispersed only after Inspector Kershaw read the Riot Act and the police opened fire, killing one person on the spot and wounding over thirty others during a series of running battles in the commercial area of the city. Seven policemen were caught unawares by a large group of rioters wielding sticks, bricks and iron pipes. They took to their heels and the crowd pursued them. "Away with the policemen!" went the cry. "Lick them! Lick them!" shouted the crowd, in hot pursuit. "Pursued by the mob like wolves pursuing their prey," the policemen made a narrow escape into Burke's rum shop at the corner of Orange and Beeston streets, downtown. A quick-witted barmaid bolted the doors behind the fleeing policemen just in time. The crowd attacked. "Murder! Murder! Help! Help!" came the desperate bawling from the bar—strange noises to be heard from Missa Kershaw's bullying policemen! It must have been music to the ears of the avenging Kingston poor. Olivier, who happened to be passing the area in his car, heard the screams, ordered his driver to stop, got out of the car and sought to relieve the trapped constables. "You are a brave man," the crowd told the governor, "but we mean to get square with these policemen." The governor remonstrated with the crowd, telling them "how surprised he was at their behaviour and asking what had come over them."[40] Soon, he too was the object of attack. He was hit twice by bricks but not seriously hurt; his aide-de-camp bundled him back into his car and they sped off. The policemen managed to escape through the rear of the bar while the crowd was distracted by its exchange with the governor.

Kingston had seen nothing of the kind before. Respectable Jamaica was shocked. "What a week of it! This is a visitation!" some cried.[41] The *Jamaica Times* trawled the history books to find out if there were any parallels for this sort of treatment of a representative of the Crown anywhere in the Empire. The *Times* discovered that Lord Elgin (who served in Jamaica between 1842 and 1845) had been pelted by English-speaking Canadians in Montreal in 1847, while he was Governor there, for the passing of an unpopular law.[42]

The papers first reported that the governor was hit by accident, that the flying bricks were not meant for Sir Sydney. But the trial of Cyril McKoy and Joel Mallacci, who were charged with the assault, told a story of intent to harm Olivier. The men had no legal representation in court and the evidence against them—including that of their own witnesses—was overwhelming. According to chief witness Charles Clarke, McKoy was one of the ringleaders of the group that besieged Burke's rum shop. When the doors were bolted behind the policemen, McKoy went and got a hatchet which he gave to another man to chop open the saloon window. When Olivier's car came along, two men got out and made their way to the window. Mallacci is said to have called out "Do you know who that is? It is Olivier. Lick him!" He hurled a brick at Olivier and McKoy sent another, hitting the governor while others in the crowd let their bricks fly at the car now speeding quickly off. Clarke, who was a schoolmate of Mallacci's, saw all this and reported it to the police. Another witness reported that McKoy boasted that he was the second man to hit the governor. Mallacci called a witness, but the man testified against Mallacci, saying he saw the accused pick up two bricks in Luke Lane that night. According to this witness, Mallacci cried out: "White give black authority to shoot and I am going to kill two before they kill me." He is said to have boasted afterwards of "licking the Governor."[43] McKoy and Mallacci were both found guilty and each sentenced to twelve months in prison.

Sir Sydney, no doubt embarrassed that such events should occur on his watch, made light of the whole affair in his telegram to his superiors at the Colonial Office in London. He blamed the disorder on "crowds of roughs" and the "dangerous and criminal class." He explained that on Monday night "[i]t became necessary" for the police to use firearms and fixed bayonets. The governor informed London that a young man was killed but did not say that the youth killed, Thomas Barclay, was an innocent party going about his lawful business when he was shot by the police. Sir Sydney reported that two officers and twenty-five policemen were injured by the mob on Monday but he lied when he wrote elliptically that there were "several persons wounded[,] a number injured principally by weapons of mob." He knew full well that the crowd targeted company property and the police and left virtually everyone else alone (one exception being a company worker, a road master). By Wednesday, February 28, when Sir Sydney dispatched his telegram, Kershaw had called for and received reinforcement from St. Catherine, Clarendon, Portland and as far away as St. James. With this and the display of force on Monday night, the city returned to its uneasy calm.[44] Olivier tried to assuage Whitehall's anxieties: "I have no reason to expect further trouble but every precaution taken. Damage not serious to property in city except broken window[,] lamps and a little shoplifting." He asked the Colonial Office to tell his wife in London that he was all right.[45]

Although the "Tramcar Riots" are seldom mentioned even in studies of Olivier, they eliminated any prospects that the governor may have had of an extension of his term. He was recalled to London in February 1913 and appointed permanent secretary to the Board of Agriculture and Fisheries, a lowly job compared to governor of Jamaica. At a salary of £1,500 it was less than a third of the £5,000 he previously earned.[46] The plantocracy and the *Gleaner*, its mouthpiece, were happy to see him go while Thomas Macdermot of the *Jamaica Times* bemoaned his departure.

The hated Deputy Inspector McCrea died suddenly of a heart attack soon after the riots.

Having been discharged from the constabulary, McKay was back in the tranquil hills of Clarendon by the time of the protest and rioting. Still, McKay made his voice heard across the island as he expressed his support for the protesters. He did not condone the rioting, but he embraced the cause of the passive resisters. He expressed his Jamaican nationalism but also articulated the defiance that came to be associated with "If We Must Die" in "Passive Resistance":

> There'll be no more riotin',
> Stonin' p'lice an' burnin' car;
> But we mean to gain our rights
> By a strong though bloodless war.

> We will show an alien trust
> Dat Jamaicans too can fight
> An' dat while our blood is hot,
> They won't crush us wi' deir might.

The poem apologizes for the inconvenience caused, but ends boldly:

> Our vict'ry day shall come.

> There are aliens in our midst
> Who would slay us for our right;
> Yet though vipers block the way
> We will rally to the fight.

> We'll keep up a bloodless war,
> We will pay the farthings-fare

An' we send the challenge forth
"Only touch us if you dare!"[47]

Significantly, McKay did not condemn the rioting, nor did he apologize for it; his "sorry" was only for "the worry given some." While the *Gleaner* and the *Jamaica Times* along with the governor denounced the rioters as "hooligans," "roughs," "the criminal elements," "the dangerous and criminal class," and other nice things, McKay referred to them as "the boys"—more evidence of his sympathy with "wrongdooers" expressed in the preface to *Constab Ballads*. He is resolutely on the side of the people; he makes himself a member of the collective "we" in whose voice the poem is enunciated. Furthermore, he repeatedly mentions the West India Electric Company as an oppressive alien presence on the island.

In investigating McKay's nationalist ideology we should note another poem of his, first published in London in April 1912. In "George William Gordon to the Oppressed Natives," McKay imagines the sentiments of Gordon, celebrated martyr of the Morant Bay Rebellion of 1865. (According to the *Gleaner*, McKay had also written a prize-winning essay in the *Jamaica Tribune* on the Morant Bay Rebellion [*Daily Gleaner*, October 12 1911]. It does not appear in the extant issues of the *Tribune*.)[48] Perhaps more than any other of his Jamaican poems, "Gordon to the Oppressed Natives" provides clear evidence that McKay's poetry of resistance written in exile was anticipated before he left the island. In McKay's rendition, Gordon's address is aimed at the exiled African nation in Jamaica:

O, you sons of Afric's soil,
    Dyin' in a foreign land,
Crushed beneat' de moil and toil,
    Break, break de oppressors' hand!

Gordon reminds the oppressed that slavery has ended and evokes Wilberforce, Sharpe, Buxton and Clarkson in their struggle for freedom. But the freedom of the African is still being denied, so

"Trample on de tyranny/Still continued by a few!" It is lawful to employ force—"use our might"—to put an end to "dis great shame." England has already compensated the slaveholders and they, too, are British subjects, and Englishmen would not tolerate such oppression:

> England paid you' ransom down!
>   Meant to save you from the pain;
> Now, freed men o' England's crown,
>   Burst de cruel tyrant's chain!
>
> Never would an English mind
>   Bow beneat' such tyranny;
> Rise, O people of my kind!
>   Struggle, struggle to be free!
>
> Shake de burden off your backs,
>   Show de tyrants dat you're strong;
> Fight for freedom's rights, you blacks,
>   Ring de slaves' old battle-song!
>
> Gordon's heart here bleeds for you,
>   He will lead to victory;
> We will conquer every foe,
>   Or togeder gladly die.[49]

In his autobiography, McKay writes that "George William Gordon became one of the legendary heroes of Jamaica that the peasants were always talking about."[50] "Gordon to the Oppressed Natives" was first published in *T. P.'s Weekly*, a magazine published by T.P. O'Connor in London, having won a prize in their international poetry competition. The Jamaican newspapers proudly reported the honor bestowed upon a native son.[51] According to McKay, when the poem was republished in Jamaica, "it created as much of a stir as 'If We Must Die' created in the United States" and it was "denounced by the leading ministers of various denominations as inciting to riot; but Mr. Jekyll wrote to the *Daily Gleaner* that it was only a poet's way of expressing his appreciation of a great personality."[52]

It is not surprising that there was a fuss over the poem. It came fresh on the heels of the "Tramcar Riots" and McKay was perhaps inspired to write it precisely because of those events—around the same time that he wrote "Passive Resistance."

5

JAMAICAN NATIONALISM
AND ITS LIMITS

McKay's position in relation to Jamaican nationalism was complex compared to his almost instinctive and visceral expression of solidarity with the black oppressed. The young poet articulates his Jamaican nationalism most explicitly in "My Native Land, My Home," published in *Songs of Jamaica*.

> Dere is no land dat can compare
>   Wid you where'er I roam;
> In all de wul' none like you fair,
>   My native land, my home.
>
> Jamaica is de nigger's place,
>   No mind whe' some declare;
> Although dem call we "no-land race,"
>   I know we home is here.[1]

In an additional six stanzas, McKay elabroates on his love and devotion to Jamaica, including a willingness to die for his beloved *patrie*:

> An' I hope none o' your sons would
>   Refuse deir strengt' to lend,
> An' drain de last drop o' deir blood
>   Their country to defend.[2]

Jamaica is seen as an island naturally endowed with all that its black inhabitants could ever need: "Your fertile soil grow all o' t'ings/To full de naygur's wants. . . ." This near-paradise is despoiled by buccra, the white ruling class (who, the poet implies, are not really a part of the nation):

> You hab all t'ings fe mek life bles',
>> But buccra 'poil de whole
> Wid gove'mint an' all de res',
>> Fe worry naygur soul.[3]

Despite this, the love remains undiminished. Such "little chupidness" [stupidness] will not nullify his devotion. But the love is not entirely unconditional:

> De time when I'll tu'n 'gains' you is
>> When you can't give me grub.[4]

There is a deliberately menacing tone in this, the final couplet. The ruling class is being warned that it should not take the "patriotism" of the black population for granted—there is a limit to how far they can go. In a poem published in the *Gleaner* in January 1912, McKay suggests that such a limit had been reached. In "Peasants' Ways o' Thinkin'," he endorses the black migration to the Isthmus, as conditions in Jamaica had become unbearable for the majority of its inhabitants. The poem informs the reader that the peasants have no illusion about conditions in Panama, but they find that they have no choice but to go if the opportunity arises. Contrary to buccra's advice against emigration, "dis is wha' we got to say:"

> We hea' a callin' from Colon,
> We hea' a callin' from Limon,
> Let's quit de t'ankless toil an' fret
> Fe where a better pay we'll get.
>
> Though ober deh de law is bad,
> An' dey no know de name o' God,
> Yet dere is nuff work fe we han's,
> Reward in gol' fe beat de ban's.[5]

McKay's enthusiastic embrace of Jamaica in "My Native Land, My Home," a veritable claiming of the island for the black "race," was a very rare posture in Jamaica at the time. It was hardly typical of the peasantry or the emergent black working class. This is because the black masses have always been suspicious of those with ambitions of national autonomy. The attitude goes back to the days of slavery when the local white ruling class (with its mulatto underlings) exercised autonomy at the expense of the enslaved. The island's assembly, an oligarchy of local slaveholders, resisted the abolition of the slave trade and fought tooth and nail against the abolition of slavery itself, which the British parliament had approved.[6] A clash occurred between the long-term interests of imperial Britain and the local interests of the planters in Jamaica and elsewhere in the British Caribbean. The abolition of both the slave trade and slavery were thus carried out over the heads of the local ruling class.

Thanks to much misinformation spread by missionaries and others, the slaves believed the ending of slavery had been brought about by the British Crown against the objection of the wicked local planters: "Victoria the Good," "Missis Queen" freed the slaves. Writing in 1921, McKay remembered that when he grew up in Jamaica, Queen Victoria was "what Lincoln is to the little American Negro child."[7] He vividly recalled that during the Diamond Jubilee celebrations in 1897 (when he was seven) his teacher and parents told him "Victoria had freed the slaves. She had mounted the throne of England with the words, 'I will be good,' on her lips. The Bible was her light. From her great love for her colored subjects she had freed them from slavery."[8] It was such mumbo-jumbo that helped to cultivate the remarkable love and devotion the Caribbean masses felt for Victoria.[9] As one historian puts it, the Queen "stood as a protective symbol and the source of their liberation from slavery."[10] Just as Afro-America's love for Abraham Lincoln has never been challenged by any other president, this love for Victoria was never extended in the same way to any other British monarch before or since her reign. Herbert Thomas, a white Jamaican who served as an inspector in the constabulary for almost half a century after joining in 1877, reported in his memoirs that among the older generation "the name of Queen Victoria was always uttered with love and reverence." News of her death was received as a personal calamity:

> I remember the old cook of a friend with whom I was staying at the time of the Queen's death coming into the room where I was sitting, folding her hands over her abdomen—which is the attitude prescribed by etiquette—bobbing me a curtsey and saying:—"Please, Inspector, is it true I hear 'missis' Queen dead?" On my answering in the affirmative, she bobbed a second curtsey, then cast both her hands and eyes heavenward, which is the gesture of despair, and heaving a deep sigh, turned and left the room without another word. They all used to think that it was Queen Victoria herself who brought about the emancipation of the slaves.[11]

McKay recalled that when Victoria died there were "strange rumours" among the Jamaican peasantry. "They said that the women's hair would be sheared off and taxation increased, for the Queen's son, Edward VII, was a spendthrift who would be demanding more and more money."[12]

Thus, right up to the middle of the twentieth century, the masses of black people in the British Caribbean believed that the imperial crown had their interests at heart and the local ruling class did not. (They were right about the latter and wrong about the former. The 1865 rebels of Morant Bay who made a desperate appeal to the "Good Queen" learned this lesson in the most painful way of all.) Given this ideological formation, nationalist pronouncements, not to mention more serious agitation against British rule, were rare. Demands for reforms? Yes. Demands for national autonomy and independence? Not until well into the twentieth century. Alexander Bustamante, the premier labor leader of early twentieth century Jamaica, summed it up: "Self-government means brown man rule."[13] That is, the local oligarchy, made up of white men and mulattoes, would take control. At the mercy of these forces, black Jamaicans would have no recourse to imperial "protection." The nature of the relationship between the imperial center and local ruling class vis-à-vis the black masses, holds the key to the enigma of the relatively late (compared to Cuba, Puerto Rico and the Dominican Republic) development of nationalism in the English-speaking Caribbean.[14]

The sentiments of "My Native Land, My Home" were therefore extraordinary. But they were in tension with those of another early poem, "Old England." In the latter, McKay longs to visit and "view de homeland England."[15] He mentions the usual tourist sights—St. Paul's Cathedral, Westminster Abbey, and so on—that he would like to see. Interestingly, among these would be Victoria's grave:

> An' I'd go to view de lone spot where in peaceful solitude
> Rests de body of our Missis Queen, Victoria de Good.[16]

There is a subversive—if somewhat confused—intent behind this sentiment, given the history of Jamaica and its relation to the British Crown. In the mythology of the black peasantry such a visit would be the equivalent of a black American child of slaves visiting the Lincoln Memorial in Washington, DC: the attachment is not to the British Crown per se but to the perceived importance of the British monarchy as a bulwark against the tyranny of the local oligarchy. Thus the traditional reading of "Old England" as an ode to colonialism and England misses the poem's greater symbolic value because it ignores that concrete, complex and over-determined *content* of the colonial relation that was in place.[17]

The poem further defies a simplistic reading in its very last line. McKay would be happy and contented after visiting these sights in England to "sail across de ocean back to my own native shore."[18] England is his "homeland"—"our home," he calls it in another poem[19]—but so also is Jamaica. In acknowledging England, he does not renounce Jamaica, and in embracing Jamaica, he does not reject England. He felt passionate about Jamaica, his "native land," but his loyalty to England was necessarily more abstract, more from the head than the heart. Significantly, all that the young colonial desires in "Old England" is to *visit* England, not to make it his real home: "I'll rest glad an' contented in me min' for evermore" with this simple visit.[20]

Despite this, however, "Our education was so directed that we really honestly believed that we were little black Britons."[21] It becomes apparent that rather than being the expression of an intellect in the ideological grip of colonialism, "Old England" is the questioning of the ideology of colonialism itself by the articulation of a divided loyalty. Indeed, Jamaica is given precedence over Britain in the poet's affective bonds. "I've never felt I was legitimately British which I am not after all," McKay wrote to a friend in the 1930s.[22] Beyond the orchestrated childhood euphoria over Victoria's Diamond Jubilee, the statement is probably true. He no doubt *thought* he was British, but it is unlikely that he *felt* British. And after his encounter with British racism while living in London between 1919 and 1921, he knew he was not British in any meaningful sense beyond the juridical, imperial one.

McKay was not alone in his ambivalence. No Jamaican was calling for independence and, except for the small group around Dr. J. Robert Love, and later Sandy Cox, virtually no one called for self-government within the British Empire, a considerably less radical request.[23] When demands for nationhood were made, U. Theo's voice was one of the earliest and clearest heard, but this was in the 1920s. McKay's friend Thomas MacDermot (who went under the pen name of Tom Redcam) occupied a similarly ambivalent position.[24] MacDermot, in fact, occupied an even more pro British position than McKay. Nonetheless, he identified a political space for pride in a Jamaican cultural identity, a kind of nationalism without the demand for statehood.[25] Redcam articulated this position in his newspaper, the *Jamaican Times*.[26]

Sandy Cox's National Club was formed in March 1909 largely because of the grievances its leader had with the Governor, Olivier. Cox, a light-skinned Jamaican civil servant, felt that the local British colonial authorities denied him promotion because he was not white. The National Club called for self-government but this call was certainly suborned to demands for much more basic reform. Cox was hounded by his colonial adversaries and by 1911 had moved to Boston and was working as a lawyer. The National Club collapsed quickly after his emigration, the objective bases for its survival simply did not exist.[27]

The position taken on the national question by Rev. C.A. Wilson typified that of the black intelligentsia in Jamaica at the time. Wilson was involved in a number of black uplift organizations in the early twentieth century. Though deeply committed to the advancement of black Jamaicans, Wilson could not find it in his heart to even so much as mention J. Robert Love and Sandy Cox in *Men With Backbone* (1913) and *Men of Vision* (1929), his praise songs to distinguished Jamaicans. Indeed, in *Men With Backbone*, he chides both Love and Cox, without mentioning them by name, for being "short-sighted" in calling for "Jamaica for Jamaicans."[28] While Wilson thought that "[m]en from abroad should not be given positions that natives are competent to fill," he nevertheless felt that black Jamaicans should count their blessings rather than agitate for self-government.[29] After all, they are much better off than the sons of Africa living under Spanish and American rule.

> With the Union Jack floating over his head, the Negro is a unit in the greatest Empire. He enjoys full liberty, and immunity from the base crimes perpetrated on the Spanish Main. . . . The barbarous and nefarious practice of lynching is unknown in Jamaica.[30]

Jamaicans, Wilson writes, "must not be content to be treated as children," but in the next breath he implicitly subscribes to the imperial notion, which Love and Cox inveighed against, that black colonials, such as those in Jamaica, were not yet "ready" for self-rule. Jamaicans, Wilson declares "must seek to grow to political manhood."[31]

Although McKay and his eldest brother would have shared some of Cox's aspirations, they most certainly would not have agreed with his attacks on Olivier, for both U. Theo and the young McKay admired the governor. Olivier had publicly praised McKay's poetry, telling the *Gleaner* "I have seen a selection of Mr. McKay's poems, and I appreciate the talent they exhibit."[32] McKay "respectfully dedicated" his first volume of poems to Olivier, "who by his sympathy with the black race has won the love and admiration of all Jamaicans."[33] McKay even refrained from publishing one of his poems, "De Gub'nor's Salary," out of his friendship with the governor and out of loyalty to Jekyll, who was himself a close friend of Olivier's. When Jekyll and McKay had showed Olivier the poem, "He dissuaded us from publishing it. He said that the politicians of Jamaica might use it to attack the position of Governor."[34] McKay did make political compromises, even then. He was, however, correct in judging that the most powerful forces arrayed against Olivier at the time were profoundly reactionary and meant the Jamaican people no good. U. Theo also admired Olivier's Fabiansm and the quality of his mind, and was grateful for his role in extending the railways into the rural areas of Clarendon. The extension was carried out in the teeth of opposition from the island's oligarchy and the *Gleaner*. It was seen as a measure aimed at helping the peasantry gain better access to markets for their produce.[35]

The McKays' admiration for Olivier was by no means unique. Black Jamaicans were sad to see him leave and were grateful for his continued interest in the island from afar. Many Jamaicans wrote to Olivier and told him so. Among them was Una Marson, the distinguished Jamaican poet and playwright. She wrote of Olivier's "wonderful love of Jamaica:"

> I have read with a great deal of interest and pleasure your articles and speeches with reference to Jamaica as they have appeared from time to time. I am taking the liberty of expressing to you my personal thanks for all you have done and are doing for our Island's welfare. . . . My late father had the honour of serving this Island devotedly for many years as Minister, Marriage Officer, Justice of the Peace, on the Parochial Board and on various Trusts and Committees, and I can remember hearing him speak of you during your administration as a very great Governor.

Mrs. Dorothea Simmons of Walker's Wood, having finished Olivier's 1936 book, *Jamaica: The Blessed Island*, wrote him straightaway: "I kept exclaiming inwardly, 'Bless him for saying that! Oh bless him for that!' You have opened the way for a better understanding of our people and problems."[36] It is a good book. But the truth is that Sydney Olivier was one of that rare breed of people who grow more radical as they get older. Some of his early policies while he was involved in colonial administration—most notably, his attempt to restrict the migration of poor Jamaicans to Panama and elsewhere—were reactionary and reprehensible, if not downright evil.[37] His policies became more sympathetic towards the peasants and workers as his governorship (1907–12) came to an end. For this the island's oligarchy was always after him. In later years, he was appalled by the deteriorating condition of workers in the British Caribbean and Jamaica in particular. In retirement and unencumbered by the protocols of office, he became more and more outspoken and anti-imperialist, especially in the 1930s, swinging back at his enemies in Jamaica in his journalism and in his book, *Jamaica*. In 1941, during the height of the Second World War, he went so far as to write (albeit in a letter to his fellow Fabian, Leonard Woolf) that "Hitler and Haw-Haw have told the truth about the British Empire, the Coloured people are still paid at starvation wages and are getting tired of it."[38] Olivier died two years later, age eighty-four.

6

EMERGENT FEMINIST
SYMPATHIES

Claude McKay's mother, who died in 1909, figured prominently in his life and memory. Some of his earlier poems were about her and he used a version of his mother's name as a nom de plume for his very first poems published in America. Living in London ten years after her death, Hannah Ann's favorite son penned some of his most moving poems in her memory. He also wrote about other Jamaican women. One of the most remarkable features of the poetry McKay wrote during his youth is the degree to which the experience of Jamaican women is woven into the overall tapestry of his work. Not an insubstantial number of his poems are written in the female voice, including "A Midnight Woman to the Bobby" and "The Apple-Woman's Complaint", two of his most accomplished poems in his entire *oeuvre*. His unforced and sympathetic portrayal of women is one of the most consistent themes in McKay's work from beginning to end, fiction as well as nonfiction, poetry as well as prose. This motif is underexplored in the critical literature on McKay.[1]

McKay's female characters are primarily of peasant and working-class background. They are young and old, they are mothers and they are childless, they are wives, they are fellow workers, they are higglers and they are prostitutes. They are depicted in love and out of love. They are seen suffering and defiantly struggling, and deep in despair. Most of all, McKay portrays with respect and compassion the precarious lives black women led in an unforgiving time.

We have already encountered Cous' Sun, the peasant higgler, and his wife in "Two-an'-Six" and their struggle to survive. In "Ribber Come-Do'n" fourteen-year-old little Milly looks after her six-week-old sibling[2] and three other brothers and sisters when they are marooned by a flooded river. Her mother had gone to a seaport to buy fish (to sell again later) and her father had been working his provision ground some distance from home when they were both cut off by the flood from their home and children. There is no food at home. It is night and the children are hungry and the parents still cannot get home. Milly seeks assistance from a neighbor:

> "Ebenin', cousin Anna,
>   Me deh beg you couple banna,
> For dem tarra one is berry hungry home;
>   We puppa ober May, ma,
>   We mumma gone a Bay, ma,
> An' we caan' tell warra time dem gwin' go come."[3]

Cousin Anna gives Milly bits of yam, some cornmeal "An' a pint o' milk fe de babe." The parents do not make it home that night, but "de picknanies went to bed/Wid a nuff nuff bellyful."[4]

Not only is "Ribber Come-Do'n" a testimony to the peasant community's structure of mutuality, it is a good illustration of the hand-to-mouth existence of the rural poor who have absolutely no reserve. The parents are not able to return home for only one night—unable to return with quarry for the day, as it were—and the children are literally stranded without food. At the centre of the drama of "Ribber Come-Do'n" is a little girl, her struggling parents and a female neighbor, all portrayed in realistic terms.

In "A Country Girl," the narrator, Fed, meets Lelia in Kingston, a girl from his own village. Finding Lelia working as a prostitute, Fed is surprised and disturbed. Asked why she stays in Kingston, Lelia explains that "Country Life . . . has no pleasures for me."[5] She wants the excitement of the city and material possessions such as pretty dresses, as well as more basic requirements. Asked as to whether she has not "swopped out your honour for gold," Lelia tells of her downward spiral:

> "Fed, it was horrid de lone country life!
> I suffered—for sometimes e'en hunger was rife;
> An' when I came, Fed, to try my chance here,
> I thought there would be no more troubles to bear.
>
> "But troubles there were an' in plenty, my lad,
> Oh, dey were bitter, an' oh, I was sad!
> . . . .
> I gave up all honour, I took a new name
> An' tried to be happy, deep sunk in de shame."[6]

Now she is too ashamed to return home and, in any case, she has become accustomed to her style of life, painful though it is:

> ". . . many gals richer than me,
> Pretty white girlies of better degree,
> Live as I do, an' are happy an' gay,
> Then why should not I be as happy as they?"[7]

McKay's childhood sweetheart, Agnes, "a light mulatto with very black hair, buxom of body and with a face that radiated sunshine," died miserably in one of Kingston's brothels.[8] This event had a major impact on McKay, reverberating in his work for the rest of his life. Almost forty years after Agnes' death, McKay could vividly remember the passion they shared. Agnes was older than Claude, but that did not prevent his becoming "fascinated" by her. They did not see each other outside of school, but during recess they would "get together in a ring and play 'Drop the Handkerchief.'" They passed notes to each other in class and Agnes started to write him long letters. McKay did not know what to write in reply so he got his friend, a stable boy who was older than he, to write letters for him.[9] U. Theo, under whose guardianship he lived at the time, discovered some of the letters.

> My brother took the letters to his wife. . . . They thought that the letters were very passionate, not the kind that children should be writing to each other. My brother whipped me for the first time. He whipped me and said he was astonished that a small boy like me could have such adult thoughts. Agnes was very angry when she heard about the beating and the finding of the letters by my brother.[10]

But "[t]he beating did not change us." Although the other school-children knew about them by then, Agnes and he "hugged our love very closely." "It was my first love. But before I could even be aware of it Agnes had blossomed into a young woman and I was still just a boy in knee-pants. Then she left the village and I never heard from her again." The next he heard of Agnes was her "miserable" death in a Kingston brothel.[11] He wrote "Agnes o' de Village Lane," and published it in the *Gleaner* in 1911:

> Fancy o' me childish will,
>   Playin' now before me eyes,
> Sadly I remember still
>   How much once your love I prize',
> As I think o' you again,
> Agnes o' de village lane.
>
> . . . .
> But dere came de partin' day,
>   An' they took me from you, dear,
> An' de passion died away,
>   But de memory was there:
> Long you've lingered in me brain,
> Plump-cheeked Agnes o' de lane.
>
> A'ter many a weary year,
>   Sad, sad news o' you I heard,
> News dat brought a scaldin' tear
>   At de sound o' every word;
> An my mind, filled wid disdain,
> Grieved for Agnes o' de lane.

> Agnes o' de lane no more,
> > For you went away, my pet,
> Agnes once so sweet an' pure,
> > To a miserable deat';
> Oh, de 'membrance brings me pain,
> Fallen Agnes o' de lane![12]

The *Gleaner* reported that within a fortnight of its publication "Agnes o' de Village Lane" was the public's "general favourite" of McKay's poems.[13] Writing *My Green Hills of Jamaica* in Chicago just a couple of years before he died, McKay could not recall any of the poem's words, but he remembered that "friends who read it said it was one of my most touching poems."[14] Agnes' story resonated precisely because it was far from unique. Her downfall was rooted in and symptomatic of the limited and terrible choices that poor people were forced to make in order to survive the hellish conditions which prevailed.

Agnes' tragedy and McKay's previous relationship with her may have informed McKay's extraordinary sympathy for prostitutes in his writing. *Banana Bottom* is the only one of his five novels, published and unpublished, which does not have a prostitute as a character. In all the others, prostitutes figure prominently. They are present also in his short stories. They are perhaps most conspicuous in some of his finest poems, including the title poem of his most celebrated collection, *Harlem Shadows*.[15] McKay uses the tragedy of the prostitute as a metaphor for the condition of black people in general.[16]

Although there were undoubtedly actual prostitutes such as Lelia and Agnes, there were others who were far from broken. McKay's admiration for the hardened but refreshing defiance of the prostitute in "A Midnight Woman to the Bobby" is self-evident. When the bobby approaches her, the woman makes a no-holds-barred, scathing and sustained verbal attack.[17]

She immediately goes on the offensive. She scorns the policeman and considers his touching her a defilement: "No palm me up, you dutty brute."[18] She audaciously suggests that he, not she, will "grunt under the law." No hick, she was born right in the heart of Spanish Town and he is out of his depth when he messes with her: "You t'ink you wise, but we wi see;/You not de fus' one fas' wid me." Her experience teaches her that

> Care how you try, you caan' do mo'
> Dan many dat was hyah befo';
> Yet weh' dey all o' dem te-day?
> De buccra dem no kick dem 'way?[19]

From start to finish she keeps up a barrage of priceless Jamaican insults. She insults his mouth ("Mash," "like ripe bread-fruit"), his nose ("jam samplatta nose") and his feet ("big an' ugly ole tu'n-foot" with "chigger," looking "like herrin' roe"). All in all, here is a "dutty ugly brute." She is not finished with him, and moves on to his background; she "traces" him. In Jamaican "tracing" has the double meaning of cursing a person as well as digging up dirt on their past which may extend to that person's lineage.[20] Before he joined the force the bobby was in a sorry state: he had never worn shoes, he never had enough to eat, he had never had clothes. Hard times pushed him into police work:

> An' when de pinch o' time you feel
> A 'pur you a you' chigger heel,
> You lef' you' district, big an' coarse,
> An' come join buccra Police Force.[21]

Now, because he is in a police uniform he feels he can throw his weight around. "'Cos you wear Mis'r Koshaw clo'es/You t'ink say you's de only man."[22] She is convinced that she will outlast her tormentor: "But wait, me frien', you' day wi come,/I'll see you go same lak a some."[23] She laughs derisively at him when he attempts to arrest her: the judge, she is certain, will not accept his word against hers without the corroboration of a witness. This is the final insult— the judiciary has no respect for the police force and a policeman's word carries no greater weight than that of a common prostitute. Or, at any rate, this is what the prostitute wants the policeman to believe.

McKay is effectively identifying prostitution with policing, giving the distinct impression that policing is the more reprehensible of the two. Both "professions" are fruits of desperation, but the policeman's is more repugnant. In his very joining of the enemy, "buccra Police Force," the policeman has betrayed his already oppressed race and beleaguered class. He started as a peasant like Lelia, then, experiencing hard times, he moves from the country to the city and becomes a prostitute: he sells himself to buccra, in this case "Mis'r Koshaw"—Lieutenant Colonel Kershaw, the inspector general. He is selling his racial (and class) loyalty (instead of his body) for a mess of pottage. The nocturnal quarrel between policeman and prostitute is a quarrel between two victims, two black victims of the same economic system.

In questioning the police force in this way—in seeing the office of constable as equivalent to that of "the oldest profession"—McKay invites his readers to question the traditional attitude to both policing and prostitution. Why should one form of prostitution (policing) be regarded as acceptable and respectable while another is proscribed and scorned? Who should be shunned and who is obscene? McKay's bobby is mute (we hear the voice of the prostitute only): his position is indefensible. And the poet reveals his hand by making the woman look upon the peasant-policeman as unclean, as a defiled abomination. "I have often wondered," McKay wrote many years later, "if it is possible to establish a really intelligent standard to determine obscenity—a standard by which one could actually measure the obscene act and define the obscene thought."[24]

"A Midnight Woman to the Bobby" is a furious, lacerating and cathartic auto-critique on McKay's part and an early instalment in his expiation. The feeling of honor sold and bought, and of remorse, is as powerfully communicated here as it is in "The Heart of a Constab" and "A Country Girl". The fact that McKay had bartered his own "innocent youth" and "swopped out" his "honour for gold" may also help to explain his humane understanding and abiding sympathy for prostitutes.

Although the prostitute in "A Midnight Woman to the Bobby" is courageous, extraordinarily eloquent, perceptive, strong and even honorable (she, after all, finds despicable any peasant who joins "buccra police force") we learn far less about her than we do about the police. She acts as a bright beam of light exposing the character and rotten innards of the police force. More than anything else, the poem is a sharply articulated critique of the constabulary. It is a measure of the contempt that McKay had for the force that he could have written such a poem. And a measure of the contempt with which he viewed himself at the time, insofar as he could have written such a poem when he was still a member of the constabulary.

From the prostitute's attack we move to "The Apple-Woman's Complaint." While we are led to admire—even cheer on—the prostitute, we feel sorry for the higgler. The world is such that the resilient and wordly-wise prostitute is more at home in it than the hard-working higgler from the country, selling apples in Kingston. She is stunned and appalled by the fact that the police ("yawnin' on his beat") has stopped her from selling her apples: "Me mus'n' car' me apple-tray." She has no reasonable alternative mode of survival, but this does not bother the police:

> Ef me no wuk, me boun' fe tief;
> S'pose dat will please de pólice chief!
> De prison dem mus' be wan' full,
> Mek dem's 'pon we like ravin' bull.[25]

She complains about the fundamental injustice of the situation, about the rank hypocrisy of the constabulary, and about the perverse pleasure that the head of the Kingston police gets from the gratuitous persecution of poor black people:

> Black nigger wukin' laka cow
> An' wipin' sweat-drops from him brow,
> Dough him is dyin' sake o' need,
> P'lice an' dem headman boun' fe feed.
>
> P'lice an' dem headman gamble too,
> Dey shuffle card an' bet fe true;

> Yet ef me Charlie gamble,—well,
> Dem try fe 'queeze him laka hell.

> De headman fe de town pólice
> Mind neber know a little peace,
> 'Cep' when him an' him heartless ban'
> Hab sufferin' nigger in dem han'.[26]

She feels that police action is aimed at pushing black women into prostitution, where they are only persecuted by the police!

> Dem wan' fe see we in de street
> Dah foller dem all 'pon dem beat;
> An' after, 'dout a drop o' shame,
> Say we be'n dah solicit dem.[27]

But her complaint falls on deaf ears. It is the complaint of the powerless, the heedless voice of one of the little people, the wailing of the condemned. And she *feels* doomed. She is desperate. She bawls for divine intervention. She lifts her head to the heavens and begs Jesus for help; she has done her best to no avail—she cannot help herself.

> We hab fe barter-out we soul
> To lib t'rough dis ungodly wul';—
> O massa Jesus! don't you see
> How pólice is oppressin' we?
>
> . . . .
> Ah massa Jesus! in you' love
> Jes' look do'n from you' t'rone above,
> An' show me how a poo' weak gal
> Can lib good life in dis ya wul'.[28]

"The Apple-Woman's Complaint," perhaps even more than "Whe' Fe Do?", is one of the most sorrowful and desperate of McKay's early poems.

But McKay's women do not only suffer and struggle. They also laugh, they play, they fall in love (even with policemen), and they fall out of love (most notably with policemen). With the significant exception of the bourgeois woman of "The Bobby to the Sneering

Lady," virtually all McKay's women are black (in the Caribbean sense of the word), overwhelmingly poor and of peasant and working-class background. In these early poems there is an intricate imbrication of oppression based on sex, race, color and class. McKay recognized the impossibility of identifying with any precision where one form of oppression ends and another begins. What is, however, most evident in these poems is the young McKay's sincere attempt to represent the lives of black Jamaican women as he observed them. Significantly, some of the most successful of McKay's early poems are written in the female authorial voice. Indeed, the best of his creole language poems is written in the female voice. For faithfulness to the Jamaican language, for rhythm, for critical social commentary, skilfully and organically embellished with humor, "A Midnight Woman to the Bobby" is unsurpassed. It would stand beside the very best creations of Jamaica's most accomplished creole language poet, Louise Bennett.[29]

How do we explain McKay's extraordinary willingness to explore important aspects of black women's experience in Jamaica at the time? How do we explain his deep compassion and empathy for the women who inhabit so many of his early poems? Can this ever be adequately explained?

McKay's close relationship with his mother and his sister ought to be paramount in any attempt at explanation. McKay observed his mother over the years—helping poor and unfortunate women at home in Clarendon. Mrs. McKay may have helped to develop her son's capacity for compassion more than anyone else, and especially compassion for suffering women. There is every indication that McKay attempted to emulate his mother's goodness.

Apart from U. Theo, with whom he had a special relationship, of all his other siblings he was closest to Rachel, his only sister. Rachel's letters to Claude are intimate and warm. "My dear Brother Claude," she opens one letter, "We were all very glad, not to see your handwriting, but to read your composition once more. I

cannot tell you the joy it gave to us all. You can only imagine."[30]
Such love, combined with his love for his mother, may have
strengthened his general respect for women.

McKay was also extremely sensitive to suffering in general. As he
wrote in one of his earliest American poems, "misery/I have the
strength to bear but not to see."[31] In his Jamaica, poor black women
(rural and urban) were the bearers of much misery and, insofar as
we may measure such a thing, women bore far more than their fair
share of it. Many women appear enduring injustice and oppression
in McKay's poems.

Another important factor suggests why women appear so fre-
quently in McKay's work. There were, quite simply, a relatively large
number of women in the population. Not only were there more
women than men then as now, during the late nineteenth and early
twentieth centuries the female population was increasing more rap-
idly than that of the male. From 1881 to 1921, the female "black"
population increased from 51.2 per cent to 53 per cent and the
"coloured" population from 53.4 per cent to 55.6 per cent.[32] The
island's sex ratio (measured by the number of males per 1000
females in the population) declined during the late nineteenth and
early twentieth centuries. From 950 in 1881 the figure dropped to
881 in 1921. For the crucial age range of 15 to 29, the fall was even
more dramatic—from 929 in 1881 to 791 in 1921. Although the
overall sex ratio for Kingston increased from 704 to 721 over the
same period, when disaggregated into age cohorts and race/color
groupings a somewhat different and more meaningful pattern
emerges. First of all, the sex ratio for those between the ages of 15
and 29 fell from an already low 700 to an almost incredible 671
between 1881 and 1921: for every hundred women there were only
67 men in this age group.[33]

Migration—internal and external—provides the primary expla-
nation for this demographic disequilibrium in Kingston in
particular and on the island as a whole. Between 1911 and 1921, 63
per cent of the migrants from rural parishes to Kingston were

women. Women also constituted two-thirds of all internal migrants to the parish of St. Andrew, a suburb of Kingston.[34] These women were the victims of the dislocation of the agrarian sector of the economy and the increasingly skewed economic and political relations in the countryside. They moved to Kingston and St. Andrew in order to escape the growing hardship of the hinterland and to seek employment in the service sector of urban Jamaica, many as domestic servants. As discussed, in the census of 1911 a quarter of all women of working age in Kingston and St. Andrew gave their occupation as domestic servant. Employers showed an overwhelming preference for female domestic servants. In 1891 eight out of ten domestic servants in Kingston and St. Andrew were female; more than nine out of ten were by 1911.[35] A significant number of the women who drifted into Kingston from the countryside ended up as prostitutes.

It is estimated that Jamaica experienced a net loss of 77,100 people through emigration between 1911 and 1921. Almost two-thirds of the emigrants were men,[36] who headed primarily to Panama and Cuba, to the heavy labor on the Panama Canal and the sugar plantations of eastern Cuba. Emigration thus exacerbated the sexual imbalance in Jamaica. The island's population was disproportionately female, and nowhere more conspicuously so than in Kingston, where (along with Spanish Town) McKay served as a constable. This female presence does not account, nor can it account, for the sympathy with which McKay portrays and discusses women in his poems. I do believe, however, that these demographic processes, which impinged upon his senses, help to explain the prominence of women in McKay's early work.

In some cases, McKay's female characters were based on women he had loved, admired and cared for. Some of these he became acquainted with during the course of his work on the beat in Spanish Town and Kingston (which we know not only from the poems themselves, but also from his autobiographical writings such as *My Green Hills of Jamaica*). It is not surprising that he should write about such people with sympathy, understanding and tenderness.

As a Fabian socialist, McKay would have been influenced by the feminist component within the movement's ideology. Annie Besant, a feminist and prominent member of the Fabian Society, was one who McKay explicitly recalled discussing with U. Theo.[37] McKay also read many of the women writers of Victorian Britain and was especially interested in the life and work of George Eliot who, apart from being a novelist, was also a prominent freethinker who translated Ludwig Feuerbach's pioneering demythologization of Christianity, *Das Wesen des Christentums* (The Essence of Christianity). (McKay reported that Jekyll, an ardent admirer of Eliot's work, tried to get acquainted with her. But Eliot, known for her aloofness, rejected him "saying she preferred not to make any new friends." The rebuff did not diminish her standing in Jekyll's pantheon of heroes and heroines. And all of this he discussed with McKay. Consequently, McKay remembered experiencing "a specially piquant human interest" in reading George Eliot.[38] McKay's exposure to feminist ideas (including those advocated by U. Theo) and what the late Victorians called "The Woman Question" probably shaped his perception of the condition of women in Jamaica.

His very advanced ideas about women, developed at a relatively young age, remained with him for the rest of his life. There is much talk in the McKay literature about his attachments to "father figures," at the expense of examining McKay's relations with women. And yet some of his closest friends and comrades were women—in his early years in America, Grace Campbell, Crystal Eastman, Louise Bryant (he dedicated his first novel, *Home to Harlem*, to Bryant); in Britain, Sylvia Pankhurst and the other women around the *Workers' Dreadnought* on which he worked; in Bolshevik Russia, Clara Zetkin; in Germany, France and North Africa, Josephine Herbst and Nancy Cunard. When he returned to the United States in 1934, among his closest friends and confidantes were Grace

Campbell, Ellen Tarry, Dorothy West, and Dorothy Day of the *Catholic Worker* movement. McKay's respect for and closeness to these women—to which the archives eloquently testify—have been all but ignored thus far.[39]

7

ON CRUELTY

Just as McKay hated to see misery and oppression, so did he hate cruelty. His extraordinary sensitivity and aversion to suffering and cruelty were important impulses that led to his deepening radicalization over time. Class, color, gender and racial oppression in Jamaica started him on his socialist journey while, more than anything else, the gigantic horrors of racism in the United States—especially lynching—deepened his black nationalism and Bolshevized his erstwhile Fabian socalism.

"Strokes of the Tamarind Switch" provides a good illustration of McKay's position. An erring young boy is sentenced by the court and is flogged with a tamarind switch. The switch, made from young branches of a tamarind tree, is pliable but hard, knotty and strong. It stings and cuts; it is designed to inflict fiery and lingering pain. Its prototype dates from the days of slavery. McKay is witness here:

> I dared not look at him,
> My eyes with tears were dim,
>   My spirit filled with hate
>   Of man's depravity,
>   I hurried through the gate.[1]

He returns with anger in his heart.

> I went but I returned,
> While in my bosom burned
>   The monstrous wrong that we
>   Oft bring upon ourselves,
>   And yet we cannot see.[2]

There is a double meaning in "ourselves." The boy is bringing misfortune upon himself, as people often do to themselves. It is also possible that when he speaks of "ourselves," McKay is not referring to the boy at all, but to black people in general and in particular, to the policemen involved in carrying out the punishment. McKay might therefore be referring to the way black people cause other black people to suffer ("And yet we cannot see"). This latter interpretation, given similar pronouncements elsewhere in his poetry, is perhaps more likely what McKay had in mind.

McKay graphically depicts the brutality of the punishment.

> The cutting tamarind switch
>   Had left its bloody mark,
>   And on his legs were streaks
>   That looked like boiling bark.

> I spoke to him the while:
> At first he tried to smile,
>   But the long pent-up tears
>   Came gushing in a flood;
>   He was but of tender years.[3]

The boy, with "eyes bloodshot and red," tells McKay that his father is dead, and explains how he fell into bad company with boys "who goaded him to wrong." He "promised to be good."

> I wished the lad good-bye,
> And left him with a sigh:
>   Again I heard him talk—
>   His limbs, he said, were sore,
>   He could not walk.[4]

McKay as narrator was "very rude" when he was small and he too was beaten. He was not beaten as brutally but he feels that such punishment was pointless: "has it done me good?" The beating comes across not only as barbaric, but mindless, gratuitous cruelty. McKay appended a note to the poem.

> This was a lad of fifteen. No doubt he deserved the flogging adminis-tered by order of the Court: still, I could not bear to see him—my own flesh—stretched out over the bench, so I went away to the Post Office near by. When I returned, all was over. I saw his naked bleeding form, and through the terrible ordeal—so they told me—he never cried. But when I spoke to him he broke down, told me between his bursts of tears how he had been led astray by bad companions, and that his mother intended sending him over-sea. He could scarcely walk, so I gave him tickets for the tram. He had a trustful face. A few minutes after, my bit-terness of spirit at the miserable necessity of such punishment came forth in song which I leave rugged and unpolished as I wrote it at the moment.[5]

McKay states that the boy "deserved the flogging;" it was a "mis-erable necessity." Yet the content, the tone, the deeply human response to the boy's suffering undermine the claimed legitimacy of his punishment. He is torn: the flogging may be legal, but it is morally wrong.

It is interesting that this tension is not present within the poem itself; or at least, it is not there in the same way. In the poem, the flogging is not a "miserable necessity"—it is not a necessity at all. By the same token, McKay's response becomes even more creditable: although he felt that the boy "deserved" the flogging, he neverthe-less had the moral courage to recognize and to declare that such punishment was barbaric. McKay is saying, then, that not even wrongdoers should be treated in this way: no human being should be treated in such a cruel and humiliating manner.

McKay writes that he "could not bear to see . . . my own flesh . . . stretched out over the bench" made ready to be flogged. There are two meanings, perhaps deliberately articulated, to "my own flesh." It means a black person, as in "fe me own black 'kin" in "The Bobby to the Sneering Lady," and "My people, my people, me owna black skin" in "The Heart of a Constab."[6] But "my own flesh" also means, quite simply, another human being like me.

McKay was similarly moved by the incident that occasioned "Jim at Sixteen" to append an authorial note to that poem too.

The poem opens with the complaint of a prisoner:

> Corpy, it pinch me so,
> > De bloomin' ole handcuff;
> A dunno warra mek
> > You put it on so rough.[7]

This is the note:

> On Friday I went to Court on duty for the first time since my enlistment. I happened to escort a prisoner, a stalwart young fellow, and as I was putting on the handcuff, which was rather small, it pinched him badly, making a raw wound. And yet he was so patient, saying he knew that I could not help it. Although it was accidentally done, I felt so sad and ashamed. The above poem grew out of this incident.[8]

McKay's aversion to cruelty *tout court* included cruelty to animals. In "De Dog-Driver's Frien'"[9] McKay admonishes his colleagues in the force for their cruelty to dogs. There is a certain amount of enlightened self-interest here—the dogs provide company for the police on patrol at night, but McKay makes a claim for their more generous treatment on moral grounds:

> Stay your hasty hands, my comrades,
> > I must speak to you again;
> For you beat de dog 'dout mussy,
> > An' dey are we night-time frien',
> Treat dem kindly, treat dem kindly,
> > For dey are God's creatures too;
> You have no more claim, dear comrades,
> > On de earth dan what dey do.[10]

The last four lines of this opening stanza serve as the refrain of the poem.

In "Killin' Nanny" two small boys, no more than two years of age, watch the capture and slaughter of a goat.

> De goat is bawlin' fe mussy,
>   An' de children watch de sight
> As de butcher re'ch his sharp knife,
>   An' 'tab wid all his might.

The narrator is intrigued and troubled by the differing responses of the children.

> Dey see the red blood flowin';
>   An' one chil' trimble an' hide
> His face in de mudder's bosom,
>   While t'udder look on wide-eyed.
>
> De tears is fallin' down hotly
>   From him on de mudder's knee;
> De udder wid joy is starin',
>   An' clappin' his han's wid glee.

Years later, "When dey had forgotten Nanny," the two are grown men and "de forehead of de laugher/Was brand' wid de mark of Cain."[11] This is perhaps too harsh and deterministic a judgement: the boy is the father of the man. Indeed, the implication is that the laughing boy was somehow born evil. McKay is also saying that exposure to and enjoyment of the slaughter of animals may lead to murder. It is obviously a big leap, but not an entirely far-fetched idea.

The most remarkable thing about "Killin' Nanny" is the fact that it was written at all. Children in the Caribbean, in the urban areas as well as in the countryside, grow up witnessing the slaughter of animals. These animals—especially goats, pigs and chickens—are frequently children's pets, with names and biographies. Little boys and girls nurse them through their ailments and anthropomorphize them only to discover that adults look at them as food. Not only are these animals coolly killed before their eyes, the children are expected to eat them. Sometimes children are even forced to catch the poor creatures that are to be turned into dinner. Such incidents are seldom forgotten as easily as McKay suggests: It is doubtful that the crying boy forgot the stab with the sharp knife and Nanny's "bawlin' fe mussy." How can the adult John forget Peggy, the frail chick, won as a prize at Sunday School, nursed back to health by the proud child, her neck wrung on a bright Sunday afternoon, turning her into the Sunday dinner? Adults talk about such traumatic events of their childhood, some bearing a permanent grudge against their parents for the death of their goat or chick, but such matters have never been registered in the literature of the Caribbean. McKay comes the closest to discussing them and no Caribbean author, to my knowledge, has written about them. To this extent, then, "Killin' Nanny" is a most remarkable artifact of the Caribbean experience and a tribute to McKay's poetic sensibilities.

On the face of it, "Snared!" is a banal story of country life—a boy sets a snare to catch a bird. But "Snared!" is understated, meditative, somber and calm. The omniscient narrator sides with the doomed bird, a John-to-whit which he calls Johnnie.

> Though, Johnnie, so sweetly you're singin',
>   Your life is jes' heng on a hinge;
> De next hour your doom will be bringin',
>   For Butty's a-settin' his springe.

It is a beautiful morning, the sun is rising over the hillside and it shines bright on the big mammee tree "An' John-t'wit is eating de red fruit,/As happy as happy can be." The opening stanza serves as a foreboding refrain. The narrator watches Butty, springe under his arm, make his way through the dewy grass and up into the mammee tree.

> An' as Butty climbe up an' climbe up,
>   He's watchin' mas' John wid one eye;
> Yet Johnnie *will* sing on so gaily,
>   Not thinkin' dat he wi' soon die.

Butty sets the snare and climbs down from the tree. Johnnie hops to his doom but, as in "Strokes of the Tamarind Switch," the narrator cannot bear to watch the dénouement:

> He's singin', an' while still a singin',
>   Him now an' again mek a hop;
> Me tu'n from de scene wid a shiver,
>   For he's hoppin' right up to the trap.[12]

Once again the Schopenhauerian moral undertones are evident—the wanton cruelty to animals, and the absurdity and cruelty of life itself. It is significant, however, that the narrator does not feel sufficiently appalled to intervene. Perhaps intervention is futile—Butty will ensnare Johnnie sooner or later. McKay merely tells of Johnnie's demise, and in so doing, perhaps inadvertently, he tells of the limits of his own compassion.

Although "Cotch Donkey," is written in a light vein its underlying message is just a serious as "Strokes of the Tamarand Switch" and "Snared!" The donkey, overloaded with produce for the market, goes on strike: it sits down in the street refusing to go any further. Its owner claims that it is lazy. But the donkey is being expected to carry more than is reasonable, and it has a sore back. Although the owner may be prosecuted for ill-treating the animal—a policeman inspects the creature's back—that won't stop the owner from continuing:

> Ef dem summons me,
>   Mek me pay few mac,
> Dat caan' mek me 'top
>   Wuk you wid sore back.[13]

Like most poor societies, Jamaica was not and is not renowned for its kindly treatment of animals. (Nor, it should be said, was it or is it notorious for the ill-treatment of animals.[14]) Dogs are generally regarded as useful guards and handy scavengers, and seldom as pets in the European or Euro-American sense of that term. They are typically fed from leftovers (if there are any). The poor and the hungry can hardly afford to be generous to animals—they have little or nothing to be generous with. Indeed, all too often they compete with animals for food. McKay's ideas on the treatment of animals were by no means typical of his fellow Jamaicans, especially those from the countryside.

So where does McKay get this attitude from? It appears that McKay's already sensitive disposition to cruelty was given reinforcement and philosophical underpinning, legitimacy and cohesion by Schopenhauer's ideas; there was an elective affinity between McKay and Schopenhauer on this particular subject.[15]

Schopenhauer regarded animals with a passionate respect unsurpassed in modern Western philosophy. We should recognize, Schopenhauer wrote, that "in all essential respects, the animal is absolutely identical with us and that the difference lies merely in the accident, the intellect, not in the substance which is the will. The world is not a piece of machinery and animals are not articles manufactured for our use."[16] Schopenhauer objected to the caging of birds and the chaining of dogs.[17] He found vivisection "cruel and shocking." The eating of animal flesh he found "unfortunate" and felt that, insofar as this had to be resorted to, "the death of the animals we eat should be rendered quite painless by the administration of chloroform and of a swift blow on the lethal spot."[18] Schopenhauer went so far as to declare that "The *greatest benefit of railways* is that millions of draught-horses are spared a miserable existence."[19] He was convinced that not only truth but morality also was on his side.

McKay was more than likely influenced or reinforced in his convictions by Schopenhauer's views. Jekyll probably had some direct impact here, too. For on top of his love of Schopenhauer, Jekyll was "a great follower of Leo Tolstoy."[20] He was also "something of a Buddhist."[21] And, according to the Oliviers, who knew him well, Jekyll was also a vegetarian.[22]

McKay's Fabian connections might also have had an effect. Henry Salt, the founder and driving force of the Humanitarian League

(1891–1919) started his political life as a Fabian. Though it developed a separate identity, the League's membership overlapped significantly with that of the early Fabians.[23] The League and the Fabians frequently put out joint publications. It advocated an end to animal cruelty, a ban on cruel sports and an end to vivisection and other forms of animal experimentation. Many of its members were leading lights in the Royal Society for the Prevention of Cruelty to Animals. League members advocated the protection of the environment. They fought for an end to flogging and the death penalty. They led the fight for penal reform. The League's founders were socialists and vegetarians. They had an all-encompassing vision of the "Good Society" and of the relationship between humanity and nature. Theirs was an ideology that freely drew upon the findings of Darwin, Marx and Spencer. Salt declared:

> [H]umanity and science between them have exploded the idea of a hard-and-fast line between white . . . and black . . . rich and poor . . . educated and uneducated . . . "good" . . . and "bad". Equally impossible to maintain in the light of newer knowledge, is the idea that there is a difference in kind and not in degree only between human and non-human intelligence.[24]

Thomas Hardy, George Bernard Shaw, Edward Aveling, Eleanor Marx, Ernest Bell, Alice Lewis and Mahatma Gandhi were League members. G.W. Foote and J.M. Wheeler, editor and sub-editor, respectively, of the *Freethinker* were also members of the League. Many dismissed Henry Salt and his colleagues as cranks and faddists, but the League's influence was far from negligible. Raphael Samuel described the League as "a Fabian *alter ego*."[25] Through his familiarity with both Fabianism and free thought, McKay would almost certainly have been exposed to the ideas advanced by the Humanitarian League and similar organizations such as the Fellowship of New Life, which flourished in the late Victorian period and perished from the savage shock of the Great War.

In the end, however, the degree to which others' ideas shaped McKay's own worldview was dependent upon the extent to which he was already receptive and predisposed to welcome and embrace them. To a significant degree, and to an extent insufficiently appreciated, people choose the kind of thinking and thinkers they want to be influenced by. The youthful McKay was no tabula rasa.

8

RELIGION AND CHRISTIANITY

Although he wrote it after converting to Catholicism,[1] *My Green Hills of Jamaica* carries McKay's fond recollections of his rationalist and freethinking childhood without the slightest hint of apology or discomfiture. Before his conversion, religion, and especially Protestant Christianity, was for him one of the greatest humbugs and one of the strongest chains keeping black humanity, in Africa as well as in the diaspora, in thrall. He directed his heaviest artillery not only at the murderous superstition of race and the cruel tyranny of capitalism, but at the "cant" of Christianity. Ray, his roving Haitian intellectual hit man, makes that abundantly clear especially in McKay's 1929 novel, *Banjo*. "As far as I have been able to think it out," Ray says to a white acquaintance, "the colored races are the special victims of biblical morality—Christian morality. Especially the race to which I belong." He goes on to say: "I don't think I loathe anything more than the morality of the Christians. It is false, treacherous, hypocritical."[2] To what extent do McKay's early poems corroborate the claims of *My Green Hills of Jamaica*, that McKay was a rationalist before he emigrated? (After all, McKay wrote the memoirs of his childhood not prior to leaving

Jamaica, but in the late 1940s.) Is there, in other words, any intimation of an incipient or maturing atheism in these poems? Any hint of his being, as he puts it, "a hard little agnostic" in his youth? The answers to these questions are that McKay's early poetry supports the claim of youthful atheism, and that this worldview was well developed, or at least confidently articulated by the young poet.

McKay's commitment to rationalism is most explicitly presented in "Old England," discussed earlier in another context. Included in the itinerary of his imagined tour of England would be a visit to St. Paul's Cathedral where he would also "hear" (not "listen to") "some of de great/Learnin' comin' from de bishops, preachin' relics of old fait'."[3] He is more interested in listening to the powerful organ and feasting his eyes on the architecture.

> I would ope me mout' wid wonder at de massive organ soun',
> An' would 'train me eyes to see de beauty lyin' all aroun'.[4]

As far as McKay is concerned then, despite their "great learnin'" the bishops could just as well have been thrown into the Thames. The massive organ with a player, plus the architectural splendor of the building itself, would do very nicely.

He goes on to make a direct contrast between, on the one hand, what he sees as the failing anachronism of religion and, on the other, the majesty of reason which has the future on its side:

> I'd go to de City Temple, where de old fait' is a wreck,
> An' de parson is a-preachin' views dat most folks will not tek;
> I'd go where de men of science meet togeder in deir hall,
> To give light unto de real truths, to obey king Reason's call.[5]

In "Cudjoe Fresh from de Lecture," McKay once again explicitly expresses his preference for a rationalist, as opposed to a religious mode of thought. The *Origin of Species* wins his support, not Genesis. Evolutionism, not Creationism, he finds persuasive. Darwin's "monkey," not the Biblical clay, is his preferred ancestor. As Cudjoe puts it:

> Yes, from monkey we spring: I believe ebery wud;
> It long time better dan f'go say we come from mud.[6]

God does not get a particularly good press in these poems: he consistently fails to answer prayers. He is either deaf, dumb, uncaring or dead. One poor mother "told of futile prayers/Said on her wearied knees."[7] The peasant of "Hard Times" says, "I ben' me knee an' pray to Gahd,/Yet t'ings same as befo'."[8] "O massa Jesus!" the apple-woman cries, "don't you see?/How pólice is oppressin' we?"[9]—and nothing happens.

McKay weaves his rationalist philosophy into his poetry seamlessly, making it organic to his art. In "Mother Dear," for instance, the dying woman is being advised to concentrate on Jesus, but instead she embraces and almost worships the enveloping natural world. Although dying, she is far more interested in this world—the concrete and the sensual that she herself has helped to fashion— than in the Other World.

> "Wife, de parson's prayin',
> Won't you listen what he's sayin',
> Spend de endin' of your day in
>   Christ our Lord?"
> But de sound of horses neighin',
> Baain' goats an' donkeys brayin',
> Twitt'rin' birds an' children playin'
>   Was all she heard.
>
> Things she had been rearin',
> Only those could claim her hearin',
> When de end we had been fearin'
>   Now had come . . . .[10]

Interested parties—at least the ones with their wits about them— did not fail to notice McKay's militant rationalism. The London-based *Literary Guide*, official organ of the Rationalist Press Association, praised *Songs of Jamaica* and went out of its way to claim McKay as one of their own, "a keen young member of the RPA. . . . The volume gives a delightful presentation of the thoughts and feelings of a black man, which in all essential points will be found precisely like our own."[11]

Like the *Literary Guide*, the *Christian Commonwealth* was generous in its review of the book. But in contrast to the *Guide*, Christian reproach came with its praise. The review in the *Commonwealth* was written by Rev. W. Marwick, an English missionary serving in Jamaica who "never loses an opportunity of doing a good turn to Jamaica and Jamaicans."[12] Still, the reverend felt obliged to chide the young Jamaican, albeit in his ever-so-English way, for the sin of rationalism. "It is to be hoped he will be able to correct his rather crude views of the teaching of the City Temple pulpit, and of the value of Rationalism, with increased knowledge and experience of the real relations of Faith and Reason."[13] What McKay thought of this review we do not know. But knowing something of their character, I can imagine him and U. Theo pouring over the passage at the dining table, reading it aloud in a good Jamaican imitation of an upperclass English accent and having a nice little African giggle. In the end, however, Marwick had the last laugh. For remarkably, both Claude and U. Theo converted to Catholicism just before they died.[14]

9

THOUGHTS ON AFRICA AND INTIMATIONS OF NÉGRITUDE

Although there is relatively little reference to Africa in the early poems, the young McKay's ambivalence towards his ancestral home is discernible. Thus the narrator in "Cudjoe Fresh from de Lecture" concedes that slavery was terrible for those who experienced it. "But, I t'ink it do good, tek we from Africa/An' lan' us in a blessed place as dis a ya."[1] Cudjoe drives his point home while giving us an indication of his perception of Africa. It is one inherited from the colonial masters, which he did not transcend. There is no irony in his words:

> Talk 'bouten Africa, we would be deh till now,
> Maybe same half-naked—all day dribe buccra cow,
> An' tearin' t'rough de bush wid all de monkey dem,
> Wile an' uncibilise', an' neber comin' tame.[2]

There is an element here that has invariably been overlooked by the critics. Cudjoe's exposure to the theory of evolution increases his pride in his blackness, in his race. As far as Cudjoe is concerned, Darwin's theory showed that human beings were fundamentally the same, that we all, regardless of color, "spring" from the monkey. The lecturer has convinced Cudjoe that human beings are essentially equal and Cudjoe has undergone an almost religious conversion; he looks upon himself with new eyes: "Him tell us 'bout we self, an' mek we fresh again."

> Me look 'pon me black 'kin, an' so me head grow big,
> Aldough me heaby han' dem hab fe plug an' dig;
> For ebery single man, no car' about dem rank,
> Him bring us ebery one an' put 'pon de same plank.[3]

This was the message, this was the news—uncommonly good tidings for black folks—that Cudjoe is trying to impart when he hails his cousin with the zeal of the newly converted:

> 'Top *one* minute, Cous' Jarge, an' sit do'n 'pon de grass,
> An' mek a tell you 'bout de news I hear at las',
> How de buccra te-day tek time an' begin teach
> All of us dat was deh in a clear open speech.[4]

Cudjoe himself recognizes that the rest, including his discourse on Africa, was a diversion. "I lef' quite 'way from wha' we be'n deh talk about,"[5] he admits. Yet it is interesting that commentators invariably notice Cudjoe's digression and ignore the essence of the poem: the scientific rejection of racism and the buttressing of black pride by science.

In "Gordon to the Oppressed Natives," McKay proudly identifies with the sons of Africa in Jamaica, if not with Africa itself, as we have seen:

> Wake de lion in your veins,
>   De gorilla in your blood;
> Show dem dat you ha' some brains,
>   Though you may be coarse an' rude.[6]

The imagery is problematic—lion in the veins, gorilla in the blood—echoing notions of the primitive African. True, the words are ostensibly Gordon's. But Gordon uttered no such words and he was in Kingston, not in Morant Bay, during the revolt. The choice of words are therefore McKay's alone. With time and education,

McKay's view of his ancestral homeland would radically alter. In "Africa," one of his finest sonnets, he celebrates her illustrious past: "The sciences were sucklings at thy breast . . . . /New peoples marvel at thy pyramids."[7] But that came a decade after leaving Jamaica.

If the young McKay had a problem with his depiction of Africa, he had none with his conception of blackness. It is little wonder that his poetry of exile and his novels, especially *Banjo* (1929), had a profound effect upon Aimé Césaire and Léopold Senghor, chief founders of the négritude movement in Paris during the 1930s; all the main protagonists in that movement—whose central ideology is the recognition and affirmation of beauty in blackness—pay homage to McKay as a primary source of inspiration. *Banjo* quickly became something of a Bible to these young black intellectuals from the Caribbean and West Africa.[8] But the respect, beauty and integrity with which black people, especially the Jamaican peasantry, are portrayed in these early poems make *Songs of Jamaica* and *Constab Ballads* founding texts in négritude, even before this ideological current had a name. (Some of the themes discussed earlier—color and class, Christianity, the black woman— would emerge as important motifs in the poetry of négritude, especially in the work of Aimé Césaire, Léopold Senghor and Léon Gontran Damas.)

This concatenation of blackness with beauty is remarkable given the times and context in which McKay wrote, for prevailing thought denied and militated against such a connection. The very definition of the African, the so-called "Negro," was the antonym of beauty. In a most explicit way, McKay went against this colonial orthodoxy— an orthodoxy that was not only intrinsic to the colonial project, but one that was generally imbibed, accepted and rearticulated by the colonized. In the Caribbean the "brown" middle class, buttressed by the educational system, were the primary domestic purveyors of such ideas, but they were not the only ones. Many ordinary black people often took for granted these negative ideas about themselves.

The astonishingly persistent phenomenon of colorism would be inexplicable in the absence of such black popular complicity.[9]

McKay links beauty with blackness in two of his love poems. In "My Pretty Dan," a woman sings of her love for a black policeman:

> I love my pólice, and he loves me too,
> An' he has promised he'll be ever true.

Her policeman lover is "de prettiest you could set eyes 'pon." Dan has a "pretty cap to match his pretty face." And "Prettiest of naygur is my dear police."[10]

"Prettiest of naygur" is nothing less than a revolutionary phrase. Nowhere in anglophone Caribbean letters, or even folklore, had beauty and "naygur" been associated in this way before. "Naygur" or "nayga" is seldom used in Jamaica and never in a positive way. It is used "by black people to condemn those of their own color. In the song 'Sammy Dead Oh' there is the line, almost a proverb, 'Nayga kean [can't] bear fe see Nayga flourish,' which Louise Bennett echoes in the poem 'Oonoo Lie!' as 'Nayga won't meck nayga prospa.' *Naygur* is often tantamount to 'good-for-nothing', and *neegrish* is 'mean or despicable.'"[11] Instead of "pretty" most Jamaicans would be familiar with hearing "dutty" [dirty] before the noun naygur. A "dutty naygur"—an epithet that still has currency—is the lowest of the low, more or less the worst insult to be found in the language. "Pretty naygur" never mind the "prettiest of naygur," is a contradiction in terms. McKay is inviting his fellow Jamaicans to reinvent the language in their own image.

In "Fe Me Sal" McKay once again challenges convention. It is the policeman's turn to sing of his love.

> In de blazin' midday heat, when I'm posted on me beat,
>   Who I t'inkin' of but fe me Sal?
> . . . .
> She's de darlin' o' me heart, an' we'll neber neber part,
>   She's de prettiest black gal in de wul';
> An' whereber you may go you won't find anedder so,
>   Wid more tender min' an' better sort o' soul.[12]

Sal is "de prettiest black gal in de wul'." This is almost as heterodox as the description of Dan. The depiction of Sal's mind and soul is also transgressional.

These motifs of négritude would be developed by McKay in his poetry, and especially in his prose, in the harsher, more racist and more alienating environments of exile.

10

THE WEAPON OF LYRIC POETRY

McKay's most passionate lyrics of rural Jamaica were written against a backdrop not of Kingston but of his experience in the police force. As I argued earlier, it is a mistake to read his poetry as simply or primarily anti-urban. His most biting social commentary is not concerned with the urban environment—Kingston or Spanish Town—but with what he depicts as the near-malevolent and destructive powers of the police and, by extension, the colonial state.

"Papine Corner" is often cited as evidence of McKay's dislike of Kingston. It is nothing of the sort. "Papine Corner" is a tongue-in-cheek description of the nocturnal events in this lively terminus where town meets country on the outskirts of Kingston. The *Gleaner* described Papine as "our local Coney Island . . . the favourite resort of the 'smart set,' especially on Sunday nights."[1] McKay's poem alludes to the hypocrisy of the Jamaican middle class and especially to that of his fellow police officers—no fewer than four of the nine stanzas are specifically directed at the carryings-on of the police at Papine Corner. But it is evident that McKay found the place exciting and that he got enormous—if somewhat vicarious, almost voyeuristic—pleasure from simply watching the behavior of the motley group of humanity milling around and at play in this part of the city.

> When you want a pleasant drive,
>   Tek Hope Gardens line;
> I can tell you, man alive,
>   It is jolly fine:
> Ef you want to feel de fun,
>   You mus' only wait
> Until when you're comin' do'n
>   An' de tram is late.[2]

As McKay remarked in his memoirs, "I didn't intend the poem as an attack on the place, because I was very fond of it." That did not stop some ministers in Kingston when the poem was published in *The Gleaner* using the poem "as a sermon to inveigh against the wickedness of life in our city."[3]

To McKay, the countryside was less an idealized counterpoint to the city than a refuge from the police force and a symbol of freedom. The countryside is home, and home is the countryside. This is illustrated most powerfully by "My Mountain Home" where his childhood in the country is defined as freedom and his time in the force is a period of suffering and captivity. The picture of home is pastoral, serene, idealized:

> De mango tree in yellow bloom,
>   De pretty akee seed,
> De mammee where de John-to-whits come
>   To have their daily feed,
>
> Show you de place where I was born,
>   Of which I am so proud,
> 'Mongst de banana-field an' corn
>   On a lone mountain-road.
> . . . .
> An' growin' up, with sweet freedom
>   About de yard I'd run;
> An' tired out I'd hide me from
>   De fierce heat of de sun.[4]

This existence ends abruptly when he becomes an adult and joins the police force.

> De early days pass quickly 'long,
>> Soon I became a man,
> An' one day found myself among
>> Strange folks in a strange lan'.

It was a psychically brutalizing form of imprisonment:

> My little joys, my wholesome min',
>> Dey bullied out o' me;
> And made me daily mourn an' pine
>> An' wish dat I was free.
>
> Dey taught me to distrust my life,
>> Dey taught me what was grief . . . .[5]

"Sukee River," written after McKay had left the force, expresses the healing power of the countryside:

> I shall love you ever,
> Dearest Sukee River:
> Dash against my broken heart,
> Nevermore from you I'll part,
>> But will stay forever,
>> Crystal Sukee River.
>
> Cool my fevered brow:
> Ah! 'tis better now,
> As I serpent-like lance t'rough
> Your broad pool o' deepest blue!
>> Dis once burnin' brow
>> Is more better now.
>
> .   .   .   .
>> Kiss my naked breast
>> In its black skin drest:
> Let your dainty silver bubbles
> Ease it of its lifelong troubles,
>> Dis my naked breast
>> In its black skin drest.

> Floatin', floatin' down
> On my back alone,
> Kiss me on my upturned face,
> Clasp me in your fond embrace,
> As I'm floatin' down
> Happy, yet alone.[6]

McKay's intense celebration of the countryside is reactive to the pain of his ordeal in the police force in Kingston. The consuming desire, the almost insatiable yearning in "De Days dat are Gone," "The Hermit," "Kite Flying," and "Heart Stirrings"[7] can only be explained as reaction to the sorrow and alienation of being on the force. To this extent McKay's pastoral and highly subjective outpourings were—to borrow Adorno's apt description of lyric poetry—"socially motivated behind the author's back."[8]

McKay celebrates his discharge in "Free" with the joy of one released from prison:

> Scarce can I believe my eyes,
> Yet before me there it lies,
> Precious paper granting me
> Quick release from misery.
>
> So farewell to Half Way Tree,
> And the plains I hate to see!
> Soon will I forget my ills,
> In my loved Clarendon hills.[9]

The counterpointing of the rural idyll with the incarcerating constabulary is a critique of the police force and all that it represented. Like the Jamaican rebel slaves of old, he abandons the plains— where the ruling class holds sway and the sugarcane grows—and escapes to the relative security of the hills, the traditional refuge of the runaway slave, maroon country.

11

PEASANTS' WAYS O' THINKIN': WHAT IS TO BE DONE?

We need not reiterate the sentiments of McKay's early poetry of revolt. We have already alluded to McKay's poem on the Morant Bay Rebellion of 1865, "George William Gordon to the Oppressed Natives," published in the Jamaican press in 1912. But what of McKay's vision, as opposed to what he was against? McKay's long poem, "Peasants' Ways o' Thinkin'," provides the most explicit answer. McKay recognizes here that what the peasants want is fairly basic (and from the tone of the poem, the demands of the peasants were also his).

The peasants are willing to reconcile themselves to some inequality between themselves and buccra:

> We may n't be rich like buccra folk;
> For us de white, for dem de yolk,
> Da's de way dat the egg divide,
> An' we content wi' de outside.

But at the heart of the peasants' demands is the need for land:

> Havin' we owna mancha-root,
> Havin' we dandy Sunday suit,
> We'll happy wi' our modest lot
> An' wont' grudge buccra wha' dem got.

> A piece o' lan' fe raise two goat,
> A little rum fe ease we t'roat,
> A little cot fe res' we head—
> An' we're contented till we dead.[1]

These modest demands are congruent with the Fabian Socialism that McKay professed at the time. They are hardly anti-capitalist but the "piece o' land" and "mancha-root" (banana tree) would hardly fall into the peasant's possessions like manna from heaven. There would have to be a struggle. Given the skewed distribution of the land in the countryside at the time, land reform would have undoubtedly challenged powerful agrarian capitalist interests. Although signalled in his early poetry, McKay's anti-capitalist revolutionary socialist positions were to develop and mature in exile.

The most astonishing feature of these early poems is the degree to which McKay's lifelong passions, concerns, hatreds and loves were conspicuously prefigured in his Jamaican years. To this extent then, what is remarkable about McKay's political trajectory in exile is not the ruptures that it manifested, but the extraordinarily distinct continuity that it had with his Jamaican youth.

THE POLITICS OF POETIC FORM AND CONTENT WITHIN THE COLONIAL CONTEXT

The form of McKay's Jamaican poetry has drawn the attention of critics, but in general the discussion is muddled and unsatisfactory. It is true that the radical content of McKay's verse is not matched by a similar daring in its form. The form need not have broken with convention just for the sake of it (as some critics imply), but it could have been more consistently effective in imparting the rhythm and metre of Jamaican. McKay's poetry is "overburdened with the remembered rhythms and diction of Romantic or Victorian English poetry" and "all too often, weak rhymes and stale poetic diction coincide."[1] It is, however, harsh and inaccurate to claim that McKay *usually* achieves "neither a harmony of voice and vision nor a meaningful tension between the two" in his poetry as a whole. His poetry is certainly uneven—especially his early Jamaican poems—but he succeeds more often than he fails as a poet and he fails more often in his early work. (The fruits of his mature years are little known, despite pretensions to the contrary. Most of his poems written in exile have never been published, let alone critically analyzed.)

Some condemn McKay for the formal traditions he follows. Edward Brathwaite criticizes McKay for using "European" metre and for writing "dialect," "bad English"—as opposed to what he calls "nation language," an unnecessary neologism meaning creole language.[2] McKay made no secret of the fact that he was wedded to the traditional European poetic forms, but he regarded them to be as much his as they were anybody else's. Was he not educated in the European tradition and was he not a product of a British colonial environment? Although the traditions of the Jamaican masses have their roots in Africa, they too are overdetermined and burdened by Europe's. The poetic forms of the Caribbean masses cannot be as easily separated from those of the colonizers as Brathwaite would like one to think.

Over the years, ordinary Jamaicans read and learned many of McKay's Jamaican poems by heart.[4] McKay recalled that when his poems started to appear in the newspapers, peasants as well as some of his comrades in the force would ask him to read for them. They liked his poems, and he reported that they used to exclaim, "Why they're just like that, they're so natural."[5] Louise Bennett, the premier Jamaican language poet, first saw the language in print in one of McKay's books. Mary Jane Hewitt writes that when Bennett was about seven years old, a teacher at Calabar School in Kingston gave her a copy of *Constab Ballads*, knowing the child was always telling her classmates anancy stories. "Here are some verses a man wrote in the Jamaican talk. You must read some of them. They're very funny!" Bennett took the book home and showed it to her Grandma Mimi who liked the poems. Bennett said it was "thrilling" to see the language in print. She memorized some of the poems and recited them to friends and relatives. McKay's early writing "reinforced Bennett's love of her primary language."[6]

Writing in 1956, J. E. Clare McFarlane, the second poet laureate of Jamaica, underscored McKay's impact upon Jamaican society. The frequent comparison between Robert Burns and McKay ("the Bobby Burns of Jamaica") "is more than superficial," McFarlane reckoned.

> Like Burns, he expresses the soul of his people in a medium created by his people. It is small wonder that his dialect poetry went immediately

to their hearts and that, although he is still unread by the majority, his name has become something of a legend among them. The masses do not read him because his work has never been issued in an edition sufficiently large and cheap to encourage its easy circulation among them; but many of his phrases have passed from lip to lip and have become household words. For McKay has caught up within his verse the spontaneous humour and infectious laughter of his people; he reflects their ability to make a jest of their dilemmas and illustrates their capacity for tender emotion.[7]

McKay's verse caught more than the "spontaneous humour and infectious laughter" of his people. It reflected much more than their ability to laugh at their dilemmas and illustrated more than their "capacity for tender emotion." McKay's project was far more encompassing. "I had," he said, "recaptured the spirit of the Jamaican peasants in verse, rendering their primitive joys, their loves and hates, their work and play, their dialect."[8] There is a tendency, discussed later, to view the Jamaican language as a medium for comedy and satire and not for serious thought. McKay demonstrated very clearly that the language could be used for a wide range of expression.

McKay's poetry resonated with the masses of his Jamaica not despite its form, but in large measure because of it; it was the form the constabs, the peasants, Grandma Mimi, little Louise and the rest of Jamaica were familiar with. Houston Baker makes a similar point in defense of Countee Cullen, the Afro-American poet. The ballad, and in particular, the Keatsian ballad, was Cullen's favorite form. For this, the critics have lambasted Cullen. Baker points out that the ballad and the sonnet were forms that resonated not only with white American audiences, but also with Afro-Americans:

It seems inconceivable that, in the first flush of pioneering urbanity and heady self-consciousness, the congregation of Reverend Frederick Cullen's well-attended Salem Methodist Episcopal Church in Harlem would have responded positively if, after the father's announcement of his son's accomplishment as *a poet*, the young Countee had produced sounds such as : "April is the cruellest month, breeding/Lilacs out of the dead land, mixing/Memory and desire, stirring/Dull roots with spring rain."

The delivery of such lines "would probably have caused consternation akin to the congregations' reaction to John in Dubois's classic story 'Of the Coming of John': 'Little had they understood of what he said, for he spoke an unknown tongue.'" Not only was the "tongue" of "such collaged allusiveness as Eliot's *unknown* to a congregation like Reverend Cullen's; it was also unnecessary, unneeded, of little use in a world bent on recognizable (rhyme, meter, form, etc.) artistic 'contributions.'"[9]

There are, however, genuine problems with the language that McKay uses in some of his Jamaican poetry. The primary problem, however, is unevenness. Some of the poems are faithful to the language, others compromise it. The issue cannot be explained away by an invoked distinction between "dialect" and "nation language." As linguists point out, there is a continuum between creole and standard English; people speak and write at different points on that continuum.[10] One of the weaknesses in McKay's use of language is that he did not always hit the right point on the continuum for the personae of his poems. This came about for a number of reasons. McKay's somewhat dual and transitory class position, his being between the peasantry and the professional black middle class, generated real problems— "interference," the linguists call it—between the two poles of the linguistic spectrum where different conventions operate. McKay may also have compromised linguistically because he was attempting to appeal simultaneously to an international, standard-English-speaking audience and a subaltern, working-class and peasant domestic readership. Walter Jekyll's elaborate preface (essentially a primer in Jamaican, and a very good one too), annotations (almost translations in some cases) and glossary would all have been superfluous were the work not intended for a larger audience.[11] McKay may also have been insufficiently confident, especially at the beginning, to use in more pristine form the language of the masses in his poems.[12] Then there was the genuine problem of transliteration. How should words in Jamaican be written; how does one write words that have hitherto only been heard and not seen? The problem of orthography exists to this very day.

Although McKay claimed to have found it easier to write poems in creole than in English, it is evident that he found it easier—perhaps even more appropriate—to articulate introspection, especially first-person introspection, in English than in creole. Evidently, he was trained to think in English and he thought in English. He apparently found English more apt for expressing sorrow. The more melancholic he became, the more he moved to the standard English pole of the linguistic continuum in his writing.[13] But McKay would not have agreed with Bennett when she said that "the nature of dialect is almost the nature of comedy" nor would he have equivocated, as Bennett did, when asked if the Jamaican language could serve a Jeremiah as well as a comic writer. Similarly, he would have demurred when McFarlane, like a good colonial, averred that "dialect," as he called the language, "is a broken tongue" with which "it is impossible to build an edifice of verse possessing the perfect symmetry of finished art . . . it may serve as an admirable record of feeling, but not as an interpreter of that record."[14] This type of argument is not only silly, it is obviously silly. For do not ordinary Jamaicans feel and express their sorrow? Do they not think about their world and interpret it? And do they not do all these things in Jamaican, the language they fashioned, know and speak? All one has to do to determine whether the language could have been used by a Jeremiah is to go to a pentecostal church in the Jamaican countryside and listen to the "testimonies" of its congregation—or, better still, listen in on a "reasoning" session of a group of Rastafarians.[15] Furthermore, McKay succeeded in capturing the pathos and thinking of ordinary Jamaicans in their own language in poems such as "Quashie to Buccra," "Whe' Fe Do?" "Hard Times," "A Midnight Woman to the Bobby," "Two-an'-Six" and "The Apple-Woman's Complaint."

McFarlane wrote that McKay "became conscious of his limitation and sought the more spacious ways of orthodox language for the full expression of his powers."[16] But there is no evidence that McKay turned to English because he thought Jamaican was limiting. I have little doubt that had he remained in the island he would have continued to write in *both* creole and English. He moved to the United States and wrote in the language that would be understood there.

Despite his political commitment to using the language of the masses, McKay found it somewhat burdensome; he wrote in creole at a price. After all, the local educated standard, the yardstick, was, as he put it, "English English." Almost forty years after leaving the island, he could still hear the patronizing and self-righteous sniggering of the anglophile, brown middle class about his "dialect" poetry. His inevitable and understandable problem was that he could not very well tell them to go to hell—literally or even to himself. Instead, like a good colonial, he would rise to their challenge and succeed as a poet in English English.

> Most of the poems that were published in Jamaica at the time were repetitious and not very good. Our poets thought it was an excellent thing if they could imitate the English poets. We had poetry societies for the nice people. There were "Browning Clubs" where the poetry of Robert Browning was studied but not understood. I had read my poems before many of these societies and the members used to say: "Well, he's very nice and pretty you know, but he's not a real poet as Browning and Byron and Tennyson are poets." I used to think I would show them something. Someday I would write poetry in straight English and amaze and confound them because they thought I was not serious, simply because I wrote poems in the dialect which they did not consider profound.[17]

Given the stigma attached to the language it comes as no surprise that only a handful of people ever had the courage to write poems in Jamaican during McKay's time. Indeed, I have seen only one poem written in the language before McKay started to publish on a regular basis in the Jamaica press.[18] Perhaps inspired by McKay's effort and the attention it drew, especially after *Songs of Jamaica* appeared, a spurt of six poems of this kind appeared in the *Jamaica*

Times in 1912.[19] But four of these were published after McKay had left for the United States. It marked the beginning of a trend that would continue in fits and starts up to the emergence of Louise Bennett in the 1940s. The poems were generally satirical and written by white Jamaicans or expatriates, principally Raglan Phillips and Norman Palmer. They generally poked fun at rather than laughed with their Jamaican characters. None of their verse had the literary merit of McKay's. No one with any serious literary ambition attempted to write poems in creole although McKay received praise in some places, especially from Thomas MacDermot (Tom Redcam). MacDermot, founder of the All Jamaica Library (an attempt to encourage an island literature and a reading public), publisher of the *Jamaica Times* and a great encourager of McKay, was a prolific poet (he was made Jamaica's first poet laureate in 1933) but he never wrote a single poem in Jamaican. Of Irish descent but a Jamaican by birth, MacDermot knew the language well and used it effectively in his pioneering novella, *Becka's Buckra Baby* (1904) and in his novel *One Brown Girl And*—(1909), but never in a poem.[20]

A black Jamaican, McFarlane founded the Jamaica Poetry League in 1923 and became its first president. He edited two major volumes of Jamaican poetry, *Voices From Summerland* (1929) and *A Treasury of Jamaican Poetry* (1949).[21] Given his views on Jamaican, it is little wonder that none of the poems in these volumes was written in creole. McKay appears, and McFarlane rejoices in his compatriot's achievements—he refers to him in 1929 as "perhaps the most outstanding literary figure of his race"[22]—but neither of these volumes carries a single poem from McKay's Jamaican years. Though Louise Bennett had published four volumes of poetry by the time *A Treasury of Jamaican Poetry* appeared in 1949, not one of her poems was included. When linguists at the University College of the West Indies began to research Jamaican and tried to establish its integrity as a language sui generis, the Poetry League objected, charging the scholars with "trying to concoct a new language."[23] Even the *Independence Anthology of*

Jamaican Literature condescends to expression in the native tongue. Louise Bennett is placed at the back of the book under a section called "Humour"—apparently an afterthought, and a bad joke. As Mervyn Morris remarked in his groundbreaking essay on Bennett, written just a year after the *Independence Anthology* came out, "By many people whose taste and judgement on other matters I respect she is regarded more or less as a local joke; a good, high-spirited joke, but, in the end, only a joke." "They preferred to accept her as a 'coon' entertainer," wrote Gordon Rohler.[24]

This cultural milieu remained stubbornly unchanged until the 1970s. It took courage for McKay to have started—and as early as 1910—and to continue writing in the local language. It took courage for Bennett too, the leading poet writing in Jamaican for decades now, considering the colonial cultural legacy. At one of her early performances in the 1940s, a voice from the audience rang out the rhetorical question "A dat yuh modder sen yuh a school fa?"[25] Even the most casual and moderately observant visitor to Jamaica, or indeed to anywhere else in the Caribbean, will know that this pathetic attitude is still pervasive, though less prevalent than it was during the 1940s. In a 1978 interview with an Afro-American scholar, Bennett was asked, "Have you ever felt the pressure to apologise [for writing poetry in Jamaican]?" Miss Lou, as she is affectionately known in Jamaica, uttered a bitter laugh as only she can:

> Ah! Massa! Oi-i-i! From I start it till now, right now, at this moment! You asking! I have done a lot, within the forty years, ha-ha! But I tell you, still there are people, still you'll find this thing of almost patronising you, you know—[Mimicking] "Oh, Miss Lou!" [Exuberant laughter] Well, of course, I don't bother with them because the people are understanding me and this is really what matters. . . .[26]

Like McKay's dismissal of the Browning Club's snobbery, the matter is not as easily laughed away as Bennett appears to have done. The lack of recognition clearly hurt and angered her. A decade before, in an interview with Jamaican poet Dennis Scott, she was more forthcoming:

My dear Dennis, I have been set apart by other creative writers a long time ago because of the language I speak and work in. From the beginning nobody ever recognised me as a writer. "Well, she is 'doing' dialect;" it wasn't even writing you know. Up to now a lot of people don't even think I write. They say "Oh, you just stand up and say these things!"

She acknowledged that in more recent times critics and other writers have come to appreciate more fully what she had been doing in the language. "Yes," she said, "and I am very gratified, very pleased that this has happened at last." Despite the belated recognition,

we have to face the fact that in the beginning this wasn't so. You know, I wasn't ever asked to a Jamaican Poetry League meeting? I was never thought good enough to be represented in that anthology *Focus*. The anthology which appeared in 1962 [*Independence Anthology of Jamaican Literature* - WJ] was the first time that anything representing the community of writers contained anything of mine in it. Most people thought that after all they couldn't discourse with me at all because I was going to talk to them in Jamaican dialect which they couldn't understand.[27]

The malady was widespread and extended well beyond Jamaica and the English-speaking Caribbean. Aimé Césaire, the great poet of négritude born some twenty-three years after McKay and brought up in a poor household in rural Martinique was, like many colonials, not allowed to speak Creole (Martinique's *lingua franca*) at home. His paternal grandmother and his father read to him the texts of the *metropole* in the language of the *metropole*, the French classics. Because of his family's strenuous effort in this endeavor, Césaire "repressed Creole in favor of French quite completely and at a very early age. He was consequently even less able than other writers of his generation to envisage Creole as a vehicle for Martinican cultural expression. Creole was never a real choice for him precisely because of the dynamics of culture and power to which he was introduced as a young child."[28]

Césaire was inculcated with the belief that, except sugar, nothing of value existed in his native island. It was not until Césaire became a student at the Lycée Schoelcher in Fort-de-France, the island's capital, that he received encouragement (from an extraordinary teacher, Eugène Revert) to see beauty in the surrounding rich flora and fauna—which were to so lavishly and effectively decorate his poetry. For the first time something about his native Martinique was affirmed. Revert's instruction was effectively extra-curricular,[29] there was no space in Césaire's science book for Martinique's plants. The centralism of the French educational system put into place by Napoleon did not allow for that, and Martinique, in more ways than geographically, was on the periphery. "We had the same curriculum and the same books as in France," Césaire told an American interviewer. "And I remember that if my grades in natural science were so low, it was because I could never find a plant from Martinique and that in my botany book I kept seeing plants from France. Everything was like that. And so we became quickly aware of the limits of official culture."[30] Césaire—still very much alive—has not written a poem in Creole so far. Undoubtedly he has been very aware of the limits of French official culture, and he has had the audacity to spectacularly transgress many of them—but not when it comes to the use of Creole for literary expression. Strangely, despite his radicalism (he was a member of the French Communist Party up to 1956 and still defines himself as a socialist), Césaire has dismissed Martinican Creole in the same words with which the much more politically conservative McFarlane did Jamaican. In a 1978 interview, Césaire infamously declared that for him,

> writing is linked to French, not Creole. . . . One aspect of Martinique's cultural retardation has to do with language, this créolité that's stayed at the stage of immediacy, incapable of elevation, of the expression of abstract ideas.[31]

It is little wonder that the *créoliste* revolt is as much against Césaire as it is against France.[32]

In marked contrast to Césaire, McKay did not doubt the capacity of his native creole. But like Césaire, he was encouraged to see beauty in his island home by an enlightened white outsider.

Although it is unlikely that McKay needed this education, Jekyll's love and enthusiasm for the Jamaican landscape clearly made a lasting impression upon him. Jekyll was a keen hiker and McKay would sometimes accompany him on his long walks over the hills. "Heaps of wildflowers spilled themselves along the roadside and Mr. Jekyll gave me lessons in higher botany, telling me the Latin names for all the flowers." Writing forty years after, McKay confessed that he had "quite forgotten" the Latin names, but, "it was nice listening to these high-sounding Latin names for our hibiscus and painted ladies, trailing feefees, bluebells, water lilies of all kinds, bell flowers, four o'clock, crotons and the rest."[33]

Again, what is remarkable is not the fact that he wrote all but one of his poems first shown to Jekyll in "straight" English, but the fact that he wrote any at all in Jamaican. McKay also had the added audacity to show the poem to a white man, a white aristocratic stranger, albeit one interested in Jamaican folklore. The poem burst out of McKay when he heard a man coaxing his harassed donkey:

> Ko how de jackass
> > Lay do'n in de road;
> An' him ondly car'
> > Little bit o' load.
>
> Kue, jackass, git up!
> > 'Tan' up 'pon you' foot!
> Dis ya load no load,
> > You's a lazy brut'.[34]

It must have taken courage for McKay to have shown it to Jekyll.

Bennett also started her poetry apprenticeship writing in "straight" English. She also had her Saul-on-the-road-to-Damascus experience through the arresting eloquence and humor of the Jamaican folk language:

One day she set out, a young teenager all dressed up for a matinee film show in Cross Roads [Kingston]. On the electric tramcars . . . , people travelling with baskets were required to sit at the back, and they were sometimes resentful of other people who, when the tram was full, tried to join them there. As Louise was boarding the tram she heard a country woman say: "Pread out yuhself, one dress-oman a come." That vivid remark made a great impression on her, and on returning home she wrote her first dialect poem, "On A Tramcar", which began:

> Pread out yuhself deh Liza, one
> Dress-oman dah look like seh
> She see de li space side-a we
> An waan foce harself een deh.

As Morris noted, this was young Louise's beginning.[35] The incident occurred in the 1930s. McKay had written his first Jamaican poem in 1909, ten years before Louise Bennett was born.[36] McKay's poetry directly influenced her artistic development.

Revert had encouraged the young Césaire to see beauty in his native Martinique, Jekyll did the same for McKay in relation to Jamaica. Above all the discussions of European philosophy and literature, music and folklore, this was Jekyll's signal contribution to the intellectual growth of the young colonial: the reassurance that there was genuine beauty in the Jamaican language and, by extension, in the culture of the ordinary Jamaican people, culture that one can celebrate without fear or favor outside of the narrow confines of upper Clarendon. McKay learned quickly to see the beauty that Jekyll had identified in his "dialect" poems and happily shared his own discovery of this beauty with others. After writing each poem, McKay sent it to Jekyll.

> [H]e wrote back to say that each one was more beautiful than the last. Beauty! A short while before I never thought that any beauty could be found in the Jamaican dialect. Now this Englishman had discovered beauty and I too could see where my poems were beautiful.[37]

McKay was especially gratified by the response of the ordinary people, the subject of his poetry. Twenty years after leaving Jamaica, and thousands of miles away in Morocco, he clung to the vivid and warm memory of the response of market women to his poems: "I remember when my first poems came out, the market women stopped me by the roadside and asked me to read to them. Those were the happiest readings I ever gave—I dislike audiences."[38]

In 1917 McKay wrote that "melody and loveliness . . . are two of the chief things I look for in poetry, a third and most important to me being thought."[39] McKay took his thinking seriously, as well as melody-making and the creation of loveliness. By and large, he succeeded in his endeavor, including his Jamaican poetry. But to judge him fairly, that is, on the basis of the primary criteria upon which he himself wrote his poetry, thought must take priority. McKay had important things to tell us about his times and the Jamaica in which he lived. Perhaps, most of all, his poetry tells us a great deal about himself, his worldview, and his political evolution. In short, if we are to understand McKay and appreciate his political development, we must first know and analyze his early poetry.

Claude McKay was a pioneer, and he bore the scars of the pioneer. It is only those who lack an historical imagination who would pit the poetic accomplishments in Jamaican of Louise Bennett, Linton Kwesi Johnson, Lorna Goodison, or Michael Smith against McKay; the more astute will recognize that it is *because* of McKay that Bennett and others have been able to supersede him—in form, if not in thought.

WHEN WAS McKAY BORN?
A CONTROVERSY, A DOCUMENT,
AND A RESOLUTION

One Sunday marnin' 'fo' de hour
Fe service-time come on,
Ma say dat I be'n born to her
Her little las'y son.

Claude McKay

Confusion reigned among his admirers on at least three continents. They wanted to pay homage to his memory. But when, they asked, should the centenary of Claude McKay's birth be celebrated, 1989 or 1990? There was no dispute about his having been born on September 15; the problem revolved around the year. In Britain and the United States, no one was sure. In India, where there has been a curiously sustained scholarly interest in McKay over the years, organizers of an international centennial conference at the University of Mysore came up with an interesting solution. In a gesture somewhat akin to Solomonic Judgement, they decided to hold their conference in January 1990, explicitly noting that "neither year was officially endorsed."[1]

In McKay's birthplace, Jamaica, there was less reticence and

Claude McKay's birth certificate, Island Record
Office, Spanish Town, Jamaica

equivocation: 1990 was the date accepted and officially promul-
gated as the centenary of his birth. Organizers, under the auspices of
the Ministry of Information and Culture, put on a grand series of
events between September and December 1990, around McKay's
life and work. Chaired by Wycliffe Bennett, an esteemed cultural
figure on the island, the celebrations began on September 15, with
an exhibition, "Celebrating Claude McKay," officially opened by
the Parliamentary Secretary in the Ministry of Information and
Culture, Senator Donna Scott-Bhoorasingh, who spoke of "McKay's
great contribution to fostering black racial pride world-wide."
McKay's last novel, *Harlem Glory*, published in 1990, was launched
by the Minister of Information and Culture, Senator the Honourable
Dr. Paul Robertson, in the presence of McKay's only offspring, Hope
McKay-Virtue, who, like McKay's literary agent, the 90-year-old
Carl Cowl, had flown in from the United States specially for the cel-
ebrations.[2] A television documentary, produced by the Creative
Production and Training Centre, outlining the poet's early years in
Jamaica and his life in the United States, Europe and Africa, was
shown. *Banana Bottom*, McKay's novel of Jamaican peasant life set at
the turn of the century, was serialized on radio. "Flame Heart," a
docu-drama based on McKay's life and work, premiered at the
island's most prestigious venue, the Ward Theatre in Kingston, and
toured May Pen, Clarendon (McKay's parish of birth), and Montego
Bay. The island's press also reported that "booklets aimed at school
children and the inauguration of a special Claude McKay award in
the Festival Literary Competition for poetry to start in Festival 91,"
would be launched. There was even talk of "Poetry in Force," a
special poetry writing scheme, in "recognition of McKay's involve-
ment with the Jamaican Police Force as a young man."[3] And
Caribbean Quarterly, a scholarly journal produced at the University
of the West Indies in Jamaica, ran a "Special Issue on Claude
McKay," recognizing 1990 as the centenary of the poet's birth.[4]

Yet all of the celebrations were, inadvertently, too late. For new
evidence, presented here, proves incontrovertibly that McKay was

born not in 1890, the year generally accepted to be the correct date, but in 1889. How did the mistake occur, and what is the evidence indicating that it is indeed a mistake?

Up to 1920, McKay had accepted and all the biographical notices about him suggested that he was born on September 15 1889. But beginning with the publication of McKay's *Harlem Shadows* in 1922, and without explanation, his date of birth was given as 1890. Between 1924 and 1927, McKay wrote a series of angry letters to Alain Locke, Professor of Philosophy at Howard University and one of the protagonists in the Harlem Renaissance, accusing Locke of cowardly and arrogant editorial policies. It was in one of these letters that McKay chided Locke for getting his date of birth wrong:

> [Y]ou ignored the date of my birth that was given in *Harlem Shadows* (my latest and most authentic biographical note is printed there) and you went and dug up an anterior date. It was after the publication of *Spring in New Hampshire* [1920] that my sister verified the date (it had been set back at Grade School so that I could be allowed to act as assistant to the school-master) and wrote me about it in London. But I suppose that you have such a passion for discovering things and acting upon your own initiative that you never considered it polite or expedient to ask for the facts.[5]

It was on the basis of this evidence that McKay scholars, such as Wayne Cooper and myself, accepted 1890 as McKay's year of birth.[6] I was somewhat troubled, however, that McKay's daughter, had been equally vehement in asserting that she vividly recalled seeing 1889 as the year of her father's birth written in the family Bible. For her, this was authoritative and definitive. She had informed the French scholar Jean Wagner of this in a letter dated November 8 1957 and she maintained this position up to her death in 1992.[7] But no one could locate the Bible and in its absence, McKay's letter to Locke carried the day. No one had a copy of McKay's birth certificate and the possibility of acquiring a copy from the Island Record Office in Spanish Town, Jamaica, had not even been raised by Wagner, Cooper or any other scholar who wrote on McKay. I assumed, largely on the thoroughness of Cooper's own biographical research on McKay, that such record, for one reason or another, did not exist. Had it existed, I thought, Cooper, a keen researcher, would more likely than not have found it. Significantly, in an essay explicitly addressing the question as to why he thought 1890 rather than 1889 was the year of McKay's birth, the question of the possible existence of birth records did not even arise. For him, the contradiction between Hope McKay-Virtue's assertion and that of McKay himself could only be resolved by precisely dating when the entry was made in the family Bible. He wrote:

> To resolve the contradiction, one would have to ascertain, if possible, when the birthdate was written in the [B]ible. Was it written shortly after his birth or was the [B]ible purchased at a later date and the birthdates written in it sometime near the time Claude began his job as an assistant to his brother U'Theo, the school master referred to in his letter to Locke? Unless scholars can with certainty date the writing in the family [B]ible to the time of McKay's birth, I believe McKay's statements [that he was born in 1890] should be accepted as the truth concerning his correct birthdate. I myself accepted 1890 as the correct date in my recent biography of him.[8]

The logic is impeccable, if only within its own, largely self-imposed parameters. Cooper wisely left open the possibility that he may have got the date wrong, but he clearly never believed that he did. "I certainly may be wrong," he averred. "But scholarship, after all, is a collective as well as an individual enterprise and if the problem of Claude McKay's 'true' birthday is ever fully resolved I will welcome either correction or confirmation of my own opinion."[9] Like him, I thought 1890 was the "true" date. But he, as well as I, was blinkered by the very way in which we set about the problem. And it so happens that there was another, even easier way to deal with the question. One had, however, to escape the existing parameters and pursue an entirely different avenue of inquiry around the problem. Like Cooper, I, too, was thoroughly persuaded by McKay's seductive argument and evidence: his older sister, Rachel, wrote to him, unsolicited, telling him that the date of birth attributed to him in a publication is incorrect; she gives a credible explanation of how the apparent error occurred, and there is no reason for her to lie about these matters; he accepts her argument, understandably defers to her authority, and acts accordingly. How could one resist this logic, especially since there was no motive or reason for falsification of this kind? How Rachel McKay made the error in the first place, I do not know. Given the detail of McKay's explanation in his letter to Locke, it is possible and plausible that the family, or members of the family, falsely claimed that McKay was a year older than he really was in order that he might teach in his brother's school at the time. But if this was the case, they would have moved his date of birth to 1888, not 1889. Rachel, apparently thinking that McKay had been going under the earlier and false date, mistakenly suggested that he moved it to 1890. Whatever the case might have been, I am now convinced that both she and McKay were wrong in their conclusions about the year of his birth.

It was effectively by accident that I discovered the error. Within a year of submitting my dissertation I became deeply immersed in its revision and expansion for publication. And it was then that I became absolutely convinced that Hope McKay-Virtue had been right all along. This was not because I had found the McKay family Bible and had carried out forensic tests along the lines suggested by Cooper and discovered that she was right—I had not. I became convinced that she was right because Claude McKay himself, in effect, revealed his date of birth in one of his autobiographical poems. Published in 1912 in his first book of poems, *Songs of Jamaica*, "My Mountain Home" has the following stanza:

> One Sunday marnin' 'fo' de hour
>   Fe service-time come on,
> Ma say dat I be'n born to her
>   Her little las'y son.[10]

McKay, the poem tells us, was born on a Sunday. I assumed that Hannah Edwards McKay remembered correctly the day on which her last and, indeed, favorite son, Claude, was born; that he was born on a Sunday morning before "service-time" at her church in the hills of Clarendon; and that, given the detail in this and other parts of the poem, there was no reason to believe that McKay had inaccurately recorded what his mother had told him. As there was no dispute about his having been born on September 15, all that I needed to do was to determine whether September 15, 1889 or September 15, 1890 fell on a Sunday. I found that September 15, 1889 was indeed a Sunday; September 15, the following year, fell on a Monday. I was therefore satisfied that the stanza was autobiographically accurate and that McKay was, indeed, born on September 15, 1889.

But were there additional documents available that could corroborate and support what I believe was good, but circumstantial, evidence? It was then that I recalled that Robert Hill and his colleagues on *The Marcus Garvey and Universal Negro Improvement Association Papers* had found the birth certificate of Marcus Garvey, who had been born in the neighboring parish of St. Ann several years before McKay himself.[11] Now, if the Island Record Office in Spanish Town, the source given for Garvey's birth certificate, had such a document for Garvey, I surmised that there was no good reason why it should not have McKay's. Apparently no one thought such documentary evidence existed and no one attempted to find it. So when I visited Jamaica in the summer of 1995, one of my primary research objectives was to find McKay's birth certificate. I found it and it confirmed what I had already been convinced was true.

The document itself has some interesting details. We can now pinpoint precisely where McKay was born. He was born in the village of Nairne Castle, which is in the James Hill district of Clarendon, and was registered eight days later on September 23 1889. He was, therefore, not born in "the village of Sunny Ville, a dependency of the parish of Clarendon," as Jean Wagner states,[12] nor in "the small community of Sunny Ville," as Cooper tells us,[13] nor in "the tiny village of Sunny Ville," as Tillery says,[14] for there are no such places. Sunny Ville was the name of the house in which the McKays lived.[15] The common misperception of Sunny Ville as a village is partly due to McKay. For in *My Green Hills of Jamaica* he largely wrote of it as if it was a village. But in an autobiographical sketch that he wrote twenty years earlier, he had noted: "I was born in a very little village high up in the hills of the parish of Clarendon in the island of Jamaica. The village was so small it hadn't a name like the larger surrounding villages. But our place was called Sunny Ville."[16] How or why he deprived Nairne Castle of its name is open to speculation; it is hard to believe that he forgot the name of the village in which he was born, especially since his Jamaican childhood and youth powerfully inhabited, if not possessed, his memory right up to his death. Clearly, though, he did not make the mistake of calling the village Sunny Ville, and he straightforwardly and accurately identified Sunny Ville as the McKay family home. I saw Sunny Ville when I visited McKay's village in 1995. It is still there and lived in by McKay's relatives. No one in Nairne Castle makes the mistake of calling the village Sunny Ville.

Thomas McKay had been a laborer before his in-laws gave him some land soon after he got married to McKay's mother. McKay never disclosed, however, that his father was unable to read and write. But the certificate reveals that, up to at least 1889, Thomas could not sign his name. Instead of a signature there is an "X" followed by the words: "The mark of Thomas Francis McKay[,] Father." Somewhat incongruously sitting beside this statement is the word "Planter," under the heading "Rank or Profession of Father." But, as shown earlier, Thomas McKay's description of himself as a planter as early as 1889 may not have been an exaggeration. The fact that Mr. McKay started out his adult life as an illiterate black laborer (a road mender) made his achievements and those of his seven sons and one daughter even more remarkable.

Surprising, too, is the fact that McKay's name is given simply as "Festus." "Claudius," the middle name—from which comes the name by which he is commonly known—is conspicuously absent from his birth certificate. It is not at all clear how or why this occurred, for McKay was apparently baptized "Festus Claudius," and this was the name that he carried in his passport. But errors and omissions of this kind were not uncommon in Jamaica.[17]

Claude McKay's birth certificate, then, provides new revelations about the author. But more than anything else, it establishes that McKay was born in 1889. The greatest irony is that McKay himself died in the firm belief that he was one year younger than he really was. Not knowing that documentary evidence existed indicating the contrary I, too, would have gone on secure in the belief that McKay was born in 1890. Had it not been the jolt of that stanza in "My Mountain Home," it is unlikely that I would have become sufficiently skeptical of the orthodoxy.

Hope McKay-Virtue, seventy-five years old and quietly steadfast in the belief that the organizers in India and Jamaica were mistaken in their timing of the centenary of her father's birth, nevertheless participated in the honoring of him. She was delighted by the commemoration. "This is, indeed, one of the high moments along my circuitous way," she told the Mysore conference. "And if I should live to be a hundred years old (and I just might!), I shall never learn to forget this delightful, delectable, delicious happening of fulfillment."[18] In a letter sent at the end of the year to her close friends, she spoke of 1990 as "a year of dreams realized, hopes fulfilled." The conference in Mysore and the celebrations in Jamaica were the high points of her year:

> In January I went half-way around the world to that vast sub-continent to attend an international conference which recognized the birth centenary of Claude McKay.
>
> On September 28, I winged across the U. S. A. en route to Jamaica to participate in a "Celebrating Claude McKay" program sponsored by the Ministry of Information and Culture.
>
> My nine days . . . in Jamaica were physically and emotionally very demanding, but oh, so satisfying and rewarding . . . 1990 was (for me) a very special year. And now, I look forward to a New Year of continued fruiting experiences in my ongoing responsibility to my heritage; embracing, along the way, fragments of the best of many worlds.[19]

Born in Jamaica in 1915, Hope McKay-Virtue was trained at Teachers' College, Columbia University, and taught in the California public school system. She corresponded with, but never met, her father; he died just weeks before their planned meeting in 1948.[20] Protective of her father's legacy, Hope McKay-Virtue died in 1992 in Long Beach, California, less than two years after her *annus mirabilis*. She never lived to a hundred and she never saw the birth certificate of her father, lodged in the Island Record Office all along, confirming her repeated claim that her father, contrary to his own mistaken assertions, was born on September 15 1889.

"Little things are big," declared Jesús Colón, the distinguished Afro-Puerto Rican writer.[21] He was right, but he was also wrong: *some* little things are big, and *some* little things *are* indeed little. Accurately dating the birth of Festus Claudius McKay, one of the most distinguished children of the African diaspora, is one of those little things that also happens to be big. For if we are to honor our heroes and heroines—and it is right and proper to honor them—we should do so on the basis of knowledge, not ignorance; on the basis of accuracy, not error or invention. Little things can be very big. For the historian, the story is also a very humbling one. It reminds us, once again, that despite our best efforts—as Karl Popper insisted many years ago—our knowledge will always be provisional; our truths, at best, nothing more than the not-yet-falsified. But, at least for the time being, I am satisfied that Claude McKay was born on September 15 1889.

Earlier versions of this appendix were published in Jamaica Journal *(September 1998) and* Black Renassance/Renaissance Noire *(vol 2, no. 2, summer 1999).*

PART III

A SELECTION OF MCKAY'S
JAMAICAN WRITING

THE WORK OF A GIFTED JAMAICAN: AN INTERVIEW WITH CLAUDE McKAY

In 1911, A. W. Stephenson, a senior writer on the Gleaner, *published a profile of McKay. The sketch, the poet's introduction to the reading public, included comments by Governor Sydney Olivier and Walter Jekyll on McKay's poetry, and four of his poems ("De Dog-Driver's Frien'," "Agnes o' de Village Lane," "Taken Aback," and "A Midnight Woman to the Bobby"). The following is Stephenson's account of his conversation with McKay. The title is Stephenson's, the sub-title has been added. The profile was published in the* Gleaner *on October 7, 1911, but McKay reports that the interview actually took place "many weeks" earlier.*

A little over a year ago, I discovered an infant prodigy who created quite a sensation. The boy is still looked upon as a marvel, and large audiences are drawn to hear him in the country.

On this occasion, I lay no claim to discovering the genius who forms the subject of this sketch; but I am pleased to be able to bring before the public a promising young Jamaican of whom more is certain to be heard in the field of literature.

I got to hear of McKay through one who had taken a great interest in the lad; and learning that he was a member of the Constabulary

Force, and stationed at Half-Way Tree, I took occasion to meet him and have a talk with him.

Modest to a degree, McKay was not inclined to say much about himself.

"I hear you are bringing out a book of poems?" I ventured.

"Yes," he replied; "through the kindness of Mr. Jekyll some of my work is being printed and will shortly be published."

"I should like to hear something about yourself, how you came to join the Police Force—something of your early career?"

The young man smiled. "What can I tell you?" he asked.

"Well, to begin, how old are you?"

"Twenty-two," he said.

"What parish are you from?"

"From Clarendon," was his monosyllabic reply.

"Tell me about your schooldays; I am sure you were a bright, clever little chap?"

"I first went to a school kept by Mr. James Hill, and then I went to Mr. Watts, and to my brother, U. Theo. McKay."

"Is Mr. McKay your brother, then?"

"Yes, and all I know I learnt from him," he said.

"Can you recall your first sucess?"

"I won a trade scholarship in 1906, and I came to Kingston in January, 1907—the Friday before the earthquake—to take it up. As a result of the earthquake I had to return home, and I was apprenticed to Mr. Campbell of Brown's Town to learn the trade of a wheel-wright. I next served under Mr. Saunders of Chapelton, but on account of illness the indenture was cancelled."

"When did you join the Police Force?"

"I enlisted last June—on the 7th of June," he said.

McKay was very reticent as to why he joined the force. It is said that the underlying cause is a pitiable love story. I hear he has poured out poem after poem on this subject, but he would not discuss the matter. "I cannot touch the public with my heart," he said, "it would be of no interest to them."

I changed the subject and asked him something about his work.

"I began writing dialect verses in 1909, my first attempt being a little thing entitled 'Hard Times'. Messrs Aston W. Gardner is publishing a volume of 50 poems entitled *Songs of Jamaica*, and I expect the book will be through the press in time for publication in December."

Mr. McKay was as diffident to speak of his works as he was to speak of himself. Those who have seen his poems express themselves in the highest terms about them. There is a charming naivete in the love poems, and humour, and pathos: rollicking fun, too, when he lets himself go. His versatility is wonderful. He treats all sorts of subjects.

Editorial note: *Some of McKay's poems published in* Songs of Jamaica *are heavily annotated. This is especially true of those that appear in the early pages of that volume. ("Two-an'-Six," for instance, has thirty-three footnotes.) The poems in* Constab Ballads *are more lightly annotated, but the volume also carries a large glossary. I have removed the annotations for various reasons—some are now superfluous, they disrupt the flow of the poems, and they take up a substantial amount of valuable space. Instead, I have provided a basic glossary for some of the more difficult terms. I have, additionally, referred readers to several texts which may prove useful.*

Except for the annotations and the insertion of a semi-colon (indicated by a square bracket) in "Christmas in de Air," the poems reproduced below are exactly as McKay published them. The poems and the comic sketch ("Bestman's Toast at a Rustic Wedding Feast") published in the press were not annotated by McKay.

FROM *SONGS OF JAMAICA*

Quashie to Buccra

You tas'e petater an' you say it sweet,
But you no know how hard we wuk fe it;
You want a basketful fe quattiewut,
'Cause you no know how 'tiff de bush fe cut.

De cowitch under which we hab de 'toop,
De shamar lyin' t'ick like pumpkin soup,
Is killin' somet'ing for a naygar man;
Much less de cutlass workin' in we han'.

De sun hot like when fire ketch a town;
Shade-tree look temptin', yet we caan' lie down,
Aldough we wouldn' eben ef we could,
Causen we job must finish soon an' good.

De bush cut done, de bank dem we deh dig,
But dem caan' 'tan' sake o' we naybor pig;
For so we moul' it up he root it do'n,
An' we caan' 'peak sake o' we naybor tongue.

Aldough de vine is little, it can bear;
It wantin' not'in' but a little care:
You see petater tear up groun', you run,
You laughin', sir, you must be t'ink a fun.

De fiel' pretty? It couldn't less 'an dat,
We wuk de bes', an' den de lan' is fat;
We dig de row dem eben in a line,
An' keep it clean—den so it *mus'* look fine.

You tas'e petater an' you say it sweet,
But you know how hard we wuk fe it;
Yet still de hardship always melt away
Wheneber it come roun' to reapin' day.

Whe' Fe Do?

Life will continue so for aye,
Some people sad, some people gay,
Some mockin' life while udders pray;
But we mus' fashion-out we way
An' sabe a mite fe rainy day—
       All we can do.

We needn' fold we han' an' cry,
Nor vex we heart wid groan and sigh;
De best we can do is fe try
To fight de déspair drawin' nigh:
Den we might conquer by an' by—
       Dat we might do.

We hab to batter in de sun
An' dat isn't a little fun,
For Lard! 'tis hellish how it bu'n:
Still dere's de big wul' to live do'n—
       So whe' fe do?

We nigger hab a tas' fe do,
To conquer prejudice dat due
To obeah, an' t'ings not a few
Dat keep we progress back fe true—
       But whe' fe do?

We've got to wuk wid might an' main,
To use we han' an' use we brain,
To toil an' worry, 'cheme an' 'train
Fe t'ings that bring more loss dan gain;

To stan' de sun an' bear de rain,
An' suck we bellyful o' pain
Widouten cry nor yet complain—
   For dat caan' do.

And though de wul' is full o' wrong,
Dat caan' prevent we sing we song
All de day as we wuk along—
   Whe' else fe do?

We happy in de hospital;
We happy when de rain deh fall;
We happy though de baby bawl
Fe food dat we no hab at all;
We happy when Deat' angel call
Fe full we cup of joy wid gall:
Our fait' in this life is not small—
   De best to do.

An' da's de way we ought to live,
For pain an' such we shouldn't grieve,
But tek de best dat Nature give—
   Da's whe' fe do.

God mek de wul' fe black an' white;
We'll wuk on in de glad sunlight,
Keep toilin' on wid all our might,
An' sleep in peace when it is night:
We must strive on to gain de height,
Aldough it may not be in sight;
An' yet perhaps de blessed right
Will never conquer in de fight—
   Still, whe' fe do?

We'll try an' live as any man,
An fight de wul' de best we can,
E'en though it hard fe understan'
   Whe' we mus' do.

For da's de way o' dis ya wul';
It's snap an' bite, an' haul an' pull,
An' we all get we bellyful—
   But whe' fe do?

King Banana

Green mancha mek fe naygur man;
    Wha' sweet so when it roas'?
Some boil it in big black pan,
    It sweeter in a toas'.

A buccra fancy when it ripe,
    Dem use it ebery day;
It scarcely give dem belly-gripe,
    Dem eat it diffran' way.

Out yonder see somoke a rise,
    An' see de fire wicket;
Deh go'p to heaben wid de nize
    Of hundred t'ousan' cricket.

De black moul' lie do'n quite prepare'
    Fe feel de hoe an' rake;
De fire bu'n, and it tek care
    Fe mek de wo'm dem wake.

Wha' lef' fe buccra teach again
    Dis time about plantation?
Dere's not'in' dat can beat de plain
    Good ole-time cultibation.

Banana dem fat all de same
    From bunches big an' 'trong;
Pure nine-han' bunch a car' de fame,—
    Ole met'od all along.

De cuttin' done same ole-time way,
    We wrap dem in a trash,
An' pack dem neatly in a dray
    So tight dat dem can't mash.

We re'ch: banana finish sell;
    Den we 'tart back fe home:
Some hab money in t'read-bag well,
    Some spen' all in a rum.

Green mancha mek fe naygur man,
    It mek fe him all way;

Our islan' is banana lan',
   Banana car' de sway.

Hard Times

De mo' me wuk, de mo' time hard,
   I don't know what fe do;
I ben' me knee an' pray to Gahd,
   Yet t'ings same as befo'.

De taxes knockin' at me door,
   I hear de bailiff's v'ice;
Me wife is sick, can't get no cure,
   But gnawin' me like mice.

De picknies hab to go to school
   Widout a bite fe taste;
An I am working like a mule,
While buccra, sittin' in de cool,
   Hab 'nuff nenyam fe waste.

De clodes is tearin' off dem back
   When money seems noa mek;
A man can't eben ketch a mac,
   Care how him 'train him neck.

De peas won't pop, de corn can't grow,
   Poor people face look sad;
Dat Gahd would cuss de lan' I'd know,
   For black naygur' too bad.

I won't gib up, I won't say die,
   For all de time is hard;
Aldough de wul' soon en', I'll try
My wutless best as time goes by,
   An' trust on in me Gahd.

Cudjoe Fresh from de Lecture

'Top *one* minute, Cous' Jarge, an' sit do'n 'pon de grass,
An' mek a tell you 'bout de news I hear at las',

How de buccra te-day tek time an' bégin teach
All of us dat was deh in a clear open speech.

You miss somet'ing fe true, but a wi' mek you know,
As much as how a can, how de business a go:
Him tell us 'bout we self, an' mek we fresh again,
An' talk about de wul' from commencement to en'.

Me look 'pon me black 'kin, an' so me head grow big,
Aldough me heaby han' dem hab fe plug an' dig;
For ebery single man, no car' about dem rank,
Him bring us ebery one an' put 'pon de same plank.

Say, parson do de same? Yes, in a diff'ren' way,
For parson tell us how de whole o' we are clay;
An' lookin' close at t'ings, we hab to pray quite hard
Fe swaller wha' him say an' don't t'ink bad 'o Gahd.

But dis man tell us 'traight 'bout how de whole t'ing came,
An' show us widout doubt how Gahd was not fe blame;
How change cause eberyt'ing fe mix up 'pon de eart',
An' dat most hardship come t'rough accident o' birt'.

Him show us all a sort o' funny 'keleton,
Wid names I won't remember under dis ya sun;
Animals queer to deat', dem bone, teet', an' head-skull,
All dem so dat did live in a de ole-time wul'.

No 'cos say we get cuss mek fe we 'kin come so,
But fe all t'ings come 'quare, same so it was to go:
Seems our lan' must ha' been a bery low-do'n place,
Mek it tek such a long time in tu'ning out a race.

Yes, from monkey we spring: I believe ebery wud;
It long time better dan f'go say we come from mud:
No need me keep back part, me hab not'in' fe gain;
It's ebery man dat born—de buccra mek it plain.

It really strange how some o' de lan' dem advance;
Man power in some ways is nummo soso chance;
But suppose eberyt'ing could tu'n right upside down,
Den p'raps we'd be on top an' givin' some one houn'.

Yes, Cous' Jarge, slabery hot fe dem dat gone befo':
We gettin' better times, for those days we no know;
But I t'ink it do good, tek we from Africa
An' lan' us in a blessed place as dis a ya.

Talk 'bouten Africa, we would be deh till now,
Maybe same half-naked—all day dribe buccra cow,
An' tearin' t'rough de bush wid all de monkey dem,
Wile an' uncibilise', an' neber comin' tame.

I lef' quite 'way from wha' we be'n deh talk about,
Yet still a couldn' help—de wuds come to me mout';
Just like how yeas' get strong an' sometimes fly de cark,
Same way me feelings grow, so I was boun' fe talk.

Yet both horse partly runnin' in de selfsame gallop,
For it is nearly so de way de buccra pull up:
Him say, how de wul' stan', dat right will neber be,
But wrong will eber gwon till dis wul' en' fe we.

Old England

I've a longin' in me dept's of heart dat I can conquer not,
'Tis a wish dat I've been havin from since I could form a t'o't,
'Tis to sail athwart the ocean an' to hear de billows roar,
When dem ride aroun' de steamer, when dem beat on England's
    shore.

Just to view de homeland England, in de streets of London walk,
An' to see de famous sights dem 'bouten which dere's so much talk,
An' to see de matches-children, dat I hear 'bout, passin' by.

I would see Sain' Paul's Cathedral, an' would hear some of de great
Learnin' comin' from de bishops, preachin' relics of old fait';
I would ope me mout' wid wonder at de massive organ soun',
An' would 'train me eyes to see de beauty lyin' all aroun'.

I'd go to de City Temple, where de old fait' is a wreck,
An' de parson is a-preachin' views dat most folks will not tek;
I'd go where de men of science meet togeder in deir hall,
To give light unto de real truths, to obey king Reason's call.

I would view Westminster Abbey, where de great of England sleep,
An' de solemn marble statues o'er deir ashes vigil keep;
I would see immortal Milton an' de wul'-famous Shakespeare,
Past'ral Wordswort', gentle Gray, an' all de great souls buried dere.

I would see de ancient chair where England's kings deir crowns put
    on,
Soon to lay dem by again when all de vanity is done;
An' I'd go to view de lone spot where in peaceful solitidue
Rests de body of our Missis Queen, Victoria de Good.

An' dese places dat I sing of now shall afterwards impart
All deir solemn sacred beauty to a weary searchin' heart;
So I'll rest glad an' contented in me min' for evermore,
When I sail across de ocean back to my own native shore.

A Midnight Woman to the Bobby

No palm me up, you dutty brute,
You' jam mout' mash like ripe bread-fruit;
You fas'n now, but wait lee ya,
I'll see you grunt under de law.

You t'ink you wise, but we wi' see;
You not de fus' one fas' wid me;
I'll lib fe see dem tu'n you out,
As sure as you got dat mash' mout'.

I born right do'n beneat' de clack
(You ugly brute, you tu'n you' back?)
Don' t'ink dat I'm a come-aroun',
I born right 'way up in 'panish Town.

Care how you try, you caan' do mo'
Dan many dat was hyah befo';
Yet whe' dey all o' dem te-day?
De buccra dem no kick dem 'way?

Ko 'pon you' jam samplatta nose:
'Cos you wear Mis'r Koshaw clo'es
You t'ink say you's de only man,
Yet fus' time ko how you be'n 'tan'.

You big an' ugly ole tu'n-foot
Be'n neber know fe wear a boot;
An chigger nyam you' tumpa toe,
Till nit full i' like herrin' roe.

You come from mountain naked-'kin,
An' Lard a mussy! you be'n thin,
For all de bread-fruit dem be'n done,
Bein' 'poil' up by de tearin' sun:

De coco couldn' bear at all,
For, Lard! de groun' was pure white-marl;
An' t'rough de rain part o' de year
De mango tree dem couldn' bear.

An' when de pinch o' time you feel
A 'pur you a you' chigger heel,
You lef' you' district, big an' coarse,
An' come join buccra Police Force.

An' now you don't wait fe you' glass,
But trouble me wid you' jam fas';
But wait, me frien', you' day wi' come,
I'll see you go same lak a some.

Say wah'?—'res' me?—You go to hell!
You t'ink Judge don't know unno well?
You t'ink him gwin' go sentance me
Widout a soul fe witness i'?

Killin' Nanny

Two little pickny is watchin',
    While a goat is led to deat';
Dey are little ones of two years,
    An' know naught of badness yet.

De goat is bawlin' fe mussy,
    An' de children watch de sight
As de butcher re'ch his sharp knife,
    An' 'tab wid all his might.

Dey see de red blood flowin';
    An' one chil' trimble an' hide
His face in de mudder's bosom,
    While t'udder look on wide-eyed.

De tears is fallin' down hotly
    From him on the mudder's knee;
De udder wid joy is starin',
    An' clappin' his han's wid glee.

When dey had forgotten Nanny,
    Grown men I see dem again;
An' de forehead of de laugher
    Was brand' wid de mark of Cain.

My Native Land, My Home

Dere is no land dat can compare
    Wid you where'er I roam;
In all de wul' none like you fair,
    My native land, my home.

Jamaica is de nigger's place,
    No mind whe' some declare;
Although dem call we "no-land race,"
    I know we home is here.

You give me life an' nourishment,
    No udder land I know;
My lub I neber can repent,
    For all to you I owe.

E'en ef you mek beggar die,
    I'll trust you all de same,
An' none de less on you rely,
    Nor saddle you wid blame.

Though you may cas' me from your breas'
    An' trample me to deat',
My heart will trus' you none de less,
    My land I won't feget.

An' I hope none o' your sons would
    Refuse deir strengt' to lend,
An' drain de last drop o' deir blood
    Their country to defend.

You draw de t'ousan' from deir shore,
    An' all 'long keep dem please';
De invalid come here fe cure,
    You heal all deir disease.

Your fertile soil grow all o' t'ings
    To full de naygur's wants,
'Tis seamed wid neber-failing springs
    To give dew to de plants.

You hab all t'ings fe mek life bles',
    But buccra 'poil de whole
Wid gove'mint an' all de res',
    Fe worry naygur soul.

Still all dem little chupidness
    Caan' tek away me lub;
De time when I'll tu'n 'gains' you is
    When you can't give me grub.

Two-an'-Six

Merry voices chatterin',
Nimble feet dem patterin',
Big an' little, faces gay,
Happy day dis market day.

Sateday! de marnin' break,
Soon, soon market-people wake;
An' de light shine from de moon
While dem boy, wid pantaloon
Roll up ober dem knee-pan,
'Tep across de buccra lan'
To de pastur whe' de harse
Feed along wid de jackass,
An' de mule cant' in de track
Wid him tail up in him back,

All de ketchin' to defy,
No ca' how dem boy might try.

In de early marnin'-tide,
When de cocks crow on de hill
An' de stars are shinin' still,
Mirrie by de fireside
Hots de coffee for de lads
Comin' ridin' on de pads
T'rown across dem animul—
Donkey, harse too, an' de mule,
Which at last had come do'n cool.
On de bit dem hol' dem full:
Racin' ober pastur' lan',
See dem comin' ebery man,
Comin' fe de streamin' tea
Ober hilly track an' lea.

Hard-wuk'd donkey on de road
Trottin' wid him ushal load,—
Hamper pack'wi' yam an' grain,
Sour-sop, an' Gub'nor cane.

Cous' Sun sits in hired dray,
Drivin' 'long de market way;
Whole week grindin' sugar-cane
T'rough de boilin' sun an' rain,
Now, a'ter de toilin' hard,
He goes seekin' his reward,
While he's thinkin' in him min'
Of de dear ones lef' behin',
Of de loved though ailin' wife,
Darlin' treasure of his life,
An' de picknies, six in all,
Whose 'nuff burdens 'pon him fall:

Seben lovin' ones in need,
Seben hungry mouths fe feed;
On deir wants he thinks alone,
Neber dreamin' of his own,
But gwin' on wid joyful face
Till him re'ch de market-place.

Sugar bears no price te-day,
Though it is de mont' o' May,
When de time is hellish hot,
An' de water-cocoanut
An' de cane bebridge is nice,
Mix' up wid a lilly ice.
Big an' little, great an' small,
Afou yam is all de call;
Sugar tup an' gill a quart,
Yet de people hab de heart
Wantin' brater top o' i',
Want de sweatin' higgler fe
Ram de pan an' pile i' up,
Yet sell i' fe so-so tup.

Cousin Sun is lookin' sad,
As de market is so bad;
'Pon him han' him res' him chin,
Quietly sit do'n thinkin'
Of de loved wife sick in bed,
An' de children to be fed—
What de labourers would say,
When dem know him couldn' pay;
Also what about de mill
Whe' him hire from ole Bill;
So him think, an' think on so,
Till him t'oughts no more could go.

Then he got up an' began
Pickin' up him sugar-pan:
In his ears rang t'rough de din
"Only two-an'-six a tin!"
What a tale he'd got to tell,
How bad, bad de sugar sell!

Tekin' out de lee amount,
Him set do'n an' begin count;'
All de time him min' deh doubt
How expenses would pay out;
Ah, it gnawed him like de ticks,
Sugar sell fe two-an'-six!

So he journeys on de way,
Feelin' sad dis market day;
No e'en buy a little cake
To gi'e baby when she wake—
Passin' 'long de candy-shop
'Douten eben make a stop
To buy drops fe las'y son,
For de lilly cash nea' done.

So him re'ch him own groun',
An' de children scamper roun',
Each one stretchin' out him han',
Lookin' to de poor sad man.

Oh, how much he felt de blow,
As he watched dem face fall low,
When dem wait an' nuttin' came
An' drew back deir han's wid shame!
But de sick wife kissed his brow:
"Sun, don't get down-hearted now;
Ef we only pay expense
We mus' wuk we common-sense,
Cut an' carve, an' carve an' cut,
Mek gill sarbe fe quattiewut';
We mus' try mek two ends meet
Neber mind how hard be it
We won't mind de haul an' pull,
While dem pickny belly full."

An' de shadow lef' him face,
An' him felt an inward peace,
As he blessed his better part
For her sweet an' gentle heart:
"Dear one o' my heart, my breat',
Won't I lub you to de deat'?
When my heart is weak an' sad,
Who but you can mek it glad?"

So dey kissed an' kissed again,
An' deir t'oughts were not on pain,
But was 'way down in de sout'
Where dey'd wedded in deir yout',

In de marnin' of deir life
Free from all de grief an' strife,
Happy in de marnin' light,
Never thinkin' of de night.

So dey k'lated eberyt'ing'
An' de profit it could bring,
A'ter all de business fix',
Was a princely two-an'-six.

Strokes of the Tamarind Switch

I dared not look at him,
My eyes with tears were dim,
   My spirit filled with hate
      Of man's depravity,
   I hurried through the gate.

I went but I returned,
While in my bosom burned
   The monstrous wrong that we
      Oft bring upon ourselves,
   And yet we cannot see.

Poor little erring wretch!
The cutting tamarind switch
   Had left its bloody mark,
      And on his legs were streaks
   That looked like boiling bark.

I spoke to him the while:
At first he tried to smile,
   But the long pent-up tears
      Came gushing in a flood;
   He was but of tender years.

With eyes bloodshot and red,
He told me of a father dead
   And lads like himself rude,
      Who goaded him to wrong:
   He for the future promised to be good.

The mother yesterday
Said she was sending him away,
   Away across the seas:
      She told of futile prayers
   Said on her wearied knees.

I wished the lad good-bye,
And left him with a sigh:
   Again I heard him talk—
      His limbs, he said, were sore,
   He could not walk.

I 'member when a smaller boy,
A mother's pride, a mother's joy,
   I too was very rude:
      They beat me too, though not the same,
   And has it done me good?

NOTE BY THE AUTHOR [McKay]—This was a lad of fifteen. No doubt he deserved the flogging administered by order of the Court: still, I could not bear to see him—my own flesh—stretched out over the bench, so I went away to the Post Office near by. When I returned, all was over. I saw his naked bleeding form, and through the terrible ordeal—so they told me—he never cried. But when I spoke to him he broke down, told me between his bursts of tears how he had been led astray by bad companions, and that his mother intended sending him over-sea. He could scarcely walk, so I gave him tickets for the tram. He had a trustful face. A few minutes after, my bitterness of spirit at the miserable necessity of such punishment came forth in song, which I leave rugged and unpolished as I wrote it at the moment.

My Pretty Dan

I have a póliceman down at de Bay,
An' he is true to me though far away.

I love my police, and he loves me too,
An' he has promised he'll be ever true.

My little bobby is a darlin' one,
An' he's de prettiest you could set eyes 'pon.

When he be'n station' up de countryside,
Fus' time I shun him sake o' foolish pride.

But as I watched him patrolling his beat,
I got to find out he was nice an' neat.

More still I foun' out he was extra kin',
An' dat his precious heart was wholly mine.

Den I became his own a true sweetheart,
An' while life last we're hopin' not fe part.

He wears a truncheon an' a handcuff case,
An' pretty cap to match his pretty face.

Dear lilly p'liceman stationed down de sout',
I feel your kisses rainin' on my mout'.

I could not give against a póliceman;
For if I do, how could I lub my Dan?

Prettiest of naygur is my dear police,
We'll lub foreber, an' our lub won't cease.

I have a póliceman down at de Bay,
An' he is true to me though far away.

A Country Girl

"Lelia gal, why in this town do you stay?
Why, tell me, why did you wander away?
Why will you aimlessly foolishly roam?
Won't you come back to your old country home?"

"Country life, Fed, has no pleasure for me,
I wanted de gay o' de city to see,
To wear ebery Sunday a prettier gown,
Da's why I came to de beautiful town."

"Well, have you gotten de joys dat you sought?
If so, were not all o' dem too dearly bought?
Yes, Liel, you do wear a prettier dress,
But have you not suffered, my girl, more or less?

"Hold up your head! look not down, tell me truth,
Have you not bartered your innocent youth?
Are you, de Lelia, true Lelia, of old,
Or have your swapped out your honour for gold?"

"Fed, it was horrid de lone country life!
I suffered—for sometimes e'en hunger was rife;
An' when I came, Fed, to try my chance here,
I thought there would be no more troubles to bear.

"But troubles there were an' in plenty, my lad,
Oh, dey were bitter, an' oh, I was sad!
Weary an' baffled an' hungry an' lone,
I gave up my spirit to sigh an' to moan.

"After dat?—O, Feddy, press me not so:
De truth?—well, I sank to de lowest of de low;
I gave up all honour, I took a new name
An' tried to be happy, deep sunk in de shame.

"Dere was no other way, Fed, I could live,
Dat was de gift dat a gay town could give;
I tried to be glad in de open daylight,
But sorrowed an' moaned in de deep o' de night.

"No, Fed, I never could go home again:
'Worse than I left it?' ah, there was de pain,
To meet up wid some o' my former schoolmates
An' listen to all o' deir taunts an' deir hates.

"Dere now, you bound me to tell you o' all,
Of all de sad suff'rings dat led to my fall;
I'm gone past reclaiming, so what must I do
But live de bad life an' mek de good go?"

"Lelia, I want you to come out de sin,
Come home an' try a new life fe begin;
Mek up you min', gal, fe wuk wid you' han',
Plant peas an' corn in de fat country lan'.

"Dere is no life, gal, so pleasant, so good,
Contented and happy, you'll eat your lee food;
No one at home knows 'bout wha' you've jes' said,
So, Liel, of exposure you needn't be 'fraid."

"Don't t'ink I care 'bout exposure, my boy!
Dat which you call sin is now fe me joy;
Country for Lelia will have no more charm,
I'll live on de same way, 'twill do me no harm.

"And after all, many gals richer than me,
Pretty white girlies of better degree,
Live as I do, an' are happy an' gay,
Then why should not I be as happy as they?"

My Mountain Home

De mango tree in yellow bloom,
    De pretty akee seed,
De mammee where de John-to-whits come
    To have their daily feed,

Show you de place where I was born,
    Of which I am so proud,
'Mongst de banana-field an' corn
    On a lone mountain-road.

One Sunday marnin' 'fo' de hour
    Fe service-time come on,
Ma say dat I be'n born to her
    Her little las'y son.

Those early days be'n neber dull,
    My heart was ebergreen;
How I did lub my little wul'
    Surrounded by pingwin!

An' growin' up, with sweet freedom
    About de yard I'd run;
An' tired out I'd hide me from
    De fierce heat of de sun.

So glad I was de fus' day when
    Ma sent me to de spring;
I was so happy feelin' then
    Dat I could do somet'ing.

De early days pass quickly 'long,
    Soon I became a man,
An' one day found myself among
    Strange folks in a strange lan'.

My little joys, my wholesome min',
    Dey bullied out o' me,
And made me daily mourn an' pine
    An' wish dat I was free.

Dey taught me to distrust my life,
    Dey taught me what was grief;
For months I travailed in de strife,
    'Fo' I could find relief.

But I'll return again, my Will,
    An' where my wild ferns grow
An' weep for me on Dawkin's Hill,
    Dere, Willie, I shall go.

An' dere is somet'ing near forgot,
    Although I lub it best;
It is de loved, de hallowed spot
    Where my dear mother rest.

Look good an' find it, Willie dear,
    See dat from bush 'tis free;
Remember that my heart is near,
    An' you say you lub me.

An' plant on it my fav'rite fern,
    Which I be'n usual wear;
In days to come I shall return
    To end my wand'rin's dere.

FROM *CONSTAB BALLADS*

Flat-Foot Drill

Fus' beginnin', flat-foot drill,
    Larnin' how fe mek right tu'n:
"'Tention! keep you' han's dem still,
Can't you tek in dat a li'l?
    Hearin' all, but larnin' none.

"But seems unno all do'n-ca',
    Won't mek up you' min' fe larn;
Drill-instructor boun' fe swea',
Dealin' wid you' class all day,
    Never see such from A barn.

"Right tu'n, you damn' bungo brut'!
    Do it *so,* you mountain man;
Car' behin' de bluff lef' foot,
Seems i' frighten fe de boot!
    Why you won't keep do'n you' han'?

"Shet you' mout'! A wan' no chat!
    Fabour say you pick up nong,
Sence you nyamin' Depôt fat
An' 'top sleep 'pon so-so mat,
    But A mean fe pull you' tongue.

"Wonder when unno wi' fit
    Fe move up in-a fus' squad,
Use carbine an' bayonet!
Wait dough,—unno wi' larn yet,—
    Me wi' drill you ti' you mad."

De Dog-Driver's Frien'

Stay your hasty hands, my comrades,
    I must speak to you again;
For you beat de dog 'dout mussy,
    An' dey are we night-time frien'.
Treat dem kindly, treat dem kindly,
    For dey are God's creatures too;
You have no more claim, dear comrades,
    On de earth dan what dey do.

'Cos you locked him up in barracks
    T'rough some failin' point o' his,
You mus' beatin' him so badly
    For de little carelessness?
Treat dem kindly, etc.

When de hours are cold an' dreary,
    An' I'm posted on me beat,
An' me tired heavy body
    Weighs upon me weary feet;

When I think of our oppressors
    Wid mixed hatred an' don'-care,
An' de ugly miau of tom-puss
    Rings out sharply on de air,

Oftentimes dem come aroun' me
    Wid dem free an' trusting soul,
Lying do'n or gambolling near me
    Wid a tender sort o' gro'l:
An' I snap my fingers at them,
    While dey wag dem tail at me;
Can you wonder dat I love dem,
    Dem, me night-time company?
Treat dem kindly, etc.

Sometimes dey're a bit too noisy
 Wid deir long leave-taking bark;
But I tell you what, it cheers me
 When de nights are extra dark.

So, dear comrades, don't ill-treat him,
 You won't mek me talk in vain;
'Member when de hours are dreary,
 He's de poor dog-driver's frien'.
Treat dem kindly, etc.

Papine Corner

When you want to meet a frien',
 Ride up to Papine,
Where dere's people to no en',
 Old, young, fat an' lean:
When you want nice gals fe court
 An' to feel jus' booze',
Go'p to Papine as a sport
 Dress' in ge'man clo'es.

When you want to be jus' broke,
 Ride up wid your chum,
Buy de best cigars to smoke
 An' Finzi old rum:
Stagger roun' de sort o' square
 On to Fong Kin bar;
Keep as much strengt' dat can bear
 You do'n in de car.

When you want know Sunday bright,
 Tek a run up deh
When 'bout eight o'clock at night
 Things are extra gay:
Ef you want to see it cram',
 Wait till night is dark,
An' beneat' your breat' you'll damn
 Coney Island Park.

When you want see gals look fine,
 You mus' go up dere,

An' you'll see them drinkin' wine
    An' all sorts o' beer:
There you'll see them walkin' out,
    Each wid a young man,
Watch them strollin' all about,
    Flirtin' all dem can.

When you want hear coarsest jokes
    Passin' rude an' vile,
Want to see de Kingston blokes,—
    Go up dere awhile:
When you want hear murderin'
    On de piano,
An' all sorts o' drunken din,
    Papine you mus' go.

Ef you want lost póliceman,
    Go dere Sunday night,
Where you'll see them, every one
    Lookin' smart an' bright:
Policeman of every rank,
    Rural ones an' all,
In de bar or on de bank,
    Each one in them sall.

Policeman dat's in his beat,
    Policeman widout,
Policeman wid him gold teet'
    Shinin' in him mout';

Policeman in uniform
    Made of English blue,
P'liceman gettin' rather warm,
    Sleuth policeman too.

Policeman on plain clo'es pass,
    Also dismissed ones;
See them standin' in a mass,
    Talkin' 'bout them plans:
Policeman "struck off de strengt'
    Physical unfit,"
Here them chattin' dere at lengt'
    'Bout a diffran' kit.

When you want meet a surprise,
   Tek de Papine track;
Dere some things will meet you' eyes
   Mek you tu'n you' back:
When you want to see mankind
   Of "class" family
In a way degra' them mind,
   Go 'p deh, you will see.

When you want a pleasant drive,
   Tek Hope Gardens line;
I can tell you, man alive,
   It is jolly fine:
Ef you want to feel de fun,
   You mus' only wait
Until when you're comin' do'n
   An' de tram is late.

Cotch Donkey

Ko how de jackass
   Lay do'n in de road;
An' him ondly car'
   Little bit o' load.

Kue, jackass, git up!
   'Tan' up 'pon you' foot!
Dis ya load no load,
   You's a lazy brut'.

Me no know wha' mek
   Pa won' swop you too;
For dere's not a t'ing
   Wut while you can do.

Ef you car' no lead,
   It is all de same;
Hamper on or no,
   'Tis de ushal game.

Póliceman a come
   Fe go mek a row,

All because o' you
    Wid you' wutless now.

"See ya, Sah, no min',
    Dis a fe me luck;
De jackass is bad,
    Him no wan' fe wuk.

"'Tek de hamper off?'
    Him no hab no cut:
Me deh tell you say
    De jackass no wut.

"Lard! me Gahd o' me!
    Him got one lee 'cratch:
Dat is not'in', Sah,
    For him always cotch.

"Do, Sah, let me off,
    Ef fe te-day one;
For a no de 'cratch
    Cause him fe lay do'n."

Now because o' you
    Dem gone bring me up;
An' wha' hu't me mos',
    You caan' wuk a tup.

Ef dem summons me,
    Mek me pay few mac,
Dat caan' mek me 'top
    Wuk you wid sore back.

A Recruit on the Corpy

Me an' de corpy drink we rum,
An' corpy larn me how fe bum;
Last night me gie 'm de last-last tup,
Yet now him come an' bring me up.

He'll carry me 'fo' officer,
An' rake up' t'ings fe charge me for;

An' all because dese couple days
Me couldn' gie 'm de usual raise.

Last night, when it come to roll-call,
Dis corpy, couldn' 'ten' at all:
We didn' mek de S.M. see 'm,
But only put things 'traight fe him.

An' we, like big fools, be'n deh fret
Ober de corpy drunk to deat':
We all treat him so very kin',
Aldough him ha' such dutty min'.

We tek him drunken off de car,
We tek him drunken out de bar,
We wake him drunken 'pon him guard,
An' yet we neber claim reward.

All bad contráry things me do,
Corpy see me an' let me go;
But 'causen me no ha' a tup,
Fe not'in 'tall him bring me up.

Pay-Day

Dere's a little anxious crowd
    Jes' outside de barrack gate,
All a-t'tinkin' deir own way
    Dat de pay is kept back late:
Faces of all types an' shades,
    Brown an' yaller, black an' gray,
Dey are waitin', waitin' dere,
    For it's póliceman pay-day.

Clearly seen among dem all
    Is a colourless white face
Anxious more dan everyone,
    Fine type of an alien race:
He is waitin' for some cash
    On de foods trust' tarra day,—
Our good frien' de Syrian,—
    For it's póliceman pay-day.

Wid a lee piece of old clot'
　'Pon her curly glossy hair,
Print frock an old bulldog boots
　Tatters all t'rough wear an' tear,
She is waitin', ober-bex',
　Our mess-woman, mudder Mell,
An' 'twould grieve you' heart to hear
　'Bouten wha' she's got to tell.

Six long fortnight come an' gone
　Since come constab hol' her up,
An', wid all de try she try,
　She can neber get a tup:
"Me wi' tell, Inspector F—
　'Bout de 'ole o' i' to-day,
An' den me wi' really see
　Ef him caan' boun' dem fe pay.

"Man dem, wid dem hungry gut,
　Six long fornight nyam me rash;
Not a gill me caan' get when
　Chiny dah dun fe him cash
Fe de plenty t'ings me trus',
　Sal' fish, pork, an' flour, an' rice,
Onion an' ingredients,
　Jes' fe mek de brukfus' nice."

See de waitin' midnight girl
　Wid her saucy cock-up lips,
An' her strongly-built black hands
　Pressed against her rounded hips:
She has passed de bound'ry line,
　An' her womanhood is sold;
Wonder not then, as you gaze
　Dat, though young, she looks so bold.

Once she roamed de country woods
　Wid a free an' stainless soul,
But she left for Kingston's slums,
　Gave herself up to de wul':
She has trod de downward course,
　Never haltin' on de way;

Dere's no better time for her
    Dan a póliceman pay-day.

Waits de slimber ball-pan man,
    Waits de little ice-cream lad,
Waits our washerwoman Sue,—
    All deh chat how pólice bad;
Each one sayin' police vile,
    Yet deir faces all betray
Dat for dem dere's no rag time
    Laka policeman pay-day.

Inside in de ord'ly room
    Things are movin' very fine'
Constab standin' in a row
    Hea' de jinglin' o' de coin;
Constab wid a solemn face,
    Constab only full o' fun,
Marchin' in de ord'ly room
    As dem name call one by one.

Quick march!—halt!—a sharp right tu'n,
    Wid de right han' smart salute,
All attention poker-stiff,
    An' a-standin' grave an' mute:
Office-clerk calls out de name,
    Office hands de amount
To Sa'an' Major standin' by,
    Who gives it a second count.

'Ter all de formalities,
    Dis an' dat an' warra not,
Salute,—'tion,—right about turn,—
    Den de precious pay is got:
Lee gone to de réward fund
    T'rough a blot' defaulter-sheet,
Run do'n by sub-officers,
    Or caught sleepin' on dem beat;

Den dere's somet'ing gone fe kit;
    Uniform mus' smart an' nice,
Else de officer won' t'ink

Dat a bobby's wutten price.
All dem way de money go;
    So de payin'-out fe some,
When de fortnight dem come roun',
    Bégin in-a ord'ly room.

Now comes payin' up de debts
    Te de miscellaneous crowd
Waitin' by de barrack-gate,
    Chattin', chattin' very loud:
Payin', payin' all de time,
    From a pou' do'n to a gill,
Whole fortnight-pay partly done,
    Yet rum-money lef' back still.

Strollin' t'rough de gate at night,
    Drinkin' Finzi tell dead drunk,
Barely standin' at tattoo,—
    After tumblin' in-a bunk;
All de two-an'-four is done,
    So-so trust nong ebery day
Tell de fortnight comes again
    An' we get de little pay.

The Apple-Woman's Complaint

While me deh walk 'long in de street,
Policeman's yawnin' on his beat;
An' dis de wud him chiefta'n say—
Me mus'n car' me apple-tray.

Ef me no wuk, me boun' fe tief;
S'pose dat will please de pólice chief!
De prison dem mus' be wan' full,
Mek dem's 'pon we like ravin' bull.

Black nigger wukin' laka cow
An' wipin' sweat-drops from him brow,
Dough him is dyin' sake o' need,
P'lice an' dem headman boun' fe feed.

P'lice an' dem headman gamble too,
Dey shuffle card an' bet fe true;
Yet ef me Charlie gamble,—well,
Dem try fe 'queeze him laka hell.

De headman fe de town police
Mind neber know a little peace,
'Cep' when him an' him heartless ban'
Hab sufferin' nigger in dem han'.

Ah son-son! dough you 're bastard, yah,
An' dere's no one you can call pa,
Jes' try to ha' you' mudder's min'
An' Police Force you'll neber jine.

But how judge bélieve pólicemen,
Dem dutty mout' wid lyin' stain'?
While we go batterin' along
Dem doin' we all sort o' wrong.

We hab fe barter-out we soul
To lib t'rough dis ungodly wul';—
O massa Jesus! don't you see
How pólice is oppressin' we?

Dem wan' fe see we in de street
Dah foller dem all 'pon dem beat;
An' after, 'dout a drop o' shame,
Say we be'n dah solicit dem.

Ah massa Jesus! in you' love
Jes' look do'n from you' t'rone above,
An' show me how a poo' weak gal
Can lib good life in dis ya wul'.

The Heart of a Constab

'Tis hatred without an' 'tis hatred within,
    An' I am so weary an' sad;
For all t'rough de tempest o' terrible strife
    Dere's not'in' to make poor me glad.

Oh! where are de faces I loved in de past,
    De frien's dat I used to hold dear?
Oh say, have dey all turned away from me now
    Becausen de red seam I wear?

I foolishly wandered away from dem all
    To dis life of anguish an' woe,
Where I mus' be hard on me own kith an' kin,
    And even to frien' mus' prove foe.

Oh! what have I gained from my too too rash act
    O' joinin' a hard Constab Force,
Save quenchin' me thirst from a vinegar cup,
    De vinegar cup o' remorse?

I t'ought of a livin' o' pure honest toil,
    To keep up dis slow-ebbin' breath;
But no, de life surely is bendin' me do'n,
    Is bendin' me do'n to de death.

'Tis grievous to think dat, while toilin' on here,
    My people won't love me again,
My people, my people, me owna black skin,—
    De wretched t'ought gives me such pain.

But I'll leave it, my people, an' come back to you,
    I'll flee from de grief an' turmoil;
I'll leave it, though flow'rs here should line my path, yet,
    An' come back to you an' de soil.

For 'tis hatred without an' 'tis hatred within,
    An' how can I live 'douten heart?
Then oh for de country, de love o' me soul,
    From which I shall nevermore part!

Fe Me Sal

In de blazin' midday heat, when I'm posted on me beat,
    Who I t'inkin' of but fe me Sal?
She is eber in me mind, ne'er a better you will find,
    She's me only lub, de best o' country gal.

When I started out fe roam from me treasured mountain-home,
    All me wanderin's were for her good;
An be'n ondly fe her sake why dis job I undertake,
    An' she cheer me when I'm sad an' out o' mood.

Any wuk I'm put to do, me jus' feel she's wid me too,
    Biddin' me fe toil bedoubten fret;
An' when all de duty's done, an' me go to sleep alone,
    'Tis but dreamin' o' me darlin' little pet.

When me deh 'pon station guard, dere is ondly one reward,
    For I get fe write her sweet lub-wuds;
Den me finish up her name wid a pile o' flourish dem,
    An' me seal de letter up wid jesmy buds.

When me go patrol a day, she's me one lee bit o' stay
    As A deh climb up Bardowie hill;
An' A somehow favour know dat, wherever I may go,
    Her soul an' heart wi' eber be mine still.

Ef me goin' to de race I'm a-t'inkin' of her face,
    An' A feel her shedah at me side;
Ef me eatin' me lee grub, I'm a-t'inkin' o' de lub
    Dat me ha' fe her alone so free an' wide.

Udder p'liceman ha' dem gal, but dere's none like fe me Sal,
    Dey can neber trus' fe dem like me;
And I needn't eber fear, ef I'm transferred anywhere,
    For me Sally is as true as true can be.

She's de darlin' o' me life, an' shall one day be me wife
    Jes' as soon as eberyt'ing is ripe;
An' me hab a feelin' strong dat it will not be too long
    'Fo' me get fe wear an Acting Corp'ral's stripe.

She's de darlin' o' me heart, an' we'll neber neber part,
    She's de prettiest black gal in de wul';
An' whereber you may go you won't find anedder so,
    Wid more tender min' an' better sort o' soul.

So de day shall soon arrive when de two o' we shall drive
    To de parish church at Half Way Tree:
An' we'll stroll back t'rough de gate, me Sal a corpy's mate,
    An' we'll be as happy-happy as can be.

The Bobby to the Sneering Lady

You may sneer at us madam,
    But our work is beastly hard;
An' while toilin' thus we scarce
    Ever get a lee reward.

Our soul's jes like fe you,
    If our work does make us rough;
Me won't 'res' you servant-gal
    When you've beaten her enough.

You may say she is me frien',
    We are used to all such prate;
Naught we meet on life's stern road
    But de usual scorn an' hate.

Say dat you wi' 'port me m'am?
    I was lookin' fe dat,—well,
Our Inspector's flinty hard,
    'Twill be few days' pay or cell.

Pains an' losses of such kind
    To we p'licemen's not'in' new;
Still A'd really like fe hear
    Wha' good it wi' do to you.

Last week, eatin' a gill bread,
    Me t'row piece out on de lea;
An' A ketch a 'port fe dat
    Which meant five roun' mac to me.

Constab-charge, civilian-charge,
    Life's a burden every way;
But reward fund mus' kep' up
    Out o' poo' policeman pay.

Ef our lot, then, is so hard,
    I mus' ever bear in mind
Dat to fe me own black 'kin
    I mus' not be too unkind.

An' p'r'aps you too will forgive
    Ef I've spoken rather free,

An' will let me somet'ing ask
 Which may soften you to me:

In de middle o' de night,
 When de blackness lies do'n deep,
Who protects your home an' stores
 While de Island is asleep?

When de dead stars cannot shine
 Sake o' rain an' cloud an' storm,
Who keeps watch out in de street
 So dat not'in' comes to harm?

Ah! you turn away your head!
 See! dere's pity in your face!
Don't, dear madam, bring on me
 This unmeritied disgrace.

A Labourer's Life Give Me

I was never ashamed o' de soil,
 So you needn't remind me of it;
I was born midst de moil an' de toil,
 An' I'll never despise it a bit.

"Sen' me back to de cutliss an' hoe!"
 I don't mind, Sir, a wud dat you say,
For little, it seems you do know
 Of de thing dat you sneer at to-day.

If I'd followed a peasant's career,
 I would now be a happier lad;
You would not be abusing me here,
 An' mekin' me sorry an' sad.

Fool! I hated my precious birthright,
 Scornin' what made my father a man;
Now I grope in de pitchy dark night,
 Hate de day when me poo' life began.

To de loved country life I'll return,
 I don't mind at all, Sir, if you smile;

As a peasant my livin' I'll earn,
    An' a labourer's life is worth while.

As a labourer livin' content,
    Wid at night a rest-place for me head,
Oh! how gaily me life will be spent,
    Wid de baneful ambition gone dead.

An' when, after a day's wukin' hard,
    I go home to a fait'ful wifee,
For my toilin' dere'll be its reward,
    A peaceful heart happy an' free.

An' me children shall grow strong an' true,
    But I'll teach dem dat life is a farce,
An' de best in dis wul' dey can do
    Is to bear with content its sad cross.

So I'll make meself happy at home,
    An my life wil be pleasanter yet;
I will take de hard knocks as dey come,
    But will conquer de worry an' fret.

Oh! a labourer's life's my desire
    In de hot sun an' pure season rains,
When de glow o' de dark-red bush fire
    Sends a new blood a-flow'n' t'rough me vains.

Sukee River

    I shall love you ever,
        Dearest Sukee River:
Dash against my broken heart,
Nevermore from you I'll part,
    But will stay forever,
    Crystal Sukee River.

    Cool my fevered brow:
        Ah! 'tis better now,
As I serpent-like lance t'rough
Your broad pool o' deepest blue!
    Dis once burnin' brow
    Is more better now.

All about me dashin',
H'is'in' up an' splashin',
Bubbles like de turtle-berries,
Jostlin' wid de yerry-yerries,
All about me dashin'
H'is'in' up an' splashin'.

Oh! dis blissful swim,
Like a fairy dream!
Jumpin' off de time-worn plank,
Pupperlicks from bank to bank,
Dis delightful swim
Is a fairy dream.

Kiss my naked breast
In its black skin drest:
Let your dainty silver bubbles
Ease it of its lifelong troubles,
Dis my naked breast
In its black skin drest.

Floatin', floatin' down
On my back alone,
Kiss me on my upturned face,
Clasp me in your fond embrace,
As I'm floatin' down
Happy, yet alone.

Wavelets laughin' hound me,
Ripples glad surround me:
Catchin' at dem light an' gay,
See dem scamper all away,
As dey playful hound me,
Or in love surround me.

T'rough de twistin' dance
Onward do I lance:
Onward under yonder cave
Comes wid me a pantin' wave,
Speedin' from de dance
Wid me as I lance.

'Neat' dis shadin' hedge
Growin' by your bridge,
I am thinkin' o' you' love,
Love dat not'in' can remove,
'Neat' dis shadin' hedge
Growin' by your bridge.

Love more pure, I ken,
Dan de love o' men,
Knowin' not de fickle mind
Nor de hatred o' my kind;
Purer far, I ken,
Dan de love o' men.

E'en when welcome deat'
Claims dis painful breat',
Of you I will ever think
Who first gave me crystal drink;
E'en when welcome deat'
Claims dis painful breat'.

For a little while
I must leave your smile:
Raindrops fallin' from de sky
Force me now to say good-bye;
Jes' lee bit o' while
I must leave your smile.

Foamin' Sukee River,
Dearer now dan ever,
I'll ne'er roam from you again
To a life o' so-so pain,
Crystal flowin' river,
Dearer now dan ever.

FROM THE *GLEANER* AND THE *JAMAICA TIMES*

Agnes o' de Village Lane

Fancy o' me childish will,
    Playin' now before me eyes,
Sadly I remember still
    How much once your love I prize',
As I think o' you again,
Agnes o' de village lane.

In de school-room worn an' old
    Fus' I saw your pretty smile,
Heard your footsteps firm an' bold,
    Loved your face so free o' guile,
An' your soul so clear of stain,
Agnes, Agnes o' de lane.

Oh, I suffered much for you,
    For dey t'umped an' beat poor me
Tell me skin tu'n black an' blue,
    Tryin' ef dey could part we;
But we closer grew we twain,
Heartfult Agnes o' de lane.

Little love t'oughts o' me breast
    I wrote by de tin lamp's light:

P'raps dey were not of de best
(Bunny showed me what to write),
Yet you never would complain,
Easy Agnes o' de lane.

But dere came de partin' day,
An' they took me from you, dear,
An' de passion died away,
But de memory was there:
Long you've lingered in me brain,
Plump-cheeked Agnes o' de lane.

A'ter many a weary year,
Sad, sad news o' you I heard,
News dat brought a scaldin' tear
At de sound o' every word;
An my mind, filled wid disdain,
Grieved for Agnes o' de lane.

Agnes o' de lane no more,
For you went away, my pet,
Agnes once so sweet an' pure,
To a miserable deat';
Oh, de 'membrance brings me pain,
Fallen Agnes o' de lane!

George William Gordon to the Oppressed Natives

O, you sons of Afric's soil,
Dyin' in a foreign land,
Crushed beneat' de moil and toil,
Break, break de oppressors' hand!

Wake de lion in your veins,
De gorilla in your blood;
Show dem dat you ha' some brains,
Though you may be coarse an' rude.

Wil'erforce has set your free,
Sharpe an' Buxton worked for you;
Trample on de tyranny
Still contined by a few!

Keep before you Clarkson's name!
   Ef your groans caan' win de fight,
Jes' to put do'n dis great shame
   Lawful 'tis to use our might.

England paid you' ransom down!
   Meant to save you from the pain;
Now, freed men o' England's crown,
   Burst de cruel tyrant's chain!

Never would an English mind
   Bow beneat' such tyranny;
Rise, O people of my kind!
   Struggle, struggle to be free!

Shake de burden off your backs,
   Show de tyrants dat you're strong;
Fight for freedom's rights, you blacks,
   Ring de slaves' old battle-song!

Gordon's heart here bleeds for you,
   He will lead to victory;
We will conquer every foe,
   Or togeder gladly die.

Passive Resistance

There'll be no more riotin',
Stonin' p'lice an' burnin' car;
But we mean to gain our rights
By a strong though bloodless war.

We will show an alien trust
Dat Jamaicans too can fight
An' dat while our blood is hot,
They won't crush us wi' deir might.

Hawks may watch us as dey like,
But we do not care a pin;
We will hold "the boys" in check,
There'll be no more riotin'.

We are sorry, sorry much
For the worry given some;

But it will not last for aye,—
Our vict'ry day shall come.

There are aliens in our midst
Who would slay us for our right;
Yet though vipers block the way
We will rally to the fight.

We'll keep up a bloodless war,
We will pay the farthings-fare
An' we send the challenge forth,
"Only touch us if you dare!"

Christmas in de Air

Dere is Christmas in de air:—
But de house is cold an' bare,
An' me wife half paralize'
Is a-dyin' wid bad eyes;
An' dere's Christmas in de air.

Oh! de time is 'tiff wid me!
Coffee parch up 'pon de tree,
All de yam-plants tek an' die
'Counten o' de awful dry:
Ah, I wonder how we'll fare,
Although Christmas in de air.

Dere's me poo' wife sick in bed
An' de children to be fed,
While de baby 'pon me knee
Is as hungry as can be[;]
Ah tough life, so cold an' drear!
Yet dere's Christmas in de air.

Wuk is shet do'n 'pon de road,
An' plantation pay no good,
Whole day ninepance for a man!
Wha' dah come to dis a lan'?
Lard, I trimble when I hear
Dat dere's Christmas in de air.

Gov'mint seem no hea' de cry
Dat de price o' food is high,
Not a single wud is said
'Bouten taxes to be paid;
Same old taxes ebery year,
Though dere's hunger in de air.

While we batter t'rough de fret,
'Tis a reg'lar pay dem get;
While we're sufferin' in pain
Dem can talk 'bout surplus-gain;
Oh me God! de sad do'n-care,
An' dere's *Hard Times* in de air.

But we'll batter on tell deat',
Holdin' life in desp'rate fait',
For we're foolish 'nough to know
Life is but a poppy show;
We feel glad de end is near,
Though dere's Christmas in de air.

O sweet life so sad, so gay,
Oh why did you come my way,
All your gaiety to vaunt
An' yet torture me wid want?
I'm a-dyin' o' despair
While dere's Christmas in de air.

Peasants' Ways o' Thinkin'

Well, boys, I'm not a gwin to preach,
Nor neider mekin' a long speech:
But only few short wuds fe say
'Bout pressin' queshtons o' de day.

I sort a be'n dah wan' fe try
To put i' in prose cut an' dry,
But a'ter all a caan' do worse
Dan dish i' up in rhymin' verse:

For 'cordin' as i' mighta run,
It may gie you a little fun,

An' mek i' nice, fur as nice goes,
Mo' dan de bare unreadin' prose.

A t'ink buccra ha' jawed enuff,
'Bout tekin' duty off foodstuff;
An as 'tis said de good's fe we,
Time's come for *our* talk 'bouten i'.

We who caan' buy a decent rug,
But wearin' mostly osnabu'g
An' caan' put gill by in a pu's',
Mus' surely know wha' good fe us.

Seems dat some folkses neber guess
Dat if de duty is made less,
On some o' our imported food,
It would do we a piles o' good.

Dem see we batter t'rough de wul'
But caan' dive deep do'n in we soul
Fe read wha' we dah feelin' dere,
An' all our pain an' all our care.

Dat poo' gal wid de sickly smile,
'Pon strugglin' wid her bastard chil',
Can tell dem how she cut an' carve
Each week fe mek a shillin' sarve.

A little cornmeal, little rice,
A little flour at lesser price
Though it be but a fardin' less,
Wi' hlep we conquer grim distress.

Perhaps dem heart would sort o' grow,
Ef dem could bring demse'f fe know
Say de young baby in we lap
Raise 'pon not'in' but cornmeal pap.

We wouldn' mind ef dem could try
Mek calico cheaper fe buy;
Tek duty off o' we blue shirt
An' also off o' we t'atch hut.

Aldough we cheerful-like an' glad,
Life well an' bitter, well an' sad;
So eben when we're mute an' dumb,
We prayin' hard dat change may come.

An' yet, dough t'ings might cheaper be,
Life caan' be much better fe we;
Jamaica do'n de hill a go,
An' neber shall be like befo'.

De pay so lee, boys; an' de wus',
De shopkeeper so cross 'pon us.
An' wid dem little trick dem rob
A fuppence out o' every bob.

We might no lub de Chinaman,
An' also de East Indian;
But of strangers de wus-wus one
A dat who dem call Syrian,

Wha sell him goods to Kingston poor,
Tekin' it quite up to dem door.
At double too de price or more
Dey'd get it in a city store.

Because t'rough circumstances dem mus'
De fripp'ries an' de fin'ries trus',
An' eber after live in fret
Fe pay off de soul-grindin' debt.

To hear in dese ya modern days
Wha' foreigners think of our ways,
Is in some fashion reder nice
An' gie to life a bit o' spice.

But fe we part we smile to see
In newspapers wha's said o' we,
An' things 'bout us in pen an' ink
Don't show de sort o' way we think.

For hardly can de buccra find
What pasin' in de black man's mind;
He tellin' us we ought to stay,
But dis is wha' we got to say:

"We hea' a callin' from Colon,
We hea' a callin' from Limon,
Let's quit de t'ankless toil an' fret
Fe where a better pay we'll get."

Though ober deh de law is bad,
An' dey no know de name o' God,
Yet dere is nuff work fe we han's,
Reward in gol' fe beat de ban's.

De freedom here we'll maybe miss,
Our ol' rum an' our Joanie's kiss,
De prattlin' of our little Nell,
De chimin' o' de village bell.

De John-t'-whits in de mammee tree,
An' all de sights we lub fe see;
All dis, I know, we must exchange
For t'ings dat will seem bad an' strange.

We'll have de beastly 'panish beer,
De never-ceasin' wear an' tear,
All Sundays wuk in cocoa-walk,
An' tryin' fe larn de country's talk;

A-meetin' mountain cow an' cat,
An' Goffs wi' plunder awful fat,
While, choppin' do'n de ru'nate wood,
Malaria suckin' out we blood.

But poo'ness deh could neber come,
An' dere'll be cash fe sen' back home
Fe de old heads, de bastard babe
An' somet'ing ober still fe sabe.

Now here dere's poo'ness eberywhere,
But den it's home an' very dear,
An' dough for years we stay away,
We're boun' to come back here some day.

We may n't be rich like buccra folk;
For us de white, for dem de yolk,
Da's de way dat the egg divide,
An' we content wi' de outside.

Havin' we owna mancha-root,
Havin' we dandy Sunday suit,
We'll happy wi' our modest lot
An' won't grudge buccra wha' dem got.

A piece o' lan' fe raise two goat,
A little rum fe ease we t'roat,
A little cot fe res' we head—
An' we're contented tell we dead.

Bestman's Toast at a Rustic Wedding Feast

Mr. and Mrs. Bride, Mr. and Mrs. Cakecutter, ladies an' gentleman, an' company. I'm call' upon to give a speech, an' I have procrastinated it with a few elegant, conjugallish, felicitous-like toasts. I am not a speechifyer, but I think I can do what the occasion demands, by producing an opportunish oration bedout great grand-flourish an' braggadocio. In de poetical words I must again say I wish you felicitous joy in dis glorious t'ing you jus' done. I t'ink married is a heabenly t'ing. I am a married man, an' can speak wid aut'ority. I no one o' those nyoungsters dat pick up de t'ing hot hot, an' when him ketch a pass him feel de weight a press him dong lak a fuppance basket o' naygar nyance a press in a you back when you dah came up Bruk Bowman Hill in a de middle day time wid de tearin' sun a lick you in a you cubbich-hole, (neck-back) an' then you feel like fling i' dong an' 'mash i' up or help i' dong or tek time gwon wid i'. No, me deh go'long wid i' fe years, an married is a good thing. Some say i' ha' teet dough. Well dat is true anuff; for a feel i' a'ready nip me like when you shove you han' under ribber rock-'tone fe ketch fish, an' a yeller-tail heng on 'pon you little finger. But *me*, me get 'way; for a tun right roun', an' pop de cla-claw slop a de root. Yet a wouldn' give it up, for married is a good t'ing. A lub i' to deat'. I don't t'ing a man a man, bedout him married. So a say again, I am a married man an' will ever remain one.

So Mr. Brammie, a welcome you as steppin' from de groun' floor on to de married platform. I don't welcome you as one o' dose

chupid chupid nyoungsters dat I jus' describe you, but as a gentle-
man married man. So we two will drink to you' healt' again, not de
lee weak weak sacriment wine, but two glass o' de real Jamaica, de
long-standin' an' delicious Daniel Finzi. Aye!

Now pass roun' de wine-glass dem, an' wid all due respectfulness to
de distinguishable company and Mrs. Brammie de lovely an' dignifuy
bride, we will drink de healt' o' Mr. an' Mrs. Brammie, an' hope dat
dem wi' live so tell we sun them in the most conjugal affections.

FROM *GINGERTOWN*

When I Pounded the Pavement

I was adding up figures and carrying over accounts in the constabulary ledger when the head clerk and sergeant entered the office and said I should go to the inspector's weekly lecture. I was surprised and annoyed. I had never gone to the lecture-room since I was transferred from the depot to that station. Because I was working in the office I had certain privileges. Lecture and ordinary drill were optional and I always exempted myself. But the inspector had desired that every man should go to the lecture.

I had always been absent conspicuously with my friend, the postman, the little constable who took the mail to and from the post-office and distributed it among sub-officers and men. He was commanded to the lecture that afternoon, also, getting there a little late, after returning from the post-office.

Our inspector had come to us from a country that has served the world well with police. Many of our sergeant-majors and some of our inspectors had come to us from the Irish Constabulary and socially and as white men they were practically nowhere in our very British-spirited colony with its insouciant mass of black and brown natives, a proud and self-sufficient mulatto aristocracy that had been building up and propagating its kind for generation upon generation, and a handful of British administrators.

But our inspector, though Irish, was not just another one of the Irish Constabulary promoted and sent out to a colony. He came from a good old Irish family, and everybody knew it. He had the aristocratic bearing. He was tall and thin and carried himself haughtily. Although he was only a third-class inspector of police, his family origin gave him precedence over his colleagues to the highest official society. It was said he was not liked among his colleagues.

Our inspector had written a book called *Police Service*. It was used as a textbook for the whole constabulary. When he lectured he had a copy on the desk before him. And he always referred to this chapter or that paragraph of his book.

That afternoon I went to the lecture. Some of the regular duty men snickered among themselves to see me there. As the inspector entered the door the sergeant-major yelled, "Shun!" We all jumped up stiff at attention. The inspector nodded acknowledgement and marched to his desk with just a suggestion of a curious smile, as if he were thinking it was all a comic show but necessary, and that he was satisfied with the exhibition.

His lecture repeated the ancient police gospel with which I was familiar. There were the preliminaries about uniforms and ceremonial duties. Obedience to superiors. Readiness to protect property. See a possible criminal in every doubtful-appearing person. Seize every opportunity to make a case.

Suddenly the inspector said that any man there who had not yet made a case should put his hand up. Three hands went up timidly above shoulders, mine, my friend the postman's, and a jolly fat-faced yellow lad who looked after the sergeant-major's horse and stable and was free from regular duty.

"Up with them!" said the inspector. And we raised our hands higher so that all the men could see. And they enjoyed seeing us humiliated because we were men with special places who did not have to mark time regularly on the beat like them.

My friend and the sergeant-major's orderly grew uncomfortable under the inspector's sneering disapproval. I felt certain I knew why we were called to the lecture and the inspector had put that question. I was at the bottom of it. For one evening when I was tipsy in Carrie Peck's bar I had boasted that I had never made a case since my enlistment and didn't intend to make any. The saloon of the bar was a rendezvous for the local officials, and my remark must have been overheard and repeated to the inspector.

We were the greater delinquents in the inspector's eyes because we had special jobs. He did not like men in special little posts which enabled them to escape the routine duties and regular discipline of the service. Such men as office clerks, orderlies, and bandsmen who could easily obtain plainclothes permits and had all their evenings free to visit the liquor shops and flirt with the barmaids. Perhaps because the inspector had been a bad boy away down from a high-class home, knocking all over the world until middle age, when he had to start in seriously as a little officer in a little British colony, he felt an aristocratic scorn for all poor little strivers after respectable little places.

The inspector told the sergeant-major to put us easy-sitting men on some sort of spade duty where we could quickly demonstrate that we were capable of performing the first duty of a policeman.

As a clerk in the office, one of my privileges had been exemption from patrol duty. Now the sergeant-major decided to put me on some sort of special patrol. I had not given a thought to the first duty of a policeman—case-making—when I joined the constabulary, and had never after been able to make myself interested in it. I had joined the constabulary under the impulse of a strong adolescent friendship.

A year before I had been an apprentice lad in a small town. But I quit the trade to go with my little friend to our capital. He was younger than myself and a great devourer of detective thrillers. All his pence were put into *Deadwood Dick* and such like tales. He had a cousin in the constabulary depot town who was a detective and he wanted also to be a detective. In the city we got jobs as errand boys. My friend's cousin wrote him that if he enlisted he would use his influence to get him in the detective service after his preliminary training. My friend said he would go, and we decided to go together.

We were both too young and too short, but a word from an influential sub-officer stretched our years and height. It was originally intended that my friend should be placed in the office, but his spelling was not very good, so they put me there. However, my friend's cousin asked the special duty sergeant to find him a permanent light job and he was given the care of the sergeant-major's sword.

It was not uncongenial, that semi-military life. Drilling and writing. My penmanship was voted as good as my aptitude for exercises. I liked the camaraderie. As the son of peasants I had grown up in an environment of individual reserve and initiative. Now I was thrown among a big depot of men of different character from bush and small town to mix in a common life with them. From my place in the office I got to know them all pretty well, newcomers who had to be measured and numbered and suited, and the older men each of whom had some occasion sometime to visit the office. And sometimes an acquaintanceship in the barracks.

Outside of my office work we did everything in common, drilling, eating, bathing, dressing, sleeping, even the ceremony of the watercloset. I remember this last thing was physically and spiritually very painful to me. My bowels just refused to function with me sitting in a long row of other men under the same necessity, and I was constipated for the first time in my life. The chief clerk and sergeant was willing that I should use the watercloset of the sub-officers, as my place in the office had made me quite one of them. But his colleagues of the drillground objected. They argued that they themselves had passed through it and that of the many things that went to the making over of a recruit into a good policeman the democratic atmosphere of the common open watercloset should not be underestimated. I solved the thing for myself by training my bowels to function when I visited the cafe in town each evening on my regular permit.

Existence at the depot was full of fun and much more satisfactory than I had imagined. The barracks life was rough and clean. And by the strangest of coincidences the drill days for my friend and me were the same and we were always put side by side during exercises. We had not ourselves thought of anything so realistically romantic happening to us. Yet there was more to come when, like a dream fully realized (after five months at the depot), a request came in from an important residential district for two bright men, and we were chosen.

The first night I was put on four hours' patrol with a very officious special constable who considered it his bounden duty that I should make a case.

We found a wharf worker drunk and sleeping it off in the portico of the old colonial government building now tenanted by bats and rain-birds. The special constable prodded the man up and wanted me to take him for being "drunk and disorderly." But the man was over-orderly under provocation. He offered no resistance and used no naughty words that could bring him under the charge of disorderly. I could not kiss the Bible before the judge that the man was disorderly. My colleague said drunkenness was enough to cover disorderly, but he was obliged to give in to me reluctantly. And while we argued the man stole quietly away.

"You'll never make a real good constable," he said, angrily. We had no other adventure for that night. Only, just before we were relieved we heard a strange tapping far down the street. We went to investigate and met an old peg-legged man well-known as a harmless and aimless nocturnal wanderer.

From the day of my first lecture I scented unpleasantness for me in the office so long as I did not make a case. I was doubly assiduous and careful at my desk. But the inspector, who was never amiable, was now coldly sneering, the sergeant-major, always jovial, grew reserved, and the sergeant and chief clerk did not conceal his disapproval of me because my boasted delinquence reflected on himself.

I knew that if I did not soon get my case I would be reduced to ordinary police duty. There were other lads with a good writing fist ready to take my place. Even if they did not have my natural aptitude and initiative, they could quickly learn the job just as well, perhaps better because of that. There were times when I fell down on the job pretty badly and went moony. If I did now, my chief would be in no mood to joke and wonder to what region my senses were fled.

Secretly I was pulling a couple of good strings to get out of the constabulary. And I wanted very much to get out without having the record of making a case. Nothing could please me more and my peasant friends and relatives who abhorred my profession.

As a son of peasants, I also had in my blood the peasant's instinctive hostility for police people. In spite of night marauders who rifled their fields and stole chickens and goats, the peasants liked the police less than the thieves. When the thieves were caught, it was invariably the peasants who did it themselves and brought them to justice. The "red seams"—so the peasants called the uniformed police—always distinguished themselves in other ways that were hateful to the peasants. They always butted in on family feuds and quarrels and made arrests when such troubles might have been easily settled by our old heads. And on popular marketing days, mostly Saturdays, when the peasants crowded the towns with their stuff, drinking rum and making merry with the rough obscene vocabulary of the fields, the uniformed police would pounce on them for disorderly conduct and thus take most of the money they made out of their pockets.

I was not only compelled to go to lecture regularly now, but also to the police court to get acquainted with the process of prosecution and trial. I learned nothing there that made me more eager to make a record. Little lawsuits were great and serious events in the existences of the peasant folk. But it was always comic to me to see my genial comrades of the barracks changed into little monsters of case-making. . . . My friend had made his case by the easiest opportunity that came to him. While he was on the beat he was accosted by a street girl that we both used to visit in common. She teased him a little for doing patrol duty, and he arrested her for "obstructing a constable on his duty." The girl had thought it was all a joke. But when the court fined her ten shillings with twenty-one days imprisonment, her smiling turned to a terrible howling.

II

The last thread of feeling attaching me to the place had snapped and all my desire now was to get out and away from it. But before I could I was compelled to face the inevitableness of making a case. . . .

One afternoon a call came for a man for special night duty at the house of an official in the Department of Public Welfare. He said there were undesirable visitors coming to his place and he wanted the police to get them. Arriving home late one evening with his wife from an Administration garden party, the official had spied a man skulking from the outhouse where the servants slept. After that he kept watch and discovered that the brown housemaid was receiving a man.

For a long time there had been quite a fuss in local newspapers and councils and pulpits about intruders at night on the properties of the wealthy and respectable. There were a trespassing law and a vagrancy law, but neither could cover these special intruders, since it was well known that they were the lovers of servant girls and let in by them. Many servant girls resided at their employers', mainly in outhouses, and chiefly the girls fresh come from the mountains. The free room was a part of their wages. They had their lovers visit them late at midnight or after, and leave early before daylight.

In some quarters it had been suggested that the Department of Public Welfare might do something about the evil. At last a bill was proposed in the Legislature to amend the vagrancy law to cover the offense. There was a big opposition from the white-collared employees against the bill. The clerks and schoolmasters, sons of the inarticulate brown-black mass. For they, with the police and soldiers, were the chief lovers of servant girls in the towns.

Especially worked up were the schoolmasters. As a group they were the greatest victims of the sexual passion. Many a black buck, after years of preparation and training in the Teacher's College, would suddenly find his career broken by an affair with a girl. And the girls bobbed up everywhere like rabbits in the fields.

It was hard enough for them to lose their careers, to be thrown back to the fields on the hoe and the machete; but they were aroused when it was proposed to add the further disgrace of cat and prison. For the amendment carried the penalty of whipping and imprisonment.

The pulpit was a strong supporter of the amendment. Life was too hot and careless in that torrid clime. And the parsons were bent upon bridling black passion. The feeling between the teachers and the preachers was sometimes a savage thing. The teachers as a body were much more intelligent than the preachers, and they did not conceal the fact that they thought so. But the preachers were their bosses, for the schools were denominational. And many a teacher's fall had been compassed by his unfriendly parson.

The amendment passed the Legislature, and some of the smart black and brown bloods of the town had already been trapped and disgraced by it.

It was Saturday night—the night that I always loved to spend with my friend in the Bijou bar-room of Essie Miller, the notorious quadroon love-girl. I took the tram out to the fashionable suburb beyond the race-track and walked down a lane of citron trees to the official's house.

It was a grand night. Warm, with the moon full of light and the big yellow citrons glowing in the trees. I thought of my comrades free down in the garden bar by the cove, lying in the grass with their girls. And here I was in uniform, bound to go prowling round a servant girl's love nest.

The official gentleman himself, Mr. Klinger, opened the door and let me into the hall. It was after ten o'clock and he had allowed the servants to retire. I saluted and bowed to him.

He was a well-set man, tall enough, with a long face, chalky-colored. Presently his wife came in and he said, "Here is the constable." She gave me a friendly nod and I bowed.

It was interesting to see her for the first time. For she had a reputation for great beauty in the colony. When she arrived there two years before, her photograph used to be the principal adornment of the society page of the local newspapers. One always read about her prominent at the fashionable affairs. The constables who went on duty to official garden parties and dances never tired of talking about the beauty of the new English lady. Her cheeks were a luscious pink, they said.

But that color was not there now. In two years the heat had drawn it out. It does that to all the people from the cool climates. Either they go pale or they tan, according to blood or occupation. The lady had gone pale, but she was strikingly beautiful still. She was of a lovely, languorous paleness. Like a languid yet lush creamy-stalked painted lady flowering in a pot in the house.

I kept watch in a corner of the veranda behind a bower of wild tanias and squat palms and climbing fee-fees. I sat there in a comfortable wicker chair and waited. Mr. Klinger felt certain that the intruder would come that night. Through the Venetian-blind we could see the lamp burning in the girl's room. He said that when the man entered the premises he should be allowed to go to his rendezvous. It would be a much better case to get him upon the act.

I kept watching the gate—a nice broad white gate, the silver gray gravel-yard spreading away from it and around the house. And around the yard growing tamarinds and gum-trees. And flowering shrubs, elders and coffee-roses and bell-flowers everywhere.

I felt exceeding comfortable in that happy surrounding, so comfortable that gate and time slipped from my consciousness and I drowsed away. . . . A hand tapped my shoulder and Mr. Klinger said, reproachfully, "You have been sleeping." I was very confused and sorry and apologetic.

"Oh, never mind. I've been watching, myself, with my wife. The rogue hasn't come yet. Strange. He's never so late. And the light is out. I wonder if we missed him. We'll wait a little longer."

It was after twelve o'clock. I must have gone off, forgetting everything, a long time. The gentleman went back in his house. It was difficult to keep alert under the warm, heavy-scented night. I tried walking on the veranda. The boards creaked, and Mr. Klinger came to the door and signed to me to sit quiet. The gravel would be quite as noisy under my patrol boots. So I sat down again and drowsiness seized me.

An hour later Mr. Klinger touched me and said we might as well try to raid. He had stolen over by the girl's room and heard nothing. But he had a presentiment that the man was there. He must have come in early in the evening before our watch began.

He beckoned to his wife and she came from inside. The three of us descended from the veranda and started to tiptoe across the yard. Now that I was really faced with the possibility of getting the man, I didn't want to do it. I didn't want to butt in on two people's celebration. For it had become something like common right to us to visit the pretty servant girls of our own class who roomed in where they worked.

I tiptoed heavily on the gravel and the gentleman clutched my arm, whispering agitatedly: "Softly, softly! They will hear you!" The outhouse was half-surrounded by a thick growth of bell-flowers, the long creamy bells, over-heavy with scent, hanging down swooning-form among the big leaves.

I broke a brittle branch and Mr. Klinger whispered in a tone that was crying to shout: "Good God, constable! You'll spoil the game!" But there was no sign of awareness in the girl's room. The door was locked, but the shutter window, whose sill was just a foot raised above the ground, was open.

Mr. Klinger stepped through first, and his wife and I followed. The couple were fast asleep, sheeted over close together in bed. The gentleman jerked the sheet off and there they were.

"Oh, look at them!" cried the lady.

"Yes, look at them!" her husband repeated. "That swine coming to indulge himself here on my premises. Arrest him, constable."

The man turned out of sleep, involuntarily drawing his hand across his forehead. Then realizing the situation, he shook the girl and jumped up, grabbing his clothes to cover his front. The girl saw her employers with a constable, and with a frightened little cry she turned over on her belly, drew the sheet over her, and covered herself entirely.

She was a pretty honey-brown country girl. I knew her by sight in the market, and used to tease her when she passed under the window of the constabulary station. The man was a big catch. He was an ambitious young black and very popular in the town among his own people. His father had made money in real estate and was the head of a native insurance building company. The son was a candidate for the Legislative Chamber. All the signs showed that he would win by popular vote. I learned later that his opponent, a European, was a friend of Mr. Klinger's; some said he was even a relative.

I had to arrest him. He dressed himself and I took him to the lock-up. The next day his father bailed him out. And he was front-page news, photograph and all. When the case was tried he received the maximum sentence. Six months in prison and twenty-one strokes of the tamarind switch. Convicted as a common criminal, his political career was broken. But I think that what broke him most of all was the switch. Policemen holding him down on a block and taking down his pants and whipping him for sleeping with a girl.

It was my first and last case. Before I could make another I managed to obtain my discharge from the constabulary.

GLOSSARY

batter	labor and sweat; work very hard; to have a difficult time
bedouten	without
bex	vex
buccra (also *buckra, backra*)	a white man or white woman; also collectively, white people
chigger (also *chiga, chiger, jigger*)	chigoe (burrowing fleas)
cotch	stand still or lie, and refuse to move
come-around	a day-laborer or casual worker, not at regular work; a loafer, a petty thief or cheat
counten	on account of
cowitch (also *cow-itch*)	the climbing vine *Mucuna pruriens* and its beans covered with fine hairs
dog-driver	policeman (derogatory)
gill	three farthings; three-quarters of a penny
fabour (also *favour*)	to resemble; to seem

Finzi	rum
ko (also *ku*, *kue*, *ki*)	look (at)
mac	abbreviation of macaroni; a shilling
mancha	nickname for the Martinique banana
mussy	mercy
nenyam	any foodstuff; food prepared for eating
nyam	eat
nuff	enough, also many
pickny (also *pickney*)	a child, especially a very young child
quattiewut	quattieworth, quattie, a quarter of sixpence
samplatta (also *samplata*, *sampata*, *sampatta*, *shumpata*)	a sandal with sole of wood or leather held on to the foot by leather or other straps
shamar	shamebush, the prickly sensitive plant (*Mimosa pudica*)
so-so	alone, sole, only; mere, ordinary
brater (also *braata*)	a little amount of the same, as of some foodstuff that one is buying, added on for good measure; similar to the thirteenth item of a baker's dozen
widouten	without

Note: For those seeking more assistance in understanding the Jamaican language, Frederic Cassidy's *Jamaica Talk: Three Hundred Years of the English Language in Jamaica*, 2nd edn (Basingstoke: Macmillan, 1971) is an authoritative resource. There are also two excellent dictionaries: F. G. Cassidy and R. B. Le Page, eds, *Dictionary of Jamaican English*, 2nd edn (Cambridge: Cambridge University Press, 1980), and Richard Allsopp, ed., *Dictionary of Caribbean English Usage* (Oxford: Oxford University Press, 1996).

LIST OF ABBREVIATIONS

ALWFH   Claude McKay, *A Long Way From Home: An Autobiography* (New York: Lee Furman, 1937).

B   Claude McKay, *Banjo: A Story Without a Plot* (New York: Harper, 1929).

BB   Claude McKay, *Banana Bottom* (New York: Harper, 1933).

CB   Claude McKay, *Constab Ballads* (London: Watts, 1912).

CMI   Claude McKay Manuscripts; Lilly Library, Indiana University, Bloomington, Indiana.

CMPJ   Claude McKay Papers; James Weldon Johnson Collection of Negro Literature and Art, American Literature Collection, Beinecke Rare Book and Manuscript Library, Yale University, New Haven.

CMPS   Claude McKay Papers; Schomburg Center for Research in Black Culture, New York Public Library, New York City.

CO   Colonial Office (files).

G   Claude McKay, *Gingertown* (New York: Harper, 1932).

GHJ   Claude McKay, "My Green Hills of Jamaica," MS; Schomburg Center for Research in Black Culture, New York Public Library, New York City.

H	Claude McKay, *Harlem: Negro Metropolis* (New York: E.P. Dutton, 1940).
HH	Claude McKay, *Home to Harlem* (New York: Harper, 1928).
MEP	Max Eastman Papers; Lilly Library, Indiana University, Bloomington, Indiana.
MGH	Claude McKay, *My Green Hills of Jamaica* (Kingston: Heinemann, 1978).
NCC	Nancy Cunard Collection; Harry Ransom Humanities Research Center, University of Texas at Austin.
NA	Claude McKay, *Negroes in America* ([1923]: Port Washington, New York: Kennikat, 1979).
PRO	Public Record Office, Kew, Surrey, United Kingdom.
SJ	Claude McKay, *Songs of Jamaica* (Kingston: Gardner, 1912).
SNH	Claude McKay, *Spring in New Hampshire* (London: Grant Richards, 1920).

NOTES

Prologue

1 Claude McKay, *A Long Way From Home* (New York: Lee Furman, Inc., 1937), hereafter abbreviated as *ALWFH*, pp. 61 and 173. "[P]oetry was my real love," he wrote, recalling his childhood, in *My Green Hills of Jamaica* (Kingston: Heinemann, 1979), hereafter abbreviated as *MGH*, p. 65.

2 Claude McKay, *Songs of Jamaica* (Kingston: Aston W. Gardner and Co., 1912), hereafter abbreviated as *SJ* and *Constab Ballads* (London: Watts and Co., 1912), hereafter abbreviated as *CB*.

3 Although he apparently read the volume, Tyrone Tillery consistently refers to *Constab Ballads* as *Constabulary Ballads*. Tyrone Tillery, *Claude McKay: A Black Poet's Struggle for Identity* (Amherst: University of Massachusetts Press, 1992).

4 See, for instance, Mervyn Morris, "Contending Values: The Prose Fiction of Claude McKay," *Jamaica Journal*, vol. 9, nos. 2 and 3, 1975; Rupert Lewis and Maureen Lewis, "Claude McKay's Jamaica," *Caribbean Quarterly*, vol. 23, nos. 2 and 3, June–September 1977; Rupert Lewis, "Claude McKay's Political Views," *Jamaica Journal*, vol. 19, no. 2, May–July 1986; Carolyn Cooper, "'Only a Nigger Gal!' Race, Gender and the Politics of Education," *Caribbean Quarterly*, vol. 38, no. 1, March 1992; Rhonda Cobham, "Jekyll and Claude: The Erotics of Patronage in Claude McKay's *Banana Bottom*," *Caribbean Quarterly*, vol. 38, no. 1, March 1992.

5 These were, however, reprinted, albeit in limited numbers, in 1972 as *The Dialect Poetry of Claude McKay: Two Volumes in One* (Plainview, New York: Books for Libraries Press, 1972), which in turn was reprinted in 1987 (Salem, New Hampshire: Ayer Company Publishers, Inc.).

6 The most significant discussions to date of McKay's Jamaican poetry are these: Jean Wagner, *Black Poets of the United States: From Paul Laurence Dunbar to Langston Hughes*, trans. Kenneth Douglas ([1963]; Urbana: University of Illinois Press, 1973), pp. 204–23 (apart from some of the problems with his analysis discussed here, Wagner seems unaware of the poems McKay published in the Jamaican press—there is no mention of them); Rupert Lewis and Maureen Lewis, "Claude McKay's Jamaica"—a pioneering discussion, though somewhat reductionist, making only scant use of McKay's poetry; Lloyd Brown, *West Indian Poetry*, 2nd ed. (London: Heinemann, 1984), pp. 41–53—in a brief but subtle discussion Brown pays too much attention to form at the expense of content, and makes no use of the poems published in the press; and Wayne Cooper, *Claude McKay: Rebel Sojourner in the Harlem Renaissance* (Baton Rouge: Louisiana University Press, 1987), pp. 36–62— the most thoroughly researched of these, but the poems are used only instrumentally for a general, biographical portrait of McKay. Between October 7 1911, and August 17 1912, McKay published at least fourteen poems in the two main newspapers on the island, the *Gleaner* and the *Jamaican Times*. Only four of these fourteen poems appear in *Songs of Jamaica* and *Constab Ballads*, the anthologies carrying two each. Cooper is the only scholar to have paid any attention to the other ten poems—and only fleetingly. Tillery, *Claude McKay*, does not so much as mention them.

7 Finished in late 1946, less than two years before he died, *MGH* was not published until 1979 (see McKay to Carl Cowl, December 25 1946; Claude McKay Papers, Beinecke Rare Book and Manuscript Library, Yale University; hereafter abbreviated as CMPJ). Because this edition departs in certain important ways from the original manuscript—it excludes, for instance, a chapter, "Personal Notes on the History of Jamaica," that McKay explicitly wanted to be included in the final version—I shall refer to the original, lodged among McKay's papers at the Schomburg Center for Research in Black Culture, New York Public Library (hereafter abbreviated as CMPS). Reference to this version will be abbreviated as GHJ.

8 McKay also published a funny little sketch, "Bestman's Toast at a Rustic Wedding Feast," which appears in Part III, below. It anticipates some of the best comic episodes in *Banana Bottom*. The sketch was published some five months after he had left the island in the Christmas number of the *Jamaica Times*, December 14 1912.

1   A Jamaican Childhood and Youth, 1889 to 1912

1 The following is a brief overview of McKay's time in Jamaica provided primarily to aid the understanding of his poetry. A substantially more detailed presentation and analysis of his Jamaican years is provided in my forthcoming study, *Claude McKay: The Making of a Black Bolshevik, 1889–1923*, from which much of the biographical information that follows is drawn.

2 Long quoted in B.W. Higman, *Jamaica Surveyed: Plantation Maps and Plans of the Eighteenth and Nineteenth Centuries* (Kingston: Institute of Jamaica Publications, 1988), p. 86.

3 *MGH*, p. 23.

4 Since 1920 there has been uncertainty as to whether McKay's year of birth was 1889 or 1890. He was in fact born in 1889: see Appendix below for details.

5 Gisela Eisner, *Jamaica, 1830–1930: A Study in Economic Growth* (Manchester: Manchester University Press, 1961), Table XLIII, pp. 244–5.

6 Ibid., Table XXXIV, p. 203.

7 Ibid., Table XLII, pp. 240–43.

8 Veront Satchell, *From Plots to Plantation: Land Transactions in Jamaica, 1866–1900* (Kingston: Institute of Social and Economic Research, University of the West Indies, 1990), Table 3.1, p. 38.

9 Ibid., pp. 42–4.

10 Eisner, *Jamaica: 1830–1930*, Table XXXIV, p. 203.

11 Ibid., Tables LVIII and LXI, pp. 294 and 302.

12 Ibid., Table XXVII, p . 171.

13 Satchell, *From Plots to Plantation*, pp. 48–9; Lord Olivier, *Jamaica: The Blessed Island* (London: Faber and Faber, 1936), pp. 377–8..

14 Ibid., p. 379.

15 Satchell, *From Plots to Plantation*, p. 48.

16 Olivier, *Jamaica: The Blessed Island*, p. 379.

17 Thomas Holt, *The Problem of Freedom: Race, Labor, and Politics in Jamaica and Britain, 1832–1938* (Baltimore: Johns Hopkins University Press, 1992), p. 353.

18 See Olivier, *Jamaica: The Blessed Island*, pp. 377–98; Ken Post, *Arise Ye Starvelings: The Jamaican Labour Rebellion of 1938 and Its Aftermath* (The Hague: Martinus Nijhoff, 1978), pp. 37–8, 63–7; Satchell, *From Plots to Plantation, passim*; Holt, *The Problem of Freedom*, pp. 347–56 where a photograph of Baker may be found on p. 351.

19 The Aliens Law Amendment of 1871 gave aliens the right to acquire and dispose of real and personal property in the island. According to Satchell, this law "had the greatest impact on land ownership, as it enabled thousands of acres of prime lands to be transferred to multinational companies and foreign individuals." The Boston Fruit Company and Lorenzo Dow Baker himself were among the main beneficiaries. Satchell, *From Plots to Plantation*, p. 79; H.A. Will, "Colonial Policy and Economic Development in the West Indies, 1895–1903," *The Economic History Review*, Second Series, vol. xxiii, no. 1, April 1970.

20 Satchell, *From Plots to Plantation*, Tables 3.1, and 3.2, pp. 38 and 41.

21 Ibid., Table 3.3, p. 41. Satchell's Table 3.3 mistakenly gives 25.6 per cent instead of 35.6 per cent for the 1900 figure for banana earnings. Cf. Table 3.3 and text on p. 49; Eisner, *Jamaica, 1830–1930*, Table XLI, p. 238.

22 Calculated from ibid., Table XXVII, p. 171.

23 Post, *Arise Ye Starvelings*, p. 37.

24 Holt, *The Problem of Freedom*, pp. 353–6; Olivier, *Jamaica: The Blessed Island*, pp. 379–98; Post, *Arise Ye Starvelings*, pp. 37, 64, 117–18.

25 Wilson Randolph Bartlett, "Lorenzo D. Baker and the Development of the

Banana Trade between Jamaica and the United States, 1881–1890," (Ph.D.Diss., American University, 1977), cited in Holt, *The Problem of Freedom*, p. 356.

26 Holt, *The Problem of Freedom*, p. 353; cf. Satchell, *From Plots to Plantation*, pp. 103, 106.

27 Eisner, *Jamaica, 1830–1930*, p. 342; emphasis added.

28 As Satchell demonstrated many so-called "squatters" had legitimate claims to the land from which they were evicted; Satchell, *From Plots to Plantation*, p. 71.

29 Ibid., pp. 106, 110; quotation from p. 106.

30 Ibid., pp. 105–6.

31 Ibid., Table 5.7, p. 100, and pp. 101–2.

32 Eisner, *Jamaica, 1830–1930*, pp. 221–2.

33 Satchell, *From Plots to Plantation*, pp. 109, 111–50.

34 See Woodville Marshall, "Notes on Peasant Development in the West Indies since 1838," *Social and Economic Studies*, vol. 17, no. 3, September 1968, pp. 252–63.

35 Satchell, *From Plots to Plantation*, p. 133.

36 Ibid., pp. 108–9.

37 *MGH*, p. 60.

38 Calculated from Satchell, *From Plots to Plantation*, Table 4.3, p. 75.

39 *MGH*, pp. 60, 25–6.

40 Eisner, *Jamaica, 1830–1930*, Table I, p. 379.

41 Cited in Patrick Bryan, *The Jamaican People, 1880–1902: Race, Class and Social Control* (London: Macmillan, 1991), pp. 268–9.

42 Ethelred Brown, "Labor conditions in Jamaica Prior to 1917," *Journal of Negro History*, October 1919, pp. 351–2.

43 Eisner, *Jamaica, 1830–1930*, Table XX, p. 163.

44 Karl Marx, *Capital*, vol. 1 (London: Lawrence and Wishart, 1974), p. 603.

45 Richard Lobdell, "Women in Jamaican Labour Force, 1881–1921," *Social and Economic Studies*, vol. 37, nos. 1 &2, March–June 1988, pp. 213–14, and Tables 9, 11, and 13, pp. 229–33.

46 Eisner, *Jamaica, 1830–1930*, p. 351.

47 H.G. De Lisser, *Twentieth-Century Jamaica* (Kingston: Jamaica Times Limited, 1913), p. 97. The move from country to town and the world of the domestic servant in Kingston is powerfully evoked in De Lisser's 1914 novel, *Jane's Career* (New York: Africana Publishing Corporation, 1971). For a general overview of the history of domestic service in the island, see B. Higman, "Domestic Service in Jamaica since 1750," in B. Higman, ed., *Trade, Government and Society in Caribbean History, 1700–1920: Essays Presented to Douglas Hall* (Kingston: Heinemann, 1983).

48 Eisner, *Jamaica, 1830–1930*, p. 350.

49 The Morant Bay Rebellion is discussed in Chapter 3.

50 Eisner, *Jamaica, 1830–1930*, p. 368, Table LXXIV, p. 369 and p. 367.

51 It is true that the figure for the first decade of the twentieth century was inflated because of the Kingston earthquake of 1907, but the average for the five-year period 1911–1915 was still high.

52 Eisner, *Jamaica, 1830–1930*, pp. 340, 137, and 342.

53 Lloyd G. Barnett, *The Constitutional Law of Jamaica* (Oxford: Oxford University Press, 1977), p. 12.

54 Hume Wrong, *Government of the West Indies* (Oxford: Clarendon Press, 1923), pp. 130–31; Wrong clearly exaggerates when he says that the vote has been "placed in reach of a very large section of the population." When he notes that "of those in possession of the qualifications only a moderate percentage register, and of those registered only a small portion trouble to go to the polls" his remarks apply almost exclusively to the white population. It is significant that for the three elections that took place between 1906 and 1920 almost half the seats returned unopposed winners. Indeed, in the elections of 1920 nine of the fourteen seats had uncontested candidates. And for the elections of 1906, 1911, and 1920 less than a third of those who were eligible voted. Calculations from Wrong, op. cit., p. 130.

55 Calculated from H.A. Will, *Constitutional Change in the British West Indies, 1880–1903* (Oxford: Clarendon Press, 1970), p. 60; the "racial composition" of the population for 1886 was calculated on the basis of half the numerical change in population for each group between the censuses of 1881 and 1891. The census figures are given in George W. Roberts, *The Population of Jamaica* (Cambridge: Cambridge University Press, 1957), Table 14, p. 65.

56 Will, *Constitutional Change*, pp. 60–66; Wrong, *Government of the West Indies*, p. 130; Bryan, *The Jamaican People*, pp. 14–20.

57 Probyn quoted in Linnette Vassell, "The Movement for the Vote for Women, 1918–1919," *Jamaican Historical Review*, vol. xviii, 1993, p. 52.

58 Frank Cundall, *Handbook of Jamaica, 1937–38* (Kingston: Government Printing Office, 1938), pp. 56–7; Barnett, *Constitutional Law of Jamaica*, pp. 12–13. Jamaican women were the first women in the British Caribbean to win the franchise: Wrong, *Government of the West Indies*, p. 130.

59 Vassell, "Movement for the Vote."

60 For the best analysis of this transition, see Ken Post's fine trilogy *Arise Ye Starvelings*, and *Strike the Iron: A Colony at War: Jamaica 1939–1945*, vols. I and II (Atlantic Highlands: Humanities Press, 1981). And, for an appreciation, see my "The Hurricane that Shook the Caribbean," *New Left Review*, no. 138, March–April 1983.

61 See Bryan, *The Jamaican People*, for a discussion of this category, pp. 216–21.

62 *MGH*, p. 60.

63 Ibid., p. 22.

64 Ibid., p. 58.

65 Ibid.; and see, for instance, the last stanza of "Strokes of the Tamarind Switch," *SJ*, p. 112.

66 *MGH*, p. 58.

67 *BB*, p. 7.

68 Telephone interview with Carl Cowl, March 18 1993.

69 Claude McKay, "My Mother," *Liberator*, March 1920, p. 24.

70 *MGH*, p. 59.

71 Ibid., p. 61.

72 T.E. McKay to McKay, undated [August 1929]; CMPJ.

73 *MGH*, p. 12. In his biography of McKay, Wayne Cooper insists that McKay's father was never a Presbyterian, and had always been a Baptist (Cooper, *Claude McKay*, p. 5). I have my doubts, however. For one thing we do not know much about Thomas's life before he moved to Nairne Castle, and second, it is unusual for McKay to make such a major error. McKay's description of his father is not figurative, as he repeated the statement in a clearly literal way elsewhere: "[M]y father was converted and educated by a Presbyterian minister." *MGH*, p. 25. Thomas McKay was probably converted to Christianity by Scottish Presbyterians and later became a Baptist.

74 *MGH*, pp. 59 and 22.

75 Ibid., pp. 22–3.

76 In his biography, Cooper overstates the antagonism that existed between McKay and his father. Cooper goes so far as to explain McKay's turn to Catholicism on the basis of what he calls McKay's "troubled relationship" with his father. "To some degree, at least," Cooper declares, "McKay's conversion to Catholicism can be considered a last act of rebellion against his sternly self-righteous father." Cooper, *Claude McKay*, pp. 364–5.

77 Thomas could not read or write so while McKay was abroad, his communication with Thomas was indirect, mediated by U. Theo and his sister Rachel. See Appendix below.

78 See note 94 below.

79 Claude McKay, "A Negro Poet and his Poems," *Pearson's Magazine*, vol. 39, no. 5, September 1918, p. 275.

80 *MGH*, pp. 11–12.

81 Ibid., p. 33.

82 *ALWFH*, p. 37.

83 *MGH*, p. 33; cf. *ALWFH*, p. 37.

84 Ibid.

85 Ibid., p. 34. McKay said that the colored minister was trained at Calabar College, but he must have meant Calabar Institution for Calabar College was not opened until 1912, and then as a secondary school attached to the Institution. See Joseph Ford and Frank Cundall, eds., *Handbook of Jamaica for 1913* (Kingston: Government Printing Office, 1913), p. 359; and "Caribbean Man: The Life and Times of Philip Sherlock," an interview conducted by Edward Baugh, *Jamaica Journal*, vol. 16, no. 3, August 1983, p. 1.

86 "Passive Resistance" is discussed in Chapter 4.

87 See, for instance, McKay's "Sufi Abdul Hamid and Organized Labor" in his *Harlem: Negro Metropolis* (New York: E.P. Dutton and Co., 1940), pp. 181ff. McKay returned to the subject of the boycott in his posthumously published novel, *Harlem Glory: A Fragment of Aframerican Life* (Chicago: Charles H. Kerr Publishing Company, 1990). The novel was written in the early 1940s, but was

only published some fifty years later. I will discuss McKay's politics in the 1930s at length in *Claude McKay: From Bolshevism to Black Nationalism*.

88 *MGH*, p. 55.

89 Ibid., p. 61 and "Original Translator's Note," *NA*, p. xvi.

90 *MGH*, p. 61.

91 "Personal Notes on the History of Jamaica," p. 10; hereafter abbreviated as "Personal Notes." (This manuscript is only partially paginated; where page numbers are clearly identifiable I have given them, otherwise the manuscript is referred to without direct reference to page.) McKay to Nancy Cunard, August 20, 1932, NCC. McKay wanted "Personal Notes on the History of Jamaica" published as a chapter of *MGH*. See McKay to Charlie Smith, October 15 [1947]; CPMS. The edition published in 1978 omitted it.

92 "Personal Notes," p. 10. According to McKay, "the obeahman . . . devoured a lot of the peasants money. He always demanded a pretty large payment for his work. So the British government was always pursuing him." It is noteworthy that Walter Jekyll held similarly negative views of obeah and obeahmen. (See Jekyll, *Jamaican Song and Story: Annancy Stories, Digging Sings, Ring Tunes, and Dancing Tunes* (London: Folklore Society, 1907; reprinted New York: Dover Publications, 1966), p. 241.) In reality, matters were not as simple as McKay made them out to have been. In any case, in *Banana Bottom* McKay would enjoy himself at the expense of his fictive obeahman. For more on the phenomenon of obeah in Jamaica see Martha Beckwith, *Black Roadways: A Study of Jamaican Folk Life* (Chapel Hill: University of North Carolina Press, 1929); Joseph Williams, *Psychic Phenomena of Jamaica* (New York: Dial Press, 1934), esp. Chapters 2 and 3; Leonard Barrett, *The Sun and the Drum: African Roots in Jamaican Folk Tradition* (London: Heinemann, 1976); and Mervyn Alleyne, *Roots of Jamaican Culture* (London: Pluto Press, 1988).

93 McKay to Nancy Cunard, August 20 1932, NCC; "Personal Notes," pp. 14–15. The phrase "without any regrets" towards the end of the passage is written in by hand—presumably an afterthought. Thomas McKay was 94, not 98 as McKay wrote, when he died on January 24 1933. (Inscription on Thomas McKay's gravestone and memorial plaque at Mount Zion Baptist Church, Nairne Castle, Clarendon.).

94 McKay may have eventually got a photograph of his father sent to him, as there is one deposited among his papers at the Beinecke Library at Yale University, but it is possible that the picture of his father may have been deposited after McKay's death by his daughter, Hope McKay-Virtue, who gave a number of items to the collection. See U. Theo McKay to Claude McKay, March 1 1929, April 26 1929, August 2 1929, May 23 1933; Rachel McKay-Cooper to McKay, August 25 1927, June 13 1929, December 26 1929; all in CMPJ; and McKay to Nancy Cunard, August 20 1932, NCC.

95 Jimmy Carnegie provides a useful portrait of U. Theo, but it is very brief (five pages) and not entirely reliable (Carnegie, "Claude McKay's Big Brother, U. Theo McKay (1872–1949)," *Caribbean Quarterly*, vol. 38, no. 1). Wayne Cooper,

in his pioneering biography, has him secondary to Walter Jekyll in McKay's development. One cannot help but be struck by the contrast between the herculean effort Cooper makes to reconstruct Jekyll's life and the relatively puny attempt to establish U. Theo's (Cooper, *Claude McKay*, Chapter 1). In *Claude McKay: A Black Poet's Struggle for Identity*, Tyrone Tillery barely mentions U. Theo, and even gets his name wrong, inexplicably referring to him repeatedly as Theophilious. He also confuses him with his brother Thomas E. McKay, an Anglican clergyman. He goes even further than Cooper in exhalting the importance of Jekyll. Jekyll's recognition of McKay's "natural attributes" as a poet, Tillery claims, "proved crucial to Claude's development as a writer and intellectual . . . the influence Jekyll exerted on McKay's intellectual development and personality was immense, the result being a peculiar combination of social inclinations." (Tillery, *Claude McKay*, pp. 10, 11–12 and 19.) Edward Brathwaite, in a scornful discussion of McKay's poetry, refers to U. Theo as McKay's "*Dan-is-the-man-in-the-van* school teacher brother" (Edward Kamau Brathwaite, *History of the Voice: The Development of National Language in Anglophone Caribbean Poetry* (London: New Beacon Books, 1984), p. 20, n. 21). The reference is to the famous calypso song by The Mighty Sparrow satirizing the idiocies of colonial education (The Mighty Sparrow [Francisco Slinger], "Dan is the Man." The lyrics are transcribed in Stewart Brown, Mervyn Morris and Gordon Rohlehr, eds., *Voice Print: An Anthology of Oral and Related Poetry from the Caribbean* (Harlow: Longman, 1989), pp. 129–30.) He describes Jekyll as McKay's Svengali. He does not tell us where he got all this from. (Brathwaite, *History of the Voice*, pp. 19, 20, 22 and 28.)

96 Stephen A. Hill, ed., *Who's Who in Jamaica, 1916*, (Kingston: The Gleaner Co. Ltd., 1916), p. 94; L.A. Thoywell-Henry, ed., *Who's Who: Jamaica, 1941–1946*, (Kingston: Who's Who (Jamaica) Ltd., 1945), p. 444; *MGH*, p. 13; Cooper, *Claude McKay*, p. 12. The University College of the West Indies (accredited by the University of London) was not established until 1948 in Kingston, Jamaica. It later became the University of the West Indies.

97 Thoywell-Henry, *Who's Who: Jamaica, 1941–1946*, p. 444.

98 *Gleaner*, August 8 1922.

99 Rev. W. Marwick, "Claude McKay, the New Jamaica Poet," *Christian Commonwealth*, March 27 1912, p. 420.

100 There is some confusion as to precisely when U. Theo gave up teaching. The 1916 edition of *Who's Who in Jamaica* stated that he "resigned teaching in 1910." But the 1945 edition of the same publication gave 1920 as the year that he stopped teaching. What is certain, however, is that, contrary to the impression given by McKay in *My Green Hills of Jamaica*, U. Theo did do some teaching after his return to Clarendon. In 1916 *Who's Who in Jamaica* stated that he taught at Mount Carey for six years, and at two Clarendon schools, Rock River (for one and a half years) and Park Hall (for "nearly eight years"). This would mean that he stopped teaching about 1910. It also appears that he combined teaching in Clarendon with farming. U. Theo might have returned to teaching after 1910 and finally stopped in 1920 but there is little evidence to support this. The 1945 *Who's*

Who might simply have made a typographical error, turning 1910 into 1920. See Hill, *Who's Who*, p. 94; Thoywell-Henry, *Who's Who*, p. 444; *MGH*, p. 21.

101 See Erna Brodber, "The Second Generation of Freemen in Jamaica, 1907–1944," (Ph.D. diss., University of the West Indies, 1984), pp. 57–70.

102 Claude McKay, "On Becoming a Roman Catholic," *Epistle*, vol. xi, no. 2, spring 1945, p. 43.

103 *MGH*, p. 19.

104 *MGH*, p. 41.

105 McKay, "On Becoming a Roman Catholic." The records of the Rationalist Press Association corroborate McKay's claimed membership. His name appears on the association's roster as a paid-up member between 1910 and 1914. See *The Rationalist Press Association Limited* 13th (1911), p. 41; 14th (1912), p. 44; 15th (1913), p. 50; 16th (1914), p. 48, annual reports, all published in London. Founded in 1899 by Charles Albert Watts, the Rationalist Press Association soon became the most successful disseminator of free thought in Britain. See F.J. Gould, *The Pioneers of Johnson's Court: A History of the Rationalist Press Association from 1899 onwards* (London: Watts, 1929); A. Gowans Whyte, *The Story of the R.P.A., 1899–1949* (London: Watts, 1949); and Edward Royle, *Radicals, Secularists and Republicans: Popular Freethought in Britain, 1866–1915* (Manchester: Manchester University Press, 1980).

106 McKay, "On Becoming a Roman Catholic."

107 For a valuable discussion of the close, if troubled, relationship between free thought and socialism in Britain at the end of the nineteenth century, see Royle, *Radicals, Secularitsts and Republicans,* esp. pp. 232–9.

108 *MGH*, p. 44. Strange and incredible though it may appear to some, McKay's claim was not far-fetched. The records of the Rationalist Party Association indicate a significant number of members on the island. Writing in 1913, C.A. Wilson remarked that "The publications of the Rationalist Press Association find a ready sale, and eager readers among the more intelligent young men and women." Wilson, *Men With Backbone And Other Pleas for Progress*, 2nd ed. (Kingston: The Educational Supply Company, 1913), p. 90.

109 *MGH*, pp. 35–40.

110 Ibid., p. 43.

111 Ibid., p. 44

112 *Gleaner*, October 7 1911.

113 *MGH*, p. 15.

114 The surviving correspondence eloquently testifies to the powerful and unique bond between them. The letters between McKay and his brother are lodged in Claude McKay Papers, James Weldon Johnson Collection of Negro Literature and Art, American Literature Collection, Beinecke Rare Book and Manuscript Library, Yale University. The correspondence will be discussed at length in my *Claude McKay: The Making of a Black Bolshevik.*

115 Author's taped interview with U. Theo's daughter, Mrs. Eloise McKay Edwards, London, August 23 1995.

116 See [R. Dingwall *et al.*], *Jamaica's Jubilee; Or, What We Are and What We Hope to Be, by Five of Themselves* (London: S.W. Partridge and Co., 1888); Wilson, *Men with Backbone* and C.A. Wilson, *Men of Vision: A Series of Biographical Sketches of Men Who Have Made Their Mark Upon Our Time* (Kingston: Gleaner Co., Ltd., [1929]); Joyce Lumsden, "Robert Love and Jamaican Politics" (Ph.D. diss., University of the West Indies, 1987); Harry Gouldbourne, *Teachers, Education and Politics in Jamaica, 1892–1972* (London: Macmillan, 1988); Bryan, *The Jamaican People*.

117 "[I]t is not in our blood," he told his more radical brother, "to be revolutionists." U. Theo McKay to McKay, March 1 1920; CMPJ.

118 U. Theo McKay, "Some Questions which Merit Consideration of Public," *Gleaner*, January 20 1919. This is a long letter to the editor that provides a valuable overview of U. Theo's ideas on a wide variety of subjects. Income taxes were imposed for the first time in 1920, and contrary to U. Theo's wishes, they were extremely regressive. Eisner, *Jamaica, 1830–1930*, pp. 23, 370–71.

119 *Gleaner*, August 8 1922, where U. Theo is reported to have said this at the Jamaica People's Association conference: "The man from over the seas could not know much about Jamaica. Jamaicans wanted their own sons to manage their affairs. The day must come when this would be so." See also U. Theo McKay, letter to the *Gleaner*, February 24 1923.

120 U. Theo McKay, "Some Questions which Merit Consideration of Public." Like virtually all black middle-class Jamaicans at the time, U. Theo did not call for universal adult suffrage. Indeed, while supporting the enfranchisement of women on the same basis as men, he suggested that "the occasion should be seized upon to raise the qualification for the franchise in general." The bill granting women the vote was passed in May 1919. However, the qualification for women was much more restrictive as discussed. The masses of black men and women were not able to vote until the introduction of universal adult suffrage in 1944. For a useful discussion of the debate over the 1918 enfranchisement bill, see Vassell, "Movement for the Vote." Unfortunately she confines her discussion to the debate in the *Gleaner*, ignoring the other and more progressive island newspaper, *Jamaica Times*. Remarkably, she missed U. Theo's important intervention even though it appeared in the *Gleaner*, and his name does not appear in her article.

121 Vassell, "Movement for the Vote," p. 45. The bill was tabled in the Legislative Council by Hubert Simpson, a light-skinned colored man who had a long and distinguished record in Jamaica's reform movement.

122 U. Theo McKay to Claude McKay, April 26 1929; CMPJ.

123 *MGH*, p. 19; McKay, "On Becoming a Roman Catholic."

124 U. Theo McKay to Claude McKay, January 24 1930; CMPJ.

125 U. Theo McKay, "The Sons of Toil," *Jamaica Times*, July 20 1912.

126 U. Theo's last sentence almost certainly refers to the massive departure of Jamaican labor to the Isthmus of Panama and elsewhere, and the debate which it had generated in the island.

127 U. Theo McKay, Letter to the Editor, "Branch Agricultural Societies," *Gleaner*, December 9 1918.

128 Ibid.; cf. James Carnegie, *Some Aspects of Jamaica's Politics, 1918–1939* (Kingston: Institute of Jamaica, 1973) p. 109 and his "Claude McKay's Big Brother," p. 8.

129 McKay ended his poem: "Like men, we'll face the murderous, cowardly pack,/Pressed to the wall, dying, but—fighting back." McKay, "If We Must Die," *Liberator*, July 1919, p. 21.

130 Carnegie, *Aspects of Jamaican Politics*, pp. 73, 100, 116.

131 "Report on Marcus Garvey by Detective Charles A. Patterson," Kingston, January 2 1928, in Robert Hill, ed., *The Marcus Garvey and Universal Negro Improvement Association Papers*, vol. vii (Berkeley: University of California Press, 1990), pp. 84–6. The colonial intelligence report does not indicate whether U. Theo spoke but it is likely he did, given that he was on the platform and not chairing the proceedings.

132 U. Theo McKay to Claude McKay, August 2 1929, CMPJ, "somebody" is underlined twice in the original.

133 *Gleaner*, August 6 1932; and his obituary, *Gleaner*, June 17 1949.

134 See especially, U. Theo McKay to Claude McKay, March 1 1929, CMPJ.

135 His brother, Herbert Jekyll, reported that when he lived in Bournemouth Jekyll made friends with Robert Louis Stevenson. See Herbert Jekyll to Frank Cundall, March 16 1929 (Waller Jekyll File, National Library of Jamaica) and detailed appreciation of Jekyll by Cundall, director of the Institute of Jamaica, and others in the *Gleaner*, August 19 1929; and Cooper, *Claude McKay*, p. 23.

136 Jekyll, *Jamaican Song and Story*. Jekyll's book, a real labor of love, is a pioneering work of enduring value.

137 *MGH*, p. 70.

138 Cooper, *Claude McKay*, pp. 23–4, 29–31. See also Rhonda Cobham, "Jekyll and Claude," pp. 55–78.

139 Jekyll's ascetic qualities are strongly brought out in the appreciation in the *Gleaner*, August 19 1929. Also see letters of Herbert Jekyll to Frank Cundall, especially that of March 16 1929 (Walter Jekyll File, National Library of Jamaica). The Oliviers developed a close friendship with Jekyll and testified to the simplicity and otherworldliness of his life in Jamaica. Margaret Olivier, ed., *Sydney Olivier: Letters and Selected Writings* (London: George Allen and Unwin Ltd., 1948), pp. 110 and 113.

140 *GHJ*, pp. 68–9; cf. *MGH*, 70, where the important reference to Tolstoy is omitted.

141 Herbert Jekyll to Frank Cundall, March 16 1929 (Walter Jekyll File, National Library of Jamaica). Jekyll definitely spent the winter of 1894 in Jamaica. An advertisement for the Queen's Hotel in Kingston carried a letter by Jekyll, dated December 1 1894, extolling the hotel's comforts. The ad ran in several issues of the *Jamaican Advocate*, including that of February 9 1895.

142 *MGH*, pp. 70–71.

143 When he died in 1876, Jekyll's father left an estate worth £140,000. Jekyll was left "£300 per annum during the life or widowhood of [his] mother." At his mother's death or remarriage, he was to receive £20,000 from his father's estate. Jekyll had settled in Jamaica soon after his mother's death. Cooper, *Claude McKay*, p. 380, n. 77, and p. 23.

144 *BB*, p. 71.

145 *MGH*, p. 70. David Levering Lewis in *When Harlem Was In Vogue* (New York: Oxford University Press, 1989, p. 58) perceived the incident to be "as revealing as improbable." Revealing, it certainly is. For what other reason would McKay recall it if it was not? Improbable? It certainly is not. Jekyll in fact was a close friend of the Oliviers and McKay had no reason to invent such a story. Lewis gives no explanation on this point. The clear implication is that McKay was lying. Lewis is not an expert on McKay nor on early-twentieth-century Jamaican history. One can only surmise that he is stretching, as so many others have done, the canvas of Afro-America over the Jamaican landscape. What Lewis and others have failed to appreciate is that the Afro-American experience is the anomaly of the Americas, the aberration, not the norm. I have come across no parallel in the Americas to the uproar caused in the United States in 1901 when a distinguished black man, Booker T. Washington, was invited to dinner by the president of the United States, Theodore Roosevelt. No other society in the New World has turned the brutal murdering of black men and women into a regional, if not a national pastime for over a century; only the United States has ever institutionalized racial segregation; only the United States has had on its statute books so-called anti-miscegenation laws. Lewis writes of McKay's rendition of the incident: "Festus Claudius McKay recalled that evening without irony, with the pleasure of a serf secure in a noblesse oblige untainted by race." Irony is a subtle literary device that is apt to be misconstrued even by Lewis.

146 U. Theo to McKay, March 1 1929, CMPJ.

147 U. Theo acknowledged receipt of the book in his last surviving letter to McKay, that of May 23 1933, CMPJ. Their correspondence after 1933 has not survived.

148 U. Theo McKay to McKay, May 23 1933, CMPJ.

149 See U. Theo to McKay: March 1, April 26, August 2, 1929, CMPJ.

150 U. Theo McKay to McKay, March 1 1929.

151 U. Theo McKay to McKay, August 2 1929.

152 McKay, "On Becoming a Roman Catholic," p.43.

153 Old Brenga, under whom he spent two years as an apprentice, hardly made an impact.

154 *Gleaner*, October 7 1911.

155 McKay, "A Negro Poet," pp. 275–6; *NA*, pp. xv–xvi.

156 Countee Cullen, ed., *Caroling Dusk* (New York: Harper and Brothers, 1927), p. 82.

157 McKay, "On Becoming a Roman Catholic."

158 *MGH*, p. 15.

159 Throughout *My Green Hills of Jamaica*, McKay's master is identified only as Brenga, or Old Brenga. However, in an interview with the *Gleaner* in 1911 McKay disclosed the name of his master as a "Mr. Campbell of Brown's Town." *Gleaner*, October 7 1911.

160 *MGH*, p. 58.

161 McKay, "My Mother," p. 22.

162 Claude McKay, "December 1919," *Cambridge Magazine*, vol. x, no. 1, summer 1920, p. 58.

163 "My Mountain Home," *SJ*, p. 125.

164 *MGH*, p. 66.

165 Ibid.

166 *ALWFH*, p. 61.

167 *ALWFH*, p. 13.

168 *MGH*, pp. 66–7. "Cotch Donkey" is almost certainly the poem in question. Its first stanza reads: "Ko how de jackass/Lay do'n in de road;/An' him ondly car'/Little bit o' load.", p. 46.

169 *MGH*, p. 67.

170 The very first chapter of *Black Skin White Masks* is entitled "The Negro and Language." "I ascribe a basic importance to the phenomenon of language," Fanon opens the chapter, "That is why I find it necessary to begin with this subject." Frantz Fanon, *Black Skin White Masks*, ([1952]; London: MacGibbon & Kee Ltd., 1968), p. 13.

171 Aimé Césaire, cited in James Baldwin, *Nobody Knows My Name* (London: Michael Joseph, 1964), p. 39.

172 Alleyne, *Roots of Jamaican Culture*, p. 15.

173 Bodilly quoted in Richard Hart, "Jamaica and Self-Determination, 1660–1970," *Race*, vol. xiii, no. 3, January 1972, p. 283; Ronald Hyam has a striking discussion of some of the key techniques through which this sense of inferiority is nurtured: Ronald Hyam, *Britain's Imperial Century, 1815–1914: A Study of Empire and Expansion* (London: B.T. Batsford, 1976), esp. pp. 156–62; an abbreviated second edition of this book was published in 1993 (Basingstoke: Macmillan Press; Lanham, MD: Barnes & Noble Books), see pp. 301–10.

174 Richard Hart, the veteran Jamaican nationalist of the 1930s, told me the story of the response of a well-educated Jamaican woman to the nationalist ferment in Jamaica in the late 1930s. Knowing that Hart was a part of the political agitation, she turned to him and asked him one day in all sincerity: "But Richard, do you really think that the French or the Germans or the Americans could do a better job of ruling Jamaica than the British?" The thought simply never occurred to her that the Jamaican people might just have wanted to, and might just have been able to rule themselves.

175 *MGH*, p. 67–8.

176 *Gleaner*, October 7 1911.

177 *MGH*, p. 68.

178 In 1910, the force had a target of 748 but only had 730 at year's end. In

1911, it had 751 but wanted 785. See Government of Jamaica, *Departmental Reports*, 1911 and 1912. The *Gleaner* blamed the difficulties of recruitment and what it saw as the diminishing quality of the island's police force on the authorities of the Panama Canal. The latter had "drained" Jamaica of the "brain and sinew of the rural population" and had recruited the most qualified members of the force. See *Gleaner*, March 11 1913, and discussion in Chapter 4 below.

179 There has been uncertainty and a great deal of confusion as to when McKay joined the constabulary and when he left. According to the Jamaica Police Force, McKay's records are no longer extant. It is, nevertheless, possible to accurately determine how long he spent in the force. In an interview published in the *Gleaner* in October 1911 McKay was asked, "When did you join the Police Force?" To which he replied: "I enlisted last June—on the 7th of June." Cooper wrongly deduces from this that McKay entered the force in June 1911, and also claims that he spent less than a year as a policeman. Both claims are wrong. We know that the first is incorrect as McKay's poem, "To Inspector W.E. Clark," clearly written *after* he had spent time in the force, is dated "21 May, 1911." McKay's "last June," therefore must have meant June 1910, not June 1911. McKay himself has been insufficiently helpful on this point. In 1918, he said he served "1910–11," which gives credence to the 1910 induction date, but hardly helps in telling us how long he stayed in the force. His Russian translator of *Negroes in America* [1923], who must have got his information from McKay himself, wrote that the poet had worked for the police as a "clerk" "for a whole year." (And did he work in another capacity for an additional period? Did McKay minimize his period and role in the force out of embarrassment before the Bolsheviks, hardly the best friends of the colonial police?) McKay in 1927 said that he served for ten months. James Weldon Johnson in 1931 said he left the force after serving for "almost a year." *My Green Hills of Jamaica* is also confusing and somewhat contradictory on this question. What we do know is that at least as late as October 21, 1911, McKay was still a member of the force as the *Gleaner* of the same date reports that "Some of his finest verses cannot be published owing to his position in the Constabulary Force, as they treat of present political questions." Within less than a fortnight, however, the *Gleaner* (November 1, 1911) informed its readers that McKay had resigned from the force, noting that he had been stationed at Half-Way Tree, attached to the clerical staff. Clearly then, McKay left the force sometime between the 21st and 31st of October 1911, and probably on the 31st. We can therefore conclude that McKay served just under seventeen months, from June 7, 1910 to October 31, 1911. McKay did not tarry in Kingston. According to the *Jamaica Times*, McKay took the train on November 13 back to Clarendon. Sources: *Gleaner*, October 7 and 21, 1911, and November 1, 1911; *Jamaica Times*, November 18, 1911; Cooper, *Claude McKay*, pp. 28, 34; "To Inspector W. E. Clark," *SJ*, p. 105; McKay, "A Negro Poet," p. 275; *NA*, p. xv; Countee Cullen, ed., *Caroling Dusk* (New York: Harper and Brothers 1927), p. 82; James Weldon Johnson, ed., *The Book of*

American Negro Poetry, rev. ed., (New York: Harcourt, Brace and World 1931), p. 165; *MGH*, pp. 72, 78–79.

180 Claude McKay, "I Shall Return," *Cambridge Magazine*, vol. x, no. 1, summer 1920, p. 58.

181 *Gleaner*, June 17 1949.

182 Cf. *ALWFH*, pp. 12, 25; and Lewis, "Claude McKay's Political Views," p. 39.

183 McKay, "On Becoming a Roman Catholic"; *MGH*, p. 23; Lord Olivier, *White Capital and Coloured Labour* ([1906]; London: The Hogarth Press, 1929).

184 *MGH*, p. 82.

185 Cited in Bryan, *The Jamaican People*, p. 220.

186 *MGH*, pp. 28–9. In "King Banana" (*SJ*, pp. 30–31), McKay celebrates the superiority of the peasant method of cultivation over the white man's science: "Wha' lef' fe buccra teach again/Dis time about plantation?/Dere's not'in' dat can beat de plain/Good ole-time cultibation."

187 McKay, "Personal Notes," p. 13.

188 *MGH*, p. 44.

189 McKay to Nancy Cunard, August 20 1932; NCC; emphasis in original.

190 Nancy Cunard, "Jamaica—The Negro Island," in her *Negro: An Anthology*, (London: Nancy Cunard at Wishart & Co., 1934), p. 449. See also Cunard to McKay, July 17 [1932], August 8 [1932], CMPJ. For similar sentiments expressed by Afro-American visitors to the island, see my *Holding Aloft the Banner of Ethiopia: Caribbean Radicalism in Early Twentieth-Century America* (London and New York: Verso, 1998), pp. 97–100.

191 *MGH*, pp. 61–3; for analysis of the substantial migration of Caribbean professionals to the United States, see my *Holding Aloft the Banner of Ethiopia*, esp. pp. 78–83.

192 *GHJ*, pp. 59–60. This is the original manuscript upon which the published version of *MGH* is based. In this particular case I felt it necessary to quote from the original version to restore elements which had been edited out for apparently no good reason; cf. *MGH*, pp. 63–4. The man referred to was Rev. A. Alexander Barclay (1876–1926), an important figure in Jamaican politics during the first three decades of the twentieth century. He had first worked as a teacher, became an activist pastor in the Presbyterian Church, serving in Clarendon at the time of McKay's mother's death in 1909, and later became a member of the legislative council. In 1920 he became the first black person nominated to the council, but was soon elected by the black voters of western St. Mary, whom he faithfully and tirelessly served until his untimely death in 1926. See Wilson, *Men of Vision*, pp. 21–40.

193 U. Theo's public objection to the ill-treatment of the laborers building the roads and the railway in Clarendon in 1912 was apparently partly induced by the memory of his father having worked as a humble road mender. (Cooper, *Claude McKay*, p. 49.)

194 McKay to James Weldon Johnson, September 5 1929; CMPJ.

195 *MGH*, p. 69.

2   Songs of Lament, Songs of Protest: An Introduction

1 *CB*, p. 7

2 *Home to Harlem* (New York: Harper & Brothers, 1928), hereafter abbreviated as *HH*; *Banjo* (New York: Harper & Brothers, 1929), hereafter abbreviated as *B*; *Gingertown* (New York: Harper & Brothers, 1932), hereafter abbreviated as *G*.

3 See, for example, *Gleaner*, October 7 1911; *Jamaica Times*, January 13 1912; Marwick, "Claude McKay, the New Jamaica Poet," p. 420.

4 Johnson, ed., *The Book of American Negro Poetry*, p. 167.

5 In his memorable polemic against Sartre and Brecht, Adorno emphasized the negative as opposed to the prescriptive role of art. "It is not the office of art," he declared, "to spotlight alternatives, but to resist by its form alone the course of the world, which permanently puts a pistol to men's heads." Theodor Adorno, "Commitment," in Ernst Bloch, et al., *Aesthetics and Politics* (London: New Left Books, 1977), p. 180.

3   The World of the Struggling Peasant

1 "Buckra," "backra," or "bockra" is derived from the Efik *mbakara*, meaning "he who surrounds or governs." In the Caribbean it soon became synonymous with white people. "Quashee" or "quashie" also has West African roots, and in the days of slavery was used by Akan-speaking slaves to describe a male born on a Sunday. It was soon extended beyond this usage. By the late eighteenth century, Quashee was taken as "a typical name for a negro," often with derogatory connotations. In the early twentieth century quashie was generally used to mean a peasant. See Cassidy and Le Page, eds., *Dictionary of Jamaican English*, 2nd edn, and Frederic Cassidy, *Jamaica Talk: Three Hundred Years of the English Language in Jamaica*, 2nd edn (Kingston and Basingstoke: The Institute of Jamaica and Macmillan Education Ltd., 1971), pp. 155–7. To obviate confusion I shall spell "buccra" the way McKay does; in more modern usage it is generally spelt "buckra."

2 "Quashie to Buccra," *SJ*, p. 13.

3 Ibid., p. 14.

4 Marx, *Capital*, vol. 1, Chapter 1.

5 "Hard Times," *SJ*, p. 53.

6 Ibid., p. 54.

7 "Fetchin' Water," *SJ*, p. 42.

8 Ibid.

9 "Retribution," *SJ*, p. 49.

10 "Two-an'-Six," *SJ*, p. 86.

11 Ibid., pp. 87–8.

12 Ibid.

13 Ibid., p. 90.

14 Ibid.

15 Ibid., p. 91.

16 Beckwith, *Black Roadways*, p. 50. "Cramouchin'" means grudging.

17 "Whe' Fe Do?" *SJ*, pp. 28–9. Schopenhauer is also explicitly echoed in

another of McKay's Jamaican poems: "De helpless playt'in of a Will, /We'll spend our short days here; an' still,/Though prisoners, feel somehow free/To live our lives o' misery." ("To W.G.G.," *CB*, p. 77.)

18 This being the suicide-contemplating "Is It Worth While?" *Pearson's Magazine*, p. 276.

19 *MGH*, p. 19; *ALWFH*, pp. 13–14; Jekyll's book of Schopenhauer's writings was published in 1911: Walter Jekyll, *The Wisdom of Schopenhauer as Revealed in Some of His Writings*, selected and translated by Walter Jekyll (London: Watts and Co., 1911). Since McKay left Jamaica in July 1912, it is probable that he read even more of Jekyll's Schopenhauer book after copies were available in 1911.

20 Arthur Schopenhauer, "Additional Remarks on the Doctrine of the Suffering of the World," in his *Parerga and Paralipomena: Short Philosophical Essays*, vol. 2, trans. E.F.J. Payne (Oxford: Clarendon Press, 1974), p. 300. This essay was among those translated by Jekyll in his selection, and therefore, one that McKay might very well have read. See Jekyll, *The Wisdom of Schopenhauer*, pp. 327–46.

21 Schopenhauer, *Parerga and Paralipomena*, p. 293.

22 Ibid., p. 300.

23 Ibid., p. 299; the italicized words were written in English by Schopenhauer.

24 Ibid., p. 300; emphasis in the original.

25 James, *Holding Aloft the Banner of Ethiopia*, pp. 32–6.

26 Max Eastman, "Biographical Note," in Claude McKay, *Selected Poems* (New York: Bookman Associates, 1953), p. 110.

27 *HH*, p. 105.

28 See "Hard Times" and "Whe' Fe Do?" *SJ*, pp. 54 and 28.

4   Constab Blues: Black Consciousness and Black Solidarity

1 *MGH*, pp. 19–20.

2 Wagner, *Black Poets of the United States*, p. 215; see also Alan McLeod, "Memory and the Edenic Myth: Claude McKay's Green Hills of Jamaica," *World Literature Written in English*, vol. 18, no. 1, April 1979.

3 *ALWFH*, p. 95. He does express some doubt, however: "Oh, that I should never draw nearer to descend into its precipitous gorges, where visions are broken and shattered and one becomes one of a million, average, ordinary, insignificant."

4 Jean Wagner Papers, Houghton Library, Harvard University.

5 The manuscript of the anthology is among McKay's papers at Yale: CMPJ.

6 The original 1963 French edition of Wagner's book has an appendix of unpublished poems—"Poèmes Inédits"—by some of the poets whose work formed the subject of Wagner's study. The appendix, which was not carried in the English translation, has eight of McKay's poems which Wagner claimed were previously unpublished (although at least two of them had been previously published). McKay's poem on cities does not appear among Wagner's selection of the poet's unpublished poems. See Jean Wagner, *Les Poèts Nègres des Etats-Unis: Le Sentiment Racial et Religieux dans la Poésie de P.L. Dunbar à L. Hughes (1890–1940)* (Paris: Librairie Istra, 1963), pp. 580–84.

7 Wagner, *Black Poets of the United States*, p. 215 and McLeod, "Memory and the Edenic Myth."

8 *MGH*, pp. 52–3.

9 *MGH*, pp. 56–7.

10 *MGH*, p. 53.

11 *CB*, pp. 40–42; 57–8.

12 *CB*, pp. 52–6; 13–14; 57–8; 71–2.

13 *CB*, pp. 50–51; 66–8.

14 *CB*, pp. 37–8.

15 See in *SJ*: "Reveille Soun'in'," pp. 61–2; "To Bennie," p. 127; "To A Comrade," p. 129; and in *CB*: "De Route March," pp. 11–12; "Bennie's Departure," pp. 15–22; "Fire Practice," pp. 26–7; "Second-Class Constable Alston," pp. 28–9; "Bound Fe Duty," p. 33. See also McKay's autobiographical story of his time in the police force, "When I Pounded the Pavement," in *G*, pp. 203–20.

16 "The Bobby to the Sneering Lady," *CB*, p. 66.

17 Ibid., see note on p. 67 of *CB*.

18 Ibid.

19 "The Heart of a Constab," *CB*, pp. 62–3. I have come across nothing in the archives or the press to indicate what U. Theo and the rest of McKay's family made of his joining the force. From McKay's own evidence, they were not consulted before he joined as it was a decision made on the spur of the moment after he had left his job at the match factory. The McKays, then, were probably faced with a fait accompli. I doubt that they would have approved. Herbert Thomas reports (*The Story of a West Indian Policeman or Forty-seven Years in the Jamaican Constabulary* [Kingston: Daily Gleaner, 1927] p. 353) that men from the more respectable families who joined the police were looked down upon by their relatives. Apart from everything else, the job meant much less status than what the family would have expected for McKay. Mrs. Icelyn McKay Binger, one of U. Theo's nieces, remembered that when she was a little girl U. Theo asked her what she wanted to be when she grew up. She told him that she wanted to become a nurse. U. Theo told her in no uncertain terms that "No McKay is ever going to wash sore." She became a teacher instead. (Author's taped interview with Mrs. Icelyn McKay Binger, May Pen, Clarendon, August 6 1995.) It is probable then, that the disapproving black people, referred to in the poem, included members of his own extended, if not immediate family. The hypothesis is supported by his story "When I Pounded the Pavement," discussed below.

20 McKay, "A Negro Poet," p. 276.

21 Claude McKay, "When I Pounded the Pavement," *G*, p. 211.

22 Ibid.

23 Ibid., p. 212.

24 Ibid.

25 Ibid., p. 219–20.

26 *Gleaner*, March 4 1913.

27 *Gleaner*, February 20 1912. The sordid tale of Jamaican tourism is very

well told by Frank Taylor in *To Hell With Paradise: A History of the Jamaican Tourist Industry* (Pittsburgh: University of Pittsburgh Press, 1993).

28 *Gleaner*, December 10 1912.

29 McKay did admit, however, that being a policeman provided him with the opportunity of "studying the type of mind that exists solely to make trouble for others because it fattened on that. And also it serve[d] me well to estimate and understand the same type among different peoples." (McKay to Nancy Cunard, April 30 1932; NCC.)

30 McKay to Nancy Cunard, August 31 1932; NCC.

31 Cassidy, *Jamaica Talk*, pp. 158–9; Cassidy and Le Page, *Dictionary of Jamaican English*, p. 80.

32 "Flat-Foot Drill," *CB*, pp. 13–14. The *Gleaner*, the mouthpiece of the Jamaican ruling class, echoed the sentiments of McKay's drill instructor. In a long editorial, "The Number and Efficiency of the Colony's Police Force," it suggested that the authorities in Panama had "drain[ed] the island of the brain and sinew of the rural population—had . . . encourage[d] resignations from the constabulary force by offering superior inducements to trained and capable policemen." The problem was, accordingly, not just quantity, but quality of recruits. The editorial was stimulated by a series of major burglaries in the business district of Kingston which led to an outcry by the merchants and a call for greater protection from the authorities. The *Gleaner* was especially peeved at the audacity of one group of burglars and the way the police dealt with them. The thieves struck in the vicinity of the *Gleaner* offices, and the paper could not "understand a gang of burglars getting into a store . . . and carting away a large haul, without being detected by the policemen on the beat." The paper did not suggest that the police-men may have been complicit in the theft, but felt that the incident showed lack of "alertness, intelligence and efficiency of the men employed." Thus the paper concluded that "If 'you cannot make a silk purse out of a sow's ear,' no more can police officers make competent constables out of uneducated rustics destitute of any real ability." *Gleaner*, March 11 1913.

33 "A Labourer's Life Give Me," *CB*, p. 71.

34 Ellen Tarry, *The Third Door: The Autobiography of An American Negro Woman* (New York: David McKay Company, Inc., 1955), p. 131.

35 "To Inspector W.E. Clark (On the Eve of His Departure for England)," *SJ*, p. 104; also see "To Inspector W.E. Clark (On His Return)," in which Clark is described as "[a]n officer so dear an' true"; *CB*, p. 89.

36 *CB*, p. 8.

37 In his report on the rioting, Kershaw stated that McCrea regretted his arrest-ing Judah and Heath "as it has engendered popular indignation against him and made matters worse and admits that the whole population of Kingston appear to openly and bitterly resent his action." (Report of Chief Inspector of Police to Colonial Secretary, 1st March, 1912, enclosed in Governor Olivier to Secretary of State for the Colonies, Lewis Harcourt, 2nd March, 1912, CO 137/690, PRO.)

38 *Gleaner*, February 22 1912.

39 See Kershaw's report to Colonial Secretary, 1st March 1912, enclosure in Olivier to Secretary of State for the Colonies, 2nd March 1912; CO 137/690, PRO.

40 *Gleaner*, February 27 1912. The campaign of passive resistance, the riot, and the trials of protesters were extensively covered by the *Gleaner* and the *Jamaica Times* between February and March 1912. I have noted only the issues of these newspapers from which I have quoted.

41 Gleaner, February 27 1912.

42 *Jamaica Times*, March 30 1912.

43 *Jamaica Times*, March 16 1912.

44 See Kershaw report; CO 137/690, PRO.

45 Sir Sydney Olivier to Lewis Harcourt, February 28 1912; CO 137/690, PRO.

46 Francis Lee, *Fabianism and Colonialism: The Life and Political Thought of Lord Sydney Olivier* (London: Defiant Books, 1988), p. 125.

47 Claude McKay, "Passive Resistance," reprinted in Cooper, *The Passion of Claude McKay*, pp. 115–16. Cooper claims that the poem was published in the *Gleaner*, April 6 1912. Despite my extensive search of holdings of the *Gleaner* in Jamaica, London and the United States, none carried the poem on the date specified by Cooper. Nor was it found in either the *Gleaner* or the *Jamaica Times* for the period of the riots and their aftermath. It is possible that it was published in the magazine section of the *Gleaner* that was not microfilmed after Cooper had carried out his research in the 1960s. There is no reason to doubt, however, the authenticity of the poem; it has all the hallmarks of McKay's work. There is further corroboration of McKay's authorship of the poem, for "Passive Resistance" is obviously the work that Max Eastman was referring to when he claimed that McKay's "first poem of political significance [was] a rally-call to the street-car men on strike in Kingston." (Max Eastman, Introduction to Claude McKay's *Harlem Shadows* [New York: Harcourt, Brace, and Co., 1922], p. xii.) The poem, of course, was not about the tramcar men (though McKay may have supported their strike, which occurred in the aftermath of the passive resistance struggle in 1912), but about the resisters; McKay never did write a poem about the strikers.

48 For more on the Morant Bay Rebellion see Lord Olivier, *The Myth of Governor Eyre* (London: The Hogarth Press, 1932); Bernard Semmel, *The Governor Eyre Controversy* (London: McKibbon and Kee, 1962); Ansel Hart, *The Life of George William Gordon* (Kingston: Institute of Jamaica, 1972); Don Robotham, *"The Notorious Riot": The Socio-Economic and Political Bases of Paul Bogle's Revolt* (Kingston: Institute of Social and Economic Research, University of the West Indies, 1981); Catherine Hall, "The Economy and Intellectual Prestige: Thomas Carlyle, John Stuart Mill, and the Case of Governor Eyre," *Cultural Critique*, vol. 12, Spring 1989; Thomas Holt, *The Problem of Freedom*, Chapter 8; Gad Heuman, *"The Killing Time": The Morant Bay Rebellion in Jamaica* (London: Macmillan Press, 1994); and Clinton Hutton, "The Defeat of the Morant Bay Rebellion," *The Jamaican Historical Review*, vol. xix, 1996.

49 Claude McKay, "George William Gordon to the Oppressed Natives," *Gleaner*, May 3 1912; and *Jamaica Times*, May 4 1912.

50 McKay, "Personal Notes."

51 See reports in *Gleaner*, May 3 1912, and *Jamaica Times*, May 4 1912.

52 McKay, "Personal Notes." If Jekyll had in fact written a letter, it was never published either in the *Gleaner* or the *Jamaica Times*.

5 Jamaican Nationalism and its Limits

1 "My Native Land, My Home," *SJ*, p. 84.

2 Ibid., p. 85

3 Ibid.

4 Ibid.

5 Claude McKay, "Peasants' Ways O' Thinkin'," *Gleaner*, January 27 1912.

6 It should be pointed out, however, that contrary to the arguments of British colonial apologists, the abolition of the slave trade and slavery itself was not brought about by the disinterested goodness of the British ruling class who had ostensibly recovered their moral posture at the end of the eighteenth and beginning of the nineteenth centuries. Rather, these progressive developments were brought about by the combination of a number of factors and forces—the frightening spectacle of emancipation from below exemplified by the Haitian Revolution (1791–1804), the emergence of new economic forces in Britain less dependent upon the slave trade and Caribbean slavery, and the agitation of abolitionists in Britain. There is a substantial literature on the subject largely revolving around the seminal work of the Caribbean scholar-politician Eric Williams, *Capitalism and Slavery* (Chapel Hill: University of North Carolina Press, 1944). The fifty-year-old debate over Williams's controversial text rages. For a good summary of the highlights see Richard B. Sheridan, "Eric Williams and *Capitalism and Slavery*: A Biographical and Historiographical Essay," in Barbara Solow and Stanley Engerman, eds., *British Capitalism and Caribbean Slavery: The Legacy of Eric Williams* (Cambridge: Cambridge University Press, 1987).

7 Claude McKay, *The Liberator*, September 1921, p. 32; the remark appears in an untitled review by McKay of Lytton Strachey's book *Queen Victoria*.

8 Ibid.

9 For further illumination of the subject see Kathleen Montieth, "The Victoria Jubilee Celebrations of 1887 in Jamaica," *Jamaica Journal*, vol. 20, no. 4, November 1987–January 1988.

10 Philip Curtin, *Two Jamaicas: The Role of Ideas in a Tropical Colony, 1830–1865* (Cambridge, Mass.: Harvard University Press, 1955), p. 197; Hart, "Jamaica and Self-Determination," p. 282–3; Gordon Lewis, *Main Currents in Caribbean Thought: The Historical Evolution of Caribbean Society in Its Ideological Aspects, 1492–1900* (Baltimore: The Johns Hopkins University Press, 1983), pp. 307–10.

11 Thomas, *Story of a West Indian Policeman*, pp. 25–6.

12 McKay, "Personal Notes," p. 7.

13 Hart, "Jamaica and Self-Determination," p. 286; George Eaton, *Alexander*

Bustamante and Modern Jamaica (Kingston: Kingston Publishers Ltd., 1975), p. 95.

14 For further discussion see my *Holding Aloft the Banner of Ethiopia*, Chapter 4. For similar reasons there has been hardly any nationalist aspiration in the French Caribbean. From time to time one hears faint cries from Guadeloupe but from the black population of Martinique, nothing but deadly silence—despite its remarkable line of black intellectuals over the centuries. For a good overview of the situation, see Richard Burton, "Between the Particular and the Universal: Dilemmas of the Martinican Intellectual," in Alistair Hennessy, ed., *Intellectuals in the Twentieth-Century Caribbean: Volume II* (London: Macmillan, 1992) and Richard Burton and Fred Reno, eds., *French and West Indian: Martinique, Guadeloupe and French Guiana Today* (London: Macmillan, 1995).

15 "Old England," *SJ*, p. 63.

16 Ibid., p. 64.

17 See, for instance, Cooper, *The Passion of Claude McKay*, pp. 4–5; Cooper, *Claude McKay*, p. 37; Wagner, *Black Poets*, p. 221; Brown, *West Indian Poetry*, pp. 43–4; and Tillery, *Claude McKay*, p. 14.

18 "Old England," p. 65.

19 "To Inspector W.E. Clark," *SJ*, p. 104.

20 "Old England," p. 64.

21 "Personal Notes," p. 7.

22 McKay to Max Eastman, June 18 1932; CMI.

23 But see the very interesting discussion that John Henderson, a British visitor to the island, had with a black Jamaican man at the turn of the century. Unnamed, he stands out on the Jamaican landscape, a cross between an apparition and a prophet. Well-groomed, dark-skinned, confident, traveled (he had lived in England for ten years and toured the Continent), prosperous (he describes himself as a planter), articulate, he called for "Jamaica for the Jamaicans." Deeply resenting the crown colony system in which the colonial governor has a built-in majority in the legislative council and de facto power of veto over the island's affairs, he nevertheless believed that the island should remain a part of the British empire. The limits of his radicalism and nationalism are captured in the following remarks:

> I would have Jamaica governed as England is governed. The people of this island have every moral right to govern themselves, to frame their own laws and to administer those laws. We are no longer barbarians; we are an educated people with ambitions, and the strength to attain our ambitions. We recognize that it is a fine thing to be part of the great Empire of Britain, but we recognize, even more clearly, that it is a finer thing to be a free, unfettered nation. England will always have our heartiest support and affection. When we have become a nation and ceased to be a crown colony, Jamaica will always feel that really she is the child of Britain.

John Henderson, *The West Indies* (London: Adam and Charles Black, 1905), pp. 145–51, citation from p. 147.

24 On the relation between MacDermot and McKay, see McKay, "Personal Notes," GHJ, p. 7; W. Adolphe Roberts, *Six Great Jamaicans: Biographical Sketches,* 2nd. ed. (Kingston: Pioneer Press, 1957) p. 91; also see U. Theo McKay to Claude McKay, August 2 1929, CMPJ. For more on MacDermot's life and work see the introduction by J.E. Clare McFarlane to Tom Redcam, *Orange Valley and Other Poems* (Kingston: The Pioneer Press, 1951); J.E. Clare McFarlane, *A Literature in the Making* (Kingston: The Pioneer Press, 1956), pp. 1–11; Kenneth Ramchand, *The West Indian Novel and its Background* (London: Faber and Faber, 1970), pp. 51–5; and Mervyn Morris, "The All Jamaica Library," *Jamaica Journal,* March 1972, pp. 47–9.

25 See, for instance, "An 'All Jamaica' Entertainment," *Jamaica Times,* June 15 1912; "Our Writers," *Jamaica Times,* August 10 1912; and "Sons and Daughters of Jamaica," front page, *Jamaica Times,* August 24 1912.

26 MacDermot deserves a biography, but has none. The most detailed portrait of him is provided by Roberts, *Six Great Jamaicans,* pp. 81–98; Lloyd Brown loses sight completely of the nationalistic side of MacDermot; see Brown, *West Indian Poetry,* pp. 28–32.

27 Before its demise, however, the National Club provided two of its officers, Marcus Garvey and W.A. Domingo, with valuable political experience. Hart, "Jamaica and Self-Determination," p. 282; Hill, ed., *The Marcus Garvey and Universal Negro Improvement Association Papers,* vol. i, pp. 20–21; Rupert Lewis, *Marcus Garvey: Anti-Colonial Champion* (London: Karia Press, 1987), pp. 42–4; Lee, *Fabianism and Colonialism,* pp. 120–24.

28 Wilson, *Men With Backbone,* p. 81.

29 Ibid., p. 82.

30 Ibid., p. 83.

31 Ibid., p. 82.

32 *Gleaner,* October 7 1911.

33 McKay's dedication reads in full: "TO/HIS EXCELLENCY/SIR SYDNEY OLIVIER,K.C.M.G.,/GOVERNOR OF JAMAICA,/WHO/BY HIS SYMPATHY WITH THE BLACK RACE/HAS WON/THE LOVE AND ADMIRATION OF ALL JAMAICANS,/THIS VOLUME IS BY PERMISSION RESPECT-FULLY DEDICATED."

34 *MGH,* p.73.

35 In *My Green Hills of Jamaica,* McKay specifically recalls U. Theo telling him that Olivier's book, *White Capital and Coloured Labour* was "very good" (*MGH,* p. 23); see also U. Theo's letters to the editor, *Gleaner,* March 13 1913, and January 20 1919, in which he credits Olivier with being the only person to have made a serious attempt to reform the Jamaican taxation system in a more equitable direction. U. Theo maintained contact with Olivier up to as late as 1938 and perhaps even later; see U. Theo's letter to Olivier in CO 950/28, September 14 1938. For more on the objection of the oligarchy to better road and rail access by the peasantry see CO 137/742, despatch 711, Governor Probyn to Viscount Milner, Secretary of State for the Colonies, October 23 1920; enclosure of report by Barclay and Cradwick, October 9, 1920; also CO 137/746, Memorial from T. Gordon

Somers and C.A. Wilson, on behalf of the Jamaica League, to Winston Churchill, Secretary of State for the Colonies, May 12 1921.

36 Una Marson to Olivier, April 8 1932; Dorothea Simmons to Olivier, January 31 1939; Sydney Olivier Papers, Rhodes House Library, Oxford University. Also see Herbert de Lisser, "Notes on Lord Olivier's Official Career in Jamaica," in Margaret Olivier, ed., *Sydney Olivier*, pp. 229–37.

37 See Newton, *The Silver Men*, pp. 59–66, and my *Holding Aloft the Banner of Ethiopia*, pp. 28–9.

38 Olivier to Leonard Woolf, February 21 1941; Sydney Olivier Papers, Rhodes House Library, Oxford University.

6 Emergent Feminist Sympathies

1 But see Cooper, "Only a Nigger Gal!"

2 The poem does not tell us whether Milly's youngest sibling is a boy or a girl.

3 "Ribber Come-Do'n," *SJ*, p. 118.

4 Ibid.

5 "A Country Girl," *SJ*, p. 119.

6 Ibid., pp. 119–20.

7 Ibid., p. 121

8 *MGH*, pp. 17–18.

9 Ibid., p. 17.

10 Ibid., pp. 17–18.

11 Ibid., p. 18.

12 Claude McKay, "Agnes o' de Village Lane," *Gleaner*, October 7 1911. The full text of this poem is produced below in Part III.

13 *Gleaner*, October 21 1911.

14 *MGH*, p. 18.

15 *Harlem Shadows* (New York: Harcourt, Brace and Company, 1922); hereafter abbreviated as *HS*.

16 See especially "Harlem Shadows," *Pearson's Magazine*, p. 276; and "Africa," *Liberator*, August 1921, p. 10. These poems were subsequently included in a number of McKay's anthologies including the posthumously published *Selected Poems*.

17 The colloquialism "bobby" is derived from the name of the founder of the modern British police force, Sir Robert Peel, Home Secretary when the force was created in 1828.

18 "A Midnight Woman to the Bobby," *SJ*, p. 74.

19 Ibid., p. 75.

20 Strangely, "trace" and "tracing" do not appear in Cassidy's *Jamaica Talk* nor in his and LePage's *Dictionary of Jamaican English* despite its local meaning and usage as a verb in the language. It is interesting that Thomas, the white Jamaican police inspector, recognizes and speaks of it. Thomas, *Story of a West Indian Policeman*, pp. 357–8.

21 "A Midnight Woman to the Bobby," p. 76.

22 Ibid., p. 75.

23 Ibid., p. 76.

24 *ALWFH*, p. 315.

25 "The Apple-Woman's Complaint," *CB*, p. 57.

26 Ibid., pp. 57–8.

27 Ibid., p. 58.

28 Ibid.

29 For examples of Bennett's work see Louise Bennett, *Jamaica Labrish* (Kingston: Sangster's Book Stores, 1966), and Louise Bennett, *Selected Poems* (Kingston: Sangster's Book Stores, 1982).

30 Rachel K. McKay-Cooper to Claude McKay, August 25 1927; CMPJ.

31 Claude McKay, "The Park in Spring," *Pearson's Magazine*, p. 267. This poem would subsequently be revised and retitled "The Castaways." See *SNH*, p. 28.

32 Eisner, *Jamaica, 1830–1930*, Tables XIV and XV, p. 155.

33 Roberts, *Population of Jamaica*, Table 17, p. 72.

34 Roberts, *Population of Jamaica*, Tables 33 and 34, pp. 145 and 146; and p. 149.

35 Richard Lobdell, "Women in the Jamaican Labour Force, 1881–1912," *Social and Economic Studies*, vol. 37, nos. 1 and 2, March–June 1988, Tables 11 and 19, pp. 231 and 239.

36 Roberts, *Population of Jamaica*, Table 32, p. 141.

37 *MGH*, p. 19. For discussions of women and Fabianism see Eric Hobsbawm, "The Fabians Reconsidered," in his *Labouring Men: Studies in the History of Labor* (London: Weidenfeld and Nicolson, 1964); Norman and Jeanne MacKenzie, *The First Fabians* (London: Weidenfeld and Nicolson, 1977); Barbara Caine, "Beatrice Webb and The Woman Question," *History Workshop Journal*, issue 14, autumn 1982; Pat Thane, "Late Victorian Women," in T.R. Gourvish and Alan O'Day, eds., *Later Victorian Britain, 1867–1900* (New York: St. Martin's Press, 1988); Sally Alexander, "Equal or Different: The Emergence of the Victorian Women's Movement," "The Fabian Women's Group, 1908–52," "Fabian Socialism and the 'Sex-Relation'," all in her *Becoming A Woman and Other Essays in 19th and 20th Century Feminist History* (London: Virago Press, 1994).

38 *ALWFH*, pp. 12 and 14.

39 I shall attempt to explore them and their meanings elsewhere. I have started the process in *Claude McKay: The Making of a Black Bolshevik, 1889–1923*, which will be continued in a second volume, *Claude McKay: From Bolshevism to Black Nationalism, 1924–1948*.

7 On Cruelty

1 "Strokes of the Tamarind Switch," *SJ*, p. 111.

2 Ibid.

3 Ibid., pp. 111–12.

4 Ibid., p. 112.

5 Ibid., p. 113.

6 "The Bobby to the Sneering Lady," *CB*, p. 67; "The Heart of a Constab," *CB*, p. 63.

7 "Jim at Sixteen," *SJ*, p. 24.

8 Ibid., p. 26.

9 In his glossary to *Constab Ballads*, McKay explained "dog-driver" simply as a "nickname for a policeman," (*CB*, p. 84) rather like "red seam." But Thomas reports that the term was less neutral than McKay makes it sound. "[T]hose of the lower orders," he writes, "speak of the police as 'dog-drivers'—which used to be the favourite term of opprobrium in my young days." Thomas, *Story of a West Indian Policeman*, pp. 351–2.

10 "De Dog-Driver's Frien'," *CB*, p. 37.

11 "Killin' Nanny," *SJ*, p. 83.

12 Claude McKay, "Snared!" *Jamaica Times*, July 27 1912.

13 "Cotch Donkey," *CB*, p. 47.

14 The American anthropologist, Martha Beckwith, however, noted in her 1929 study of Jamaican folk life that Bryan Edwards, an eighteenth-century Jamaican planter-historian, "complains of the cruelty the Negroes showed towards animals, and I am afraid," she remarked, "they are not much improved in the ways of pity today." Beckwith, *Black Roadways*, p. 118.

15 I am not saying that McKay swallowed Schopenhauer's philosophical and ideological positions whole. He clearly did not. There is, most conspicuously, none of Schopenhauer's militant misogyny in McKay's work or political outlook. For evidence of this misogyny see for instance, Schopenhauer's essay "On Women," *Parerga and Paralipomena*, vol. ii. pp. 614–26. Interestingly, Jekyll did not include this essay in his anthology of Schopenhauer's writings.

16 Schopenhauer, "On Religion," in *Parerga and Paralipomena*, vol. ii, p. 375. Much, but not all of this essay is carried in Jekyll's book. The passages quoted are included in his translation; see *Wisdom of Schopenhauer*, pp. 356–72.

17 Schopenhauer, *Parerga and Paralipomena*, vol. ii. p. 297.

18 Ibid., p. 375. It is not insignificant that even when Schopenhauer berated his poodle he referred to him as "you, sir." Rudiger Safranski, *Schopenhauer and the Wild Years of Philosophy*, trans. Ewald Osers (Cambridge, Mass: Harvard University Press, 1990), p. 284.

19 Schopenhauer, "On Religion," p. 375; emphasis in original.

20 This is quoted from McKay's original manuscript: "He [Jekyll] was a great follower of Leo Tolstoy, and a pessimist." It is somehow omitted from the published version. See GHJ, p. 68; cf. MGH, p. 70. Tolstoy, like Jekyll, was a great admirer of Schopenhauer. This is most explicit in Leo Tolstoy, "A Confession," in *A Confession and Other Religious Writings*, trans. Jane Kentish (Harmondsworth: Penguin Books, 1987), pp. 17–80.

21 *MGH*, p. 68.

22 See Olivier, ed., *Sydney Olivier*, pp. 110 and 113. For further indication of the depth of the friendship between Jekyll and the Oliviers see Jekyll to Sydney

Olivier, 21 February 1928, Olivier Papers, Rhodes House. There is no evidence that McKay followed Jekyll's example in his eating habits.

23 The following remarks on Salt and the League draw upon the MacKenzies, *The First Fabians* and, especially, Dan Weinbren, "Against *All* Cruelty: The Humanitarian League, 1891–1919," *History Workshop*, issue 38, autumn 1994.

24 Quoted in Weinbren, "Against *All* Cruelty," p. 90.

25 Quoted in Weinbren, "Against *All* Cruelty," p. 102, n. 8.

8   Religion and Christianity

1 McKay was baptized a Catholic on October 11 1944 in Chicago; McKay, "On Becoming a Roman Catholic," p. 43.

2 *B*, p. 268. Earlier in the novel, McKay writes that Banjo, the chief protagonist, despite his plight, "instinctively turned" his back against "the Helping-Hand brotherhood of Christian charity with all its sanctimonious cant." Ibid., p. 242.

3 "Old England," *SJ*, p. 63.

4 Ibid., p. 64.

5 Ibid.

6 "Cudjoe Fresh From De Lecture," *SJ*, p. 57.

7 "Strokes of the Tamarind Switch," *SJ*, p. 112.

8 "Hard Times," *SJ*, p. 53.

9 "The Apple-Woman's Complaint," *CB*, p. 58.

10 "Mother Dear," *SJ*, p. 78. McKay recalled that after reading Spinoza's *Ethics*, he for a time considered himself a pantheist. "Mother Dear" was perhaps written during this period. See *ALWFH*, p. 14.

11 *Literary Guide*, January 1 1912; review reprinted in the *Gleaner*, January 13 1912, from which I have quoted. It is significant that McKay's second volume of poetry, *Constab Ballads* was published by Watts & Co, the publishing arm of the Rationalist Press Association. Watts had published Jekyll's *The Wisdom of Schopenhauer*, in 1911, the year before *CB* came out. (Jekyll, of course, made the arrangements on McKay's behalf with Watts & Co.)

12 Thomas MacDermot, editor of the *Jamaica Times*; see *Jamaica Times*, May 4 1912.

13 Marwick, "Claude McKay, the New Jamaica Poet," p. 420.

14 I was told of U. Theo's surprising conversion to Catholicism by his daughter. Like McKay, he too converted shortly before he died. Author's taped interview with Mrs. Eloise McKay Edwards, London, August 23 1995.

9   Thoughts of Africa and Intimations of Négritude

1 "Cudjoe Fresh from de Lecture," *SJ*, p. 57.

2 Ibid.

3 Ibid., p. 55.

4 Ibid.

5 Ibid., p. 58.

6 McKay, "George William Gordon to the Oppressed Natives."

7 Claude McKay, "Africa," *Liberator*, August 1921, p. 10.

8 Lilyan Kesteloot, *Les Ecrivains Noirs de Langue Française: Naissance d'une Littérature* (Brussels: Editions de l'Institut de Sociologie de l'Université Libre de Bruxelles, 1963); see also Jacques Louis Hymans, *Léopold Sédar Senghor: An Intellectual Biography* (Edinburgh: Edinburgh University Press, 1971); Edward O. Ako, "*L'Etudiant Noir* and the Myth of the Genesis of the Négritude Movement," *Research in African Literatures*, vol. 15, no. 3, 1984; Martin Steins, "Brown France vs. Black Africa: The Tide Turned in 1932," *Research in African Literatures*, vol. 14, no. 4, 1983; Liliane Blary, "Claude McKay and Africa: *Banjo*," *Commonwealth: Essays and Studies*, vol. 5, 1981–1982; Michel Fabre, "Beyond *Banjo*: Claude McKay's African Experience," ibid.; Bridget Jones, "With *Banjo* By My Bed: Black French Writers Reading Claude McKay," *Caribbean Quarterly*, vol. 38, no. 1, March 1992.

9 The classic statement of the problem is, of course, Frantz Fanon, *Black Skin, White Masks*. I have attempted, albeit briefly, to supplement Fanon's analysis with a less psychological and more materialist exploration in my "Migration, Racism and Identity Formation: The Caribbean Experience in Britain," in Winston James and Clive Harris, eds., *Inside Babylon: The Caribbean Diaspora in Britain* (London: Verso, 1993), esp. pp. 233–9.

10 "My Pretty Dan," *SJ*, pp. 114–15.

11 Cassidy, *Jamaica Talk*, pp. 156–7; cf. Cassidy and Le Page, eds., *Dictionary of Jamaican English*; Izett Anderson and Frank Cundall, eds., *Jamaica Proverbs and Sayings* (rev. ed. 1927; Kingston and Shannon: Sangster's Book Stores Ltd. and Irish University Press, 1972), p. 90.

12 "Fe Me Sal," *CB*, pp. 64, 65.

10 The Weapon of Lyric Poetry

1 *Gleaner*, October 28 1911.

2 "Papine Corner," *CB*, p. 42.

3 *MGH*, p. 73. There might very well have been a fuss over the poem, but if there was, it was not carried in the *Gleaner* as McKay claimed. The poem was first published in the *Gleaner*, October 28 1911.

4 "My Mountain Home," *SJ*, p. 124.

5 Ibid., p. 125.

6 "Sukee River," *CB*, pp. 78 and 79. McKay's river bathing did not end after he left the island. While living in North Africa in the early 1930s, one of the things he treasured about his little house near Tangiers was its closeness to a river suitable for bathing. "I am not much of a swimmer," he wrote a friend, "but very fond of floating in deep water and at high tide the sea drives up the river which is always calm and excellent for bathing when the sea is often rough because of the strait and Levant winds." McKay to Nancy Cunard, August 20 1932; NCC.

7 All published in *SJ*: pp. 59–60; 41; 79–80; 69–71, respectively.

8 Theodor Adorno, *Notes to Literature*, vol. 1, trans. Shierry Weber Nicholson (New York: Columbia University Press, 1991), p. 43.

9 "Free," *CB*, p. 73.

11 Peasants' Ways o' Thinkin': What is to be Done?

1 "Peasants' Ways o' Thinkin'," *Gleaner*, January 27 1912.

Epilogue

1 Mervyn Morris, "Contending Values: The Prose Fiction of Claude McKay," *Jamaica Journal*, vol. 9, nos. 2 & 3, 1975, p. 36.

2 Brathwaite, *History of the Voice*, pp. 13, 19–22.

3 McKay discusses these issues most explicitly in McKay to Joel E. Springarn, January 9 1917, and June 18 1917; and his "Author's Word," in *HS*, pp. xix–xxi.

4 Even some enlightened members of the island's middle class knew and loved these poems. Richard Hart recently surprised me by reciting from memory a large section of "The Midnight Woman to the Bobby," which he had first read as a boy growing up in Jamaica in the 1920s. He had been born into one of Jamaica's most prominent families. Conversation with Richard Hart, London, July 3 1998.

5 *MGH*, p. 69.

6 Brathwaite, *History of the Voice*, p. 28, n. 35; Mary Jane Hewitt, "A Comparative Study of the Careers of Zora Neal Hurston and Louise Bennett as Cultural Conservators," (Ph.D.diss., University of the West Indies, 1986), pp. 26–7.

7 McFarlane, *A Literature in the Making*, p. 84.

8 Claude McKay, "A Negro to His Critics," *New York Herald Tribune Books*, March 6 1932, pp. 1 and 6.

9 Houston Baker, *Modernism and the Harlem Renaissance* (Chicago: University of Chicago Press, 1987), pp. 86–7; emphases in original.

10 See especially Mervyn Alleyne, "A Linguistic Perspective on the Caribbean," in Sidney Mintz and Sally Price, eds., *Caribbean Contours* (Baltimore: Johns Hopkins University Press, 1985), pp. 155–79; and Alleyne, *Roots of Jamaican Culture*, esp. pp. 120–48.

11 *Songs of Jamaica*, apart from the preface, has detailed annotations. *Constab Ballads* is not as heavily annotated but boasts a fourteen-page glossary.

12 Brown, *West Indian Poetry*, pp. 42–3. Although it has its problems (it, for instance, spends too much time discussing form rather than content), of the existing literature on the subject, Brown's is by far the most astute discussion of McKay's Jamaican poetry.

13 In *SJ*, for example, see "The Hermit," "De Days Dat Are Gone," "Mother Dear," "Kite-Flying," "Strokes of the Tamarind Switch," "To Bennie."

14 "Bennett on Bennett" [Louise Bennett interviewed by Dennis Scott], *Caribbean Quarterly*, vol. 14, nos. 1 and 2, March–June 1968, p. 97; and McFarlane, *A Literature in the Making*, pp. 84–5.

15 For good analyses of the language of Rastafari, see Joseph Owens, *Dread: The Rastafarians of Jamaica* (Kingston: Sangsters, 1976); Barry Chevannes, *Rastafari: Roots and Ideology* (Syracuse: Syracuse University Press, 1994), esp. Chapter 8; John Homiak, "Dub History: Soundings on Rastafari Livity and Language," in Barry Chevannes, ed., *Rastafari and Other African-Caribbean Worldviews* (New

Brunswick: Rutgers University Press, 1998); and especially Velma Pollard, *Dread Talk: The Language of Rastafari* (Kingston: Canoe Press, 1994).

16 McFarlane, *A Literature in the Making*, p. 85. Brathwaite similarly claimed, tendentiously, that "In order to be 'universal' McKay forsook his nation language, forsook his early mode of poetry, and went to the sonnet." Brathwaite, *History of the Voice*, p. 20.

17 *MGH*, pp. 86–7.

18 A.N. Stuart, "William Knibb," *Jamaica Times*, August 21 1909.

19 See, in *Jamaica Times*, by Norman Palmer, "De Tourist" (March 2 1912), "Monday Morning" (March 30 1912), "The Iconoclast" (December 14 1912); and, by Raglan Phillips, "De Tourist Dem: A Reply" (March 30 1912), "Experience" and "De P'menta Price" (October 12 1912); and, by L.A.M. Robertson, "O Sing Nightingale" (December 14 1912). Raglan Philips also wrote some jingoistic verses in Jamaican during the First World War: see, for example, "Victoria First Gran-Pickney" and "De War-Time Solo," *Jamaica Times*, Christmas Number, December 1914.

20 Tom Redcam, *Becka's Buckra Baby* (Kingston: Jamaica Times Printery, 1904) and *One Brown Girl And—: A Jamaica Story* (Kingston: Jamaica Times Printery, 1909). The most comprehensive collection of Redcam's poetry is "The Poetical Works of Tom Redcam, Poet Laureate of Jamaica, 1910–1933" (Manuscript presented to the Institute of Jamaica by the Poetry League 1957), National Library of Jamaica, Kingston; and the posthumously published *Orange Valley and Other Poems* .

21 J.E. Clare McFarlane, ed., *Voices From Summerland: An Anthology of Jamaican Poetry* (London: Fowler Wright, Ltd., 1929), and *A Treasury of Jamaican Poetry* (London: University of London Press, 1949). McFarlane's definition of Jamaican was rather idiosyncratic. Many of the contributors were British and Irish expatriates living in Jamaica, yet strangely, although Lionel Robertson was highly regarded as a poet (his *Flormel* [Kingston: Times Printery, 1908] was especially praised) none of his poetry was represented in the volumes. It appears doubtful that he was excluded because of the quality of his work. (McFarlane's hero, MacDermot, thought highly of Robertson and indeed published his 1908 volume.) One wonders if he was kept out because he was not born in Jamaica. Though Guyanese by birth, he had roots in Jamaica as well as Trinidad and had lived in Jamaica for most of his adult life. The fact that he was a black Guyanese and not a white Britisher might have counted against him.

22 McFarlane *Voices From Summerland*, p. 304.

23 Ivy Baxter, *The Arts of an Island: The Development of the Culture and the Folk and Creative Arts in Jamaica, 1492–1962* (Metuchen: The Scarecrow Press, Inc., 1970), p. 158.

24 A.L. Hendriks and Cedric Lindo, eds., *Independence Anthology of Jamaican Literature* (Kingston: The Arts Celebration Committee of the Ministry of Development and Welfare, 1962); and Mervyn Morris, "On Reading Louise

Bennett Seriously," [1963] *Jamaica Journal*, December 1967, p. 69; Gordon Rohler, *My Strangled City and Other Essays*, (Port-of-Spain: Longman Trinidad, 1992), p. 70.

25 Cited in Mervyn Morris, "Introduction," Louise Bennett, *Selected Poems*, pp. xii–xiii. Literal translation: "Is that what your mother sent you to school for?")

26 Daryl Cumber Dance, *New World Adams: Conversations with Contemporary West Indian Writers* (Leeds: Peepal Tree Books, 1992), p. 27.

27 "Bennett on Bennett," p. 98

28 A. James Arnold, *Modernism and Negritude: The Poetry and Poetics of Aimée Césaire* (Cambridge, Mass: Harvard University Press, 1981), p. 5. Cf. Introduction by Clayton Eshleman and Annette Smith in Aimé Césaire, *The Collected Poetry* (Berkeley: University of California Press, 1983), p. 1.

29 Arnold, *Modernism and Negritude*, pp. 7–8.

30 Charles Rowell, "It is Through Poetry that One Copes with Solitude: An Interview with Aimé Césaire," *Callaloo*, vol. 12, no. 1, winter 1989, p. 59. Born in the French-controlled sister island of Guadeloupe more than a generation after Césaire, Maryse Condé wrote that when she was a child "I could not name one of the mountains of Guadeloupe, because I was taught about the Alps and the Pyrinees." Vèvè A. Clark, "'I Have Made Peace With My Island': An Interview with Maryse Condé," *Callaloo*, vol 12, no. 1, winter 1989, p. 113. Also see Madeleine Cottenet-Hage and Kevin Meehan, "'Our Ancestors the Gauls . . .': Schools and Schooling in Two Caribbean Novels," *Callaloo*, vol. 15, no. 1, winter 1992.

31 Césaire quoted in Lucien Taylor, "Créolité Bites: A Conversation with Patrick Chamoiseau, Raphael Confian, and Jean Bernabé," *Transitions*, issue 74, 1999, p. 129; Arnold, *Modernism and Negritude*, p. 73.

32 Edouard Glissant, *Caribbean Discourse: Selected Essays* ([1981] Charlottesville: University Press of Virginia, 1989); Jean Barnabé, Patrick Chamoiseau and Raphael Confiant, *Eloge de la créolité* (Paris: Gallimard, 1989); "The Literature of Guadeloupe and Martinique," special issue of *Callaloo* (vol. 15, no. 1, winter 1992), ed. Maryse Condé; Derek Walcott, "A Letter to Chamoiseau," *New York Review of Books*, August 14 1997, reprinted in his *What the Twilight Says: Essays* (New York: Farrar, Straus and Giroux, 1998); J. Michael Dash, *The Other America: Caribbean Literature in a New World Context* (Charlottesville: University of Virginia Press, 1998); and Taylor, "Créolité Bites".

33 *MGH*, p. 76.

34 *MGH*, p. 66–7. I have quoted the opening stanzas to "Cotch Donkey". First published in the *Gleaner*, October 21 1911, the poem was reprinted in *CB*, pp. 46–7.

35 Morris, "Introduction," to Bennett, *Selected Poems*, pp. iv–v.

36 In a 1911 interview McKay said: "I began writing dialect verses in 1909, my first attempt being a little thing entitled 'Hard Times.'" *Gleaner*, October 7 1911. "Hard Times" was published in *SJ*, pp. 53–4.

37 *MGH*, p. 69.

38 McKay to Nancy Cunard, August 20 1932; NCC.

39 McKay to J.E. Springarn, June 18 1917; Joel Springarn Papers, Manuscripts and Archives Section, New York Public Library.

Appendix

1 A.L. McLeod, "Preface," in McLeod, ed., *Claude McKay: Centennial Studies* (New Delhi: Sterling Publishers Private Limited, 1992), p. vi.

2 Written by McKay in the early 1940s, *Harlem Glory: A Fragment of Aframerican Life* remained unpublished for almost half a century. Cowl, who died in 1997, like the Jamaican organizers of the commemoration, accepted 1990 as the centenary of McKay's birth. In his preface to the book Cowl saluted the publishers, Charles H. Kerr Company, "for seizing this moment to honor Claude McKay on the hundredth anniversary of his birth." In the end, then, the timing of the publication of the book was made to coincide with the "centenary" and its celebration. See Carl Cowl, Preface to Claude McKay, *Harlem Glory*, pp. 5–7.

3 *Sunday Gleaner*, September 9 1990; *Daily Gleaner*, September 19 1990; *Sunday Gleaner*, September 23 1990; *Daily Gleaner*, October 5 1990.

4 *Caribbean Quarterly*, vol. 38, no. 1, March 1992.

5 McKay to Alain Locke, June 4 1927; Alain Locke Papers, Moorland–Spingarn Research Center, Howard University.

6 Wayne Cooper, *Claude McKay*; Winston James, "Claude McKay: A Political Portrait in his Jamaican and American Contexts, 1890–1920," Ph.D. diss., London School of Economics and Political Science, University of London, 1993.

7 Wagner, *Black Poets of the United States*, p. 198, n. 2; McLeod, "Preface," p. vi.

8 Cooper, "Claude McKay's Birthday," p. 2.

9 Ibid., p. 3.

10 Claude McKay, "My Mountain Home," *SJ*, p. 124; "las'y" in the poem means lasty, the diminutive of "last." McKay was his mother's last child. "I was the baby of the family and the favourite of my mother," he wrote. Claude McKay, *MGH*, p. 58.

11 Robert Hill, ed., *The Marcus Garvey and Universal Negro Improvement Association Papers*, vol. i (Berkeley: University of California Press, 1983), p. 14.

12 Wagner, *Black Poets of the United States*, p. 198.

13 Cooper, *Claude McKay*, pp. 6–7.

14 Tillery, *Claude McKay*, p. 3.

15 Mervyn Morris is the only McKay commentator to accurately grasp this basic fact. Morris, "Introduction," to McKay, *MGH*, p. xiii.

16 See McKay's biographical note, written by himself, in Cullen, ed., *Caroling Dusk*, pp. 81–2.

17 As late as the 1950s and 1960s many Jamaicans who migrated to Britain did not know or discover their "official" name until they applied for a passport and had to produce their birth certificates. Two sisters, for example, were mistakenly registered with the same first name on their birth certificates, even though they had always been known by different names. This discovery did not occur until one

had applied to go to England and encountered difficulty when it came to light that she had been confused with the other by the authorities.

18 Hope McKay-Virtue quoted in McLeod, "Preface," p. vii.

19 Copy in the author's possession.

20 Tarry, *The Third Door*, pp. 268–70.

21 Jesús Colón, *A Puerto Rican in New York and Other Sketches* (New York: International Publishers, 1982), pp. 115–17.